HAIL TO UNCP!

A 125-Year History of the University of North Carolina at Pembroke

David K. Eliades

Lawrence T. Locklear

Linda E. Oxendine

Welcome to UNCP!
Lum Lm
Linda E. Oxendine

CHAPEL HILL
PRESS, INC.

FRONT COVER PHOTO: Historic Old Main, on the campus of the University of North Carolina at Pembroke, with 125th anniversary celebration banners.
PHOTO TAKEN BY RAUL RUBIERA JR., UNIVERSITY PHOTOGRAPHER, UNC PEMBROKE.

BACK COVER PHOTO: First building of Croatan Normal School. The structure, built in 1888 by the Lumbee people, was located in the Pates community, one and a half miles west of Pembroke.

Please address any questions concerning this book to:
University Communications and Marketing
UNC Pembroke | Post Office Box 1510 | Pembroke, NC 28372

Phone: 910.521.6533
Web: http://www.uncp.edu/ucm
Email: ucm@uncp.edu

Second Printing, 2015
Printed in the United States of America

Library of Congress Cataloging-In-Publication Data (Prepared by The Donohue Group, Inc.)

Eliades, David K., 1938–
    Hail to UNCP! : a 125-year history of the University of North Carolina at Pembroke / David K. Eliades, Lawrence T. Locklear, Linda E. Oxendine.
    pages : illustrations, maps ; cm
    Includes bibliographical references and index.
    ISBN: 978-1-59715-098-9
    1. University of North Carolina at Pembroke—History. 2. Universities and colleges—North Carolina—Pembroke—History. I. Locklear, Lawrence T. II. Oxendine, Linda. E. III. Title.

LD3952.5 .E45 2014
378.756/332   2014934647

For the Braves—
past, present, and future.

Contents

Illustrations and Maps

ILLUSTRATIONS

Preface

> *Where Carolina's lofty pine trees*
> *Pierce the southern blue,*
> *Proudly stands our Alma Mater*
> *Courageous, strong and true;*
> *Black and gold float on forever*
> *Symbol of loyalty,*
> *Pembroke, our Alma Mater,*
> *Hail to UNCP!*

> Ira Pate Lowry '29
> and Reba M. Lowry,
> first verse of "Hail to
> UNCP" (1954)

An air of celebration, reflection, and nostalgia filled the campus of the University of North Carolina at Pembroke in the spring of 2012 as the university kicked off a fourteen-month-long celebration of its 125th anniversary. That May, graduates, along with their families, and faculty gathered in the Quad, nestled between historic Old Main and the lofty pine trees, to celebrate their graduation during Commencement exercises. Special guest and keynote speaker Kevin Gover, the director of the Smithsonian's National Museum of the American Indian, spoke to the significance of "time-honored rituals of Commencement." Gover, a member of the Pawnee Indian Tribe, proclaimed, "I am a big fan of ritual and ceremony. And that is because these are the ways that a culture, a people, express their values. Gathering and dressing up and marching are how we say what is happening today is important to us. It is how we say you have achieved something we respect.... We honor these things in our culture...." With these remarks, Gover acknowledged the cultural and educational significance of that day's ceremony. More importantly, he foreshadowed the upcoming events of the anniversary celebration. The fourteen-month "ceremony" would highlight the institution's value to the Lumbee Indians and southeastern North Carolina while honoring and showcasing 125 noteworthy years of rich history and heritage filled with achievement, adversity, and triumph.

It would be very difficult to overestimate the educational, economic, cultural, and social importance of UNC Pembroke to the people and the region it serves. The institution was chartered on March 7, 1887, as a normal school for the Lumbee Indians of Robeson County, North Carolina. For three generations it was an exclusively Indian institution, representing opportunity and hope to a people experiencing the burdens, oppression, and restrictions of segregation and prejudice. Then, in 1954, it was opened to all citizens of all races, and its role broadened to provide opportunity for all qualified applicants. Since the 1960s, it has experienced rapid growth in its curriculum and physical plant, and its impact on southeastern North Carolina has been impressive. At the conclusion of its first 125 years, UNC Pembroke soars toward the future, positioning itself for the next 125 years of even greater growth, engagement, and service.

If the past is prologue to the future, the future will no doubt continue to be one of struggle and accomplishment. That is nothing new to an institution that was born in adversity. At this point, it is only fitting to look back to the origins of the institution and to trace its evolution from the narrowly focused Croatan Normal School into the University of North Carolina at Pembroke, a regionally recognized constituent institution of the University of North Carolina system.

Hail to UNCP! A 125-Year History of the University of North Carolina at Pembroke explores the university's history from its establishment in 1887 to the conclusion of its 125th anniversary celebration in 2013. This is a new, updated, and expanded edition of *Pembroke State University: A Centennial History* (1986), coauthored by David K. Eliades and Linda Ellen Oxendine. The first edition focused on the history of the institution from 1887 to 1985, as it was preparing for its Centennial Celebration. Although Eliades passed away in 2007, Lawrence T. Locklear '05, '12 and Oxendine collaborated to write *Hail to UNCP!* The new edition weaves additional details into the period between 1887 and 1985, while including important developments from 1985 to the spring undergraduate Commencement on May 4, 2013, the close of the 125th anniversary celebration.

The authors have tried to write an interesting, informative, and readable book that recaptures details of a unique institution and history once lost to memory. Although not neglecting the legal and organizational influences that shape a university, a conscious effort has been made to emphasize the social history of the campus community, broadly speaking—to focus on what the institution has meant and still means to the Lumbee people, to students past and present, and to the people of the area that it serves—while highlighting luminaries from the institution's history and the defining moments in its evolution from a normal school to a four-year institution of higher education. Few institutions of higher education have had greater impact on their immediate region than UNC Pembroke. Although many of the institution's leaders, including the trustees, were male through most of the twentieth century, women were important as students, teachers, and, in turn, mothers of students and supporters of the school. Recognizing that many people had lifelong relationships with the institution, the authors acknowledged changes in women's names through marriage by denoting their maiden names in parentheses. Also, when available, the graduation year for alumni of the institution is listed immediately following the individual's name. All photographs and images, unless otherwise noted, are courtesy of UNC Pembroke. This book is organized chronologically into eight chapters that summarize the transformative tenures of the institution's chief executives. Any mistakes are those of the authors.

The Lowry Bell Tower, a university landmark wrapped in black and gold and situated in the Quad between historic Old Main and the Mary Livermore Library, serenades the campus daily with the sweet music of the university's alma mater. Written in 1954 by professors Ira Pate Lowry '29 and his wife Reba M. Lowry, the aptly titled tune conjures up feelings of pride in our alma mater as we proudly proclaim, "Hail to UNCP!"

Acknowledgments

Reconstructing the past of the University of North Carolina at Pembroke using a documentary record, at times nonexistent or fragmented, proved to be a challenge and required a great deal of assistance. The authors have been generously helped by many individuals who gave us their time, loaned us materials, or encouraged and supported our efforts.

While we cannot mention everyone who helped make this book a reality, numerous people merit specific mention for their contributions to the first edition, *Pembroke State University: A Centennial History.* Thanks to former university staff member Donnie Roberts and his fellow faculty and staff who have passed away since its publication in 1986: Grace G. Britt '84; Dr. Dalton Brooks '60; Dr. Adolph L. Dial '43; Chancellor Emeritus Paul R. Givens; Dr. Robert Hersch; Elmer Hunt '53; Dr. Clifton Oxendine '24; Gary Spitler; and Gene Warren. Others who warrant special attention include Bruce Barton '86, the late Julian Pierce '66 and the Legal Aid of North Carolina–Pembroke Office, and Shari Lohela Eliades.

A variety of individuals deserve special acknowledgment for contributions to *Hail to UNCP! A 125-Year History of the University of North Carolina at Pembroke.* Special thanks to university staff members Kristen Anderson; Frank Britt; Ginger Brooks; Chancellor Kyle R. Carter; Rhonda Chavis '13; Carlene Cummings '88; Amber Dial '98, '08; Susan Evans; Kimberly Hunt; Tom Jackson '85, '06; Dr. Beverly King; Terry Locklear '03; Cynthia Oxendine '83, '94; Terry Oxendine '80; Raul Rubiera Jr.; Marty Spitzer; Wendy Sweat; Whitney Swesey; Blake Tyner '05; and David Ybarra. Thanks to faculty and staff Sandy Briscar, Dr. Jane Haladay, Dr. Mary Ann Jacobs, Dr. Charles Jenkins, and Dr. Rose Stremlau for your editorial assistance. The authors are especially grateful to staff member Scott Bigelow for his editorial assistance and advice on the manuscript. Our sincerest appreciation goes out to Bruce Barton '86, Dorothy L. Blue '55, Barbara Braveboy-Locklear '90, Isaac Timothy "Tim" Brayboy '64, Ruth L. Dial, James A. Jacobs Jr., Delton Ray Locklear '54, Chancellor Emeritus Allen C. Meadors, Chancellor Emeritus Joseph B. Oxendine, Michael Schaeffer, and Mary Alice (Pinchbeck) Teets '58, along with student Megan McMillan '14, for their contributions. Thanks also to Natasha B. Locklear for your support.

The staff of the following libraries, archives, museums, and genealogical societies provided invaluable assistance and information to this edition: Gary Fenton Barefoot, Moye Library at Mount Olive College; Eric Blevins, NC Museum of History; Carlene Cummings '88, Mary Livermore Library at UNC Pembroke; Keith Longiotti, Wilson Library at UNC–Chapel Hill; Cathy L. Martin, legislative librarian with the North Carolina General Assembly; Burl McCuiston, Carl A. Rudisill Library at Lenoir-Rhyne University; Amy McDonald with Duke University Archives; Laura Smith, Archives of Appalachia at East Tennessee State University; and Marcy Thompson, Transylvania County (North Carolina) Library. Thanks also to Carol M. Forbes, Wilson County (North Carolina) Genealogical Society; genealogists William S. Lamm and Wanda Causby Rabb; Dr. Michael Pelt, retired professor, Mount Olive College; and Linda Laton, legislative assistant to State Representative Charles Graham.

To these people, plus the many others not named, we express our deep appreciation.

HAIL TO UNCP!

Introduction

THE UNIVERSITY OF NORTH CAROLINA
AT PEMBROKE TODAY

UNCP continues to evolve as a regional comprehensive university that serves all of southeastern North Carolina.

Dr. Kyle R. Carter, chancellor,
University of North Carolina at Pembroke,
Installation Program (2011)

In 2013 the University of North Carolina at Pembroke possesses all the qualities of a distinguished institution of higher education: personal learning in a small campus setting, engaged learners, service-minded students, nationally recognized scholars, championship athletics, a diverse study body, affordability, a beautiful campus, a rich history and heritage, and a historic mission of service to the Lumbee Tribe and southeastern North Carolina.

Unique from its humble beginnings in 1887 UNC Pembroke has emerged in the twenty-first century as a vibrant, comprehensive regional university that is charting a course for continued growth and service to southeastern North Carolina and the state. UNC Pembroke is a master's level degree-granting university and one of seventeen schools that make up the University of North Carolina system. The institution counts more than twenty-two thousand alumni and an enrollment of more than sixty-two hundred students, from North Carolina and beyond, among its constituencies. The university offers forty-one undergraduate and eighteen graduate degree programs, including the recent addition of a master of science in nursing. With 230 acres and forty-nine buildings, the campus has grown to serve an increasingly residential student body. In the past decade, the university experienced rapid growth of enrollment, programs, and campus construction, and students have been the primary beneficiaries. The entire region is profiting from the university's growing economic impact and engaged outreach.

UNC Pembroke continues to translate its mantra—"where learning gets personal"—into student success. Small class size and close interaction with faculty continue to define the Pembroke experience. The average class size is twenty-one students and the student-to-faculty ratio is 15:1. Faculty take tremendous care to ensure the success and growth of their students. There is objective evidence that learning happens here, and student outcomes are outstanding. Results of the most recent Collegiate Learning Assessment placed students in the eighty-fifth percentile among one hundred peer institutions for learning gained between freshman and senior years. According to the most recent survey, 90 percent of graduating seniors either had a job or were planning to go to graduate school. One-third of the graduates surveyed planned to continue their education at UNC Pembroke.

UNC Pembroke's current student body can make a strong case that it is the smartest ever, and that undergraduate study here is more rigorous than ever. Requirements for admissions and academic standing are higher than at any other point in the institution's history, and there are more opportunities for students to take their studies to the next level. The Esther G. Maynor Honors College offers select courses, travel and research opportunities, and a living-learning community. To facilitate research, the Pembroke Undergraduate Research and Creativity (PURC) Center connects students with faculty and funding. The Biotechnology Research and Training Center

offers opportunities for engaged, mentored student research with nationally recognized scholars. The Office of International Programs continues
to expand options for study abroad, with semester, yearlong, and summer
programs. International students, who come to Pembroke from around the
globe, add to what *US News & World Report* ranks as the most diverse
student body in North Carolina and the southern United States.

The university has leveraged technology to build on its reputation for
teaching and learning. UNC Pembroke is a leader among all UNC institutions in the use of technology. This goes far beyond SMART Boards,
wireless Internet, and online library resources. More than one-fifth of the
credit hours offered during the 2012–2013 academic year were delivered

FIGURE IN.I. *UNC Pembroke students are engaged learners
who conduct research with nationally recognized scholars.*

online. Over half of the 2012 summer school credits were earned online. Online instruction and other technologies, including interactive video classrooms, allow UNC Pembroke to more effectively reach out to students in locations from the Sandhills to the beach and at Fort Bragg as well.

Outreach, both educational and civic, is the hallmark of the exceptional university. With the growth of online education, four satellite campuses (Sandhills, Cape Fear, and Richmond community colleges and Fort Bragg) and classrooms at other community colleges across the region, UNC Pembroke is constructing seamless pathways to undergraduate and graduate degrees. The Bachelor of Interdisciplinary Studies Program was created specifically for community college graduates who may take the majority of their classes online or at off-campus sites, possibly never seeing the main campus until graduation day. The master of public administration is available entirely online. Veterans and active-duty soldiers are another special focus of UNC Pembroke's engaged outreach. In addition to a full-time staff and classrooms at Fort Bragg, the Office of Military and Veterans Services on campus employees a full-time coordinator. For its efforts, UNC Pembroke was named a "military friendly" university in 2013 by two national publications.

While the economic impact of the university exceeds $200 million annually, UNC Pembroke's influence is multidimensional. With a 2012–2013 operating budget of more than $81 million, the university employs almost nine hundred full-time faculty and staff. The Thomas Family Center for Entrepreneurship and the Small Business and Technology Development Center (SBTDC) assist new and expanding businesses. Teams of master of business administration (MBA) candidates also provide consulting for businesses, governments, and nonprofits. Academic programs in entrepreneurship and sustainable agriculture are training the next generation of enterprisers. The Regional Center contributes an array of programs for economic, community, and professional development, hosting annual symposia in support of community health, biotechnology, agribusiness, and entrepreneurship.

UNC Pembroke's students are community service–oriented. Providing more than eleven thousand volunteer hours in 2012–2013, the university was named to the President's Higher Education Community Service Honor Roll for the fifth time since 2007. While the spirit of community service is a constant, the nature of community service is changing as faculty build opportunities for service-learning classes into the curriculum. Here, learning leaps from classroom to community in wide-ranging projects from literacy programs to sophisticated marketing support of nonprofit organizations. More than twenty service-learning classes are offered each semester.

Without question, a university's most significant contribution to society is the value it adds to human capital. While continuing its historic mission to train public school teachers, the university's graduates include bankers, research scientists, accountants, entrepreneurs, doctors, professional athletes, broadcasters, and more. UNC Pembroke graduates enrich their profession and local communities. One area in which UNC Pembroke really shines is its undergraduate training for dozens of doctors and other health-care professionals, many of whom return to their home communities to practice after receiving advanced training elsewhere. However, the university is beginning to train health-care professionals here. In the $29 million Health Sciences Building, completed in 2012, the university's growing nursing program is increasing its four-year licensure program to two hundred students. The new Master of Science in Nursing Program opened in fall 2013 to train the nurse educators and leaders of the future. The nursing program is truly outstanding. UNC Pembroke is the only public university in North Carolina with a 100 percent passing rate of its graduates on the NCLEX-RN exam in 2011 and 2012. As part of their training, nursing students engage with faculty and the region to provide health education, screenings, and research. Programs in social work and counseling have also expanded. With the master of social work program and the nationally accredited Clinical Mental Health and School Counseling Programs, UNC Pembroke is contributing significantly to the health and welfare of the region.

FIGURE IN.2. *Health Sciences Building.*

While the university looks outward, it does so from one of the most beautiful campuses in North Carolina, with its historic Old Main—listed on the National Register of Historic Places—to the ultramodern Health Sciences Building, which has been transformed into a student-friendly residential setting. More than three thousand students live on campus and in three private apartment complexes in Pembroke. Student life comes with many lifestyle amenities. Students may choose from traditional single- and double-occupancy rooms, suites, and apartments. Campus dining has diversified as well, with a renovation of the dining hall that was completed in 2012. Starbucks, Papa John's, and Einstein Brothers Bagels are the newest additions to the menu. Campus entertainment is also important to student life and a robust campus experience, and Givens Performing Arts Center (GPAC) continues its tradition of offering diverse programming and world-renowned performers. Students can see Broadway musicals, stand-up comedy, distinguished speakers, student productions, and more. Campus events such as the annual Pembroke Day bring the campus and local community together in the Quad. Students also take advantage of active student organizations, the Campbell Wellness Center, and the Campus Recreation Program.

Outstanding athletic programs are another campus attraction. UNC Pembroke offers sixteen sports that compete in the Peach Belt Conference at the NCAA Division II level. After its first season in 2007, Braves football has not had a losing season. The program set a record by earning an NCAA tournament bid in just its third year of competition. Braves athletics are experiencing a renaissance in virtually every sport. Men's basketball has gone to the NCAA tournament in two of the last three years (2011 and 2013). Individual excellence is also evident. Wrestler Mike Williams won a 2012 national championship, and golfer Meaghan Moore finished second in the 2012 NCAA Division II National Championships. Excellence on the playing fields continues in the classroom. Between 2010 and 2012, UNC Pembroke's student-athletes twice won the Peach Belt Conference President's Cup for the highest overall grade point average.

One thing about the university that has not changed is the need for external funding. The Office of Sponsored Research and Programs has been successful winning federal, state, and foundation grant funding to

FIGURE IN.3. *Old Main with Arrowhead.*

support student research and provide support for students. Although UNC Pembroke remains one of the most affordable universities in the nation, the demand for need-based financial aid is greater than ever. The endowment, which climbed to $17.1 million in 2012, provides approximately $250,000 in donor-funded scholarships annually. With 88 percent of the student body receiving financial aid in some form—and tuition and student debt rising—the need is substantial. The Office of Advancement looks to its friends and alumni for support now more than ever. UNC Pembroke's corporate and other friends have stepped up their support by endowing professorships. Thanks to friends like BB&T, Irwin Belk, James Thomas, Martha Beach '62, the family of Howard Brooks '63, and C. D. Spangler and William C. Friday, both former presidents of the University of North Carolina system, the university has added eleven endowed professorships. Typically between $500,000 and $1 million, these special endowments help attract outstanding scholars and teachers, like Dr. Ben Bahr, who conducts world-class research on Alzheimer's disease. All but one of these endowments was established in the last sixteen years. Others corporate partners, like Lumbee Guaranty Bank, Pembroke Hardware, Duke Energy, and the Robeson County Farm Bureau, support programs and scholarships annually.

The university's planned twelfth endowed professorship, in American Indian studies, brings this introduction full circle. As the university kicked off the celebration of its first 125 years in 2012, Chancellor Kyle R. Carter announced the formation of the Southeast American Indian Studies (SAIS) Program. It will become UNC Pembroke's signature academic program, capitalizing on the university's unique history and its position as the leading institution of higher education for Indians of the eastern United States. Headquartered in Old Main, SAIS will leverage existing and future resources to establish a premier teaching and research center, with a focus on southeastern Indians that will attract students and scholars from near and far. UNC Pembroke confers more undergraduate degrees

FIGURE IN.4. *Water feature and amphitheatre.*

to Indians than any institution east of the Mississippi and is in the top 10 nationally. With its location at the heart of the Lumbee Tribe, this program will distinguish UNC Pembroke for the next 125 years and beyond.

What will the future hold for the little school that opened its doors with fifteen students and one teacher in 1888? Overcoming adversity and challenges marked every step along the journey of this remarkable university. As this story demonstrates, inspired leadership and community support are key ingredients to UNC Pembroke's success. Like the founders, we continue to believe that education uplifts individuals and communities. The global economy and the exploding information technology age make a college education more important than ever. By reading *Hail to UNCP!*, readers can grasp the extraordinary spirit of this institution and the people who contributed to its success.

—Scott Bigelow, University Communications and Marketing

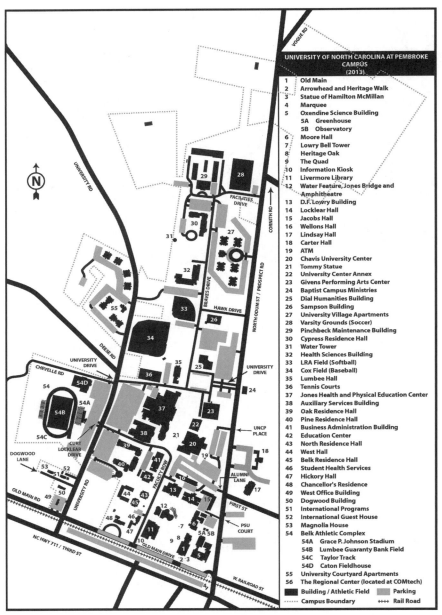

UNIVERSITY OF NORTH CAROLINA AT PEMBROKE
CAMPUS
(2013)

1   Old Main
2   Arrowhead and Heritage Walk
3   Statue of Hamilton McMillan
4   Marquee
5   Oxendine Science Building
     5A   Greenhouse
     5B   Observatory
6   Moore Hall
7   Lowry Bell Tower
8   Heritage Oak
9   The Quad
10   Information Kiosk
11   Livermore Library
12   Water Feature, Jones Bridge and
     Amphitheatre
13   D.F. Lowry Building
14   Locklear Hall
15   Jacobs Hall
16   Wellons Hall
17   Lindsay Hall
18   Carter Hall
19   ATM
20   Chavis University Center
21   Tommy Statue
22   University Center Annex
23   Givens Performing Arts Center
24   Baptist Campus Ministries
25   Dial Humanities Building
26   Sampson Building
27   University Village Apartments
28   Varsity Grounds (Soccer)
29   Pinchbeck Maintenance Building
30   Cypress Residence Hall
31   Water Tower
32   Health Sciences Building
33   LRA Field (Softball)
34   Cox Field (Baseball)
35   Lumbee Hall
36   Tennis Courts
37   Jones Health and Physical Education Center
38   Auxiliary Services Building
39   Oak Residence Hall
40   Pine Residence Hall
41   Business Administration Building
42   Education Center
43   North Residence Hall
44   West Hall
45   Belk Residence Hall
46   Student Health Services
47   Hickory Hall
48   Chancellor's Residence
49   West Office Building
50   Dogwood Building
51   International Programs
52   International Guest House
53   Magnolia House
54   Belk Athletic Complex
     54A   Grace P. Johnson Stadium
     54B   Lumbee Guaranty Bank Field
     54C   Taylor Track
     54D   Caton Fieldhouse
55   University Courtyard Apartments
56   The Regional Center (located at COMtech)

■ Building / Athletic Field   ▮ Parking
······· Campus Boundary   ++++ Rail Road

MAP IN.I. *University of North Carolina at Pembroke campus (2013).*

Chapter One

1887–1909
THE FOUNDATION IS LAID

Our present generation reaching a higher stage still contends for the education of the head, hand and heart and only by the cultivation of these three may we hope to reach that high standard that God in his wisdom planned for us when man was made.

Never before has the necessity of education been so great.

T.C. Henderson, principal,
Croatan Normal School, letter to the
Croatan Indians in *The Robesonian*
(September 28, 1900)

The University of North Carolina at Pembroke was originally established for the educational benefit of the Lumbee Indians of North Carolina. Since their contact with Europeans, the history of the Lumbees has been one of great struggle—struggle to establish a legal and political identity, gain an education, and acquire first-class citizenship. The history of the university is inseparable from that struggle and central to the success of the Lumbee people. The intertwined history of both the people and the institution is a story of success, often against great odds.

To understand the history of the university, it is first necessary to know some relevant background information concerning the Lumbees.

UNC Pembroke is located in the heart of the Lumbee Tribe of North Carolina. More than fifty-five thousand Lumbees make their home in southeastern North Carolina. They are the largest of North Carolina's eight tribes and one of the largest in the United States. Lumbees reside mainly in Robeson and adjoining Cumberland, Hoke, and Scotland Counties. While the town of Pembroke is the social and political center of the tribe, the oldest Indian communities are Fairgrove, Prospect, Saddletree, and Union Chapel. Kinship ties along with relationships to community, church, and the land are central to the Lumbee identity. The ancestors of the present-day Lumbee—remnants of Eastern Woodland tribes from North Carolina, South Carolina, and Virginia decimated from disease and warfare with Europeans—coalesced and settled in the swamps of Robeson County during the eighteenth century, seeking a familiar refuge to escape the encroachment of white settlers. Indians, according to archaeological records, have resided in Robeson and surrounding counties for thousands of years, thus retaining a familiarity with the county's waterway, swamplands, and innumerable resources. White settlers found the county's swamplands undesirable, making Robeson County one of the last areas settled by non-Indians. Although the last speakers of a traditional language died at the end of the nineteenth century, the Lumbee maintain a dialect of English that distinguishes them from the white and African American communities of the region. Each year on the Saturday closest to July 4, over twenty thousand Lumbees gather in Pembroke for the annual weeklong Lumbee Homecoming to celebrate their history and culture.

The Indians of Robeson and surrounding counties have been known at various times in their history as Croatans (1885–1911), Indians of Robeson County (1911–1913), and Cherokee Indians of Robeson County (1913–1952), all due to lingering questions of historical tribal origin. In 1952, tribal members held a referendum and selected "Lumbee Indians of North Carolina" as the name for the tribe. The new name was derived from the Indians' name of "Lumbee" for the county's main waterway—legally designated Lumber River in 1809 by the North Carolina General Assembly. This naming pattern is in the same tradition of other southeastern U.S. tribes that share names with rivers, such as the Pee Dee, Congaree, and Wateree. The Reverend D. F. Lowry '05, a prominent figure in the university's history and proponent of the name change, reasoned, "Because the tribe is composed originally of members from different tribes, no one historical name is appropriate. Rather, ... the tribe should take its name from a geographical name, [like] earlier tribes in the area [did]." In 1953 the North Carolina General Assembly recognized the tribe's sovereign act by enacting legislation that legally changed the tribal name to "Lumbee Indians of North Carolina." On June 7, 1956, President Dwight D. Eisenhower signed into law the Lumbee Act, which recognized the tribal name change but simultaneously

FIGURE 1.1. *Seal of the Lumbee Tribe of North Carolina.*

denied its members the benefits and services of federal recognition. Today, the Lumbee continue their quest for full federal recognition. Tribal affairs are managed by a three-branch government, headquartered in Pembroke, with a chairperson, Tribal Council, and Supreme Court.

The first contacts with Lumbee ancestors in Robeson County came during the 1730s and 1740s when Scottish immigrants began to move into the Cape Fear River Valley of southeastern North Carolina. In the eighteenth and early nineteenth centuries, the Lumbees, though sometimes viewed as a contentious people, were first-class citizens, having the right to bear arms, vote, and fulfill civic obligations. Unfortunately, in the 1830s, several developments combined to cast them into a new and inferior social and political status. Against a backdrop of racial concerns over slave insurrection and Indian removal, North Carolina held the Constitutional Convention of 1835, which proved to be a turning point in Lumbee history. Although the convention took steps to make the state government more democratic for whites, it also took steps to deny nonwhites political privileges and to control their lives; the convention decreed that "free persons of color" were no longer able to vote, hold any public office, bear arms, or possess the other privileges of first-class citizenship. While these provisions were directly aimed at "free blacks," Lumbees were trapped by their nonwhite status and the prevailing climate of fear that demanded that nonwhites be rendered politically powerless.

From 1835 until 1885 the Lumbees experienced discrimination, mistreatment, and disdain. All of this reached a climax in the 1864–1874 period with the bloody "Lowrie War." For much of that ten-year period, Indian Henry Berry Lowrie led a triracial band against the white establishment, partly to defend Indian rights and partly as an act of personal vengeance for the murder of his father, Allen, and brother William at the end of the Civil War in 1865. Though whites viewed Lowrie as an outlaw, the Lumbees have long held him up as a folk hero because he fought back against injustice. From the Indian standpoint, Henry Berry Lowrie's actions were in response to crimes committed against his people. By 1874 Lowrie had mysteriously disappeared and the Lowrie War was over, though the bitterness and hatreds generated by that experience would long influence the history of race relations in southeastern North Carolina. The Lowrie War, however, marked a turning point in Indian-white relations in Robeson County as Indians asserted themselves, challenging the racial status quo. Historian and Robeson County native W. McKee Evans wrote, "What is more evident is how much the Spencer rifles of the Lowry band contributed to the perceptions of the dominant white group: white historians expended considerably more energy in the late nineteenth and early twentieth century demonstrating that the Lumbees were Indians than they had expended in the previous half-century demonstrating that they were not."

The chaos and problems of the 1860s and 1870s were compounded first by the horrors and destruction of the Civil War and then by the bitterness of Reconstruction. In the midst of this tumultuous era, a Republican-dominated convention met to give North Carolina a new constitution. The North Carolina constitution of 1868 affected the Lumbees in two major ways. First, it restored political equality to all males, decreeing that anyone who met the legal requirements was eligible to vote and to hold office—regardless of race. Consequently, that same year, James "Big Jim" Oxendine, a Lumbee and future member of the institution's original Board of Trustees, became the first Indian to be elected a county commissioner for Robeson County; he served from 1868 to 1876. Second, the 1868 constitution established a public school system, not segregated by race, which was to operate a minimum of four months each year. North Carolinians refused to send their children to integrated schools, and the system foundered.

By 1875 Reconstruction ended in North Carolina, and Democrats amended the 1868 constitution. Thirty amendments were attached to the document, most of which were reactionary in nature and designed to assure white supremacy in the state. One of the amendments stated that the public schools of North Carolina were to be established on a "separate but equal" basis. As it turned out, the state provided public schools for whites and blacks, but none for Indians. For the next ten years, the Lumbees were not only denied schools of their own but made brutally aware of their lack of political and legal equality. While they found themselves unacceptable to the white community, they were determined not to be forced to join the black community because they recognized that they would lose their status and perceived Indianness if they did so. To maintain their separate identity, most Indians chose to attend poor-quality Indian subscription schools or not attend school at all, thereby encumbering high illiteracy rates among Lumbees. Anderson Locklear, namesake for UNC Pembroke's Locklear Hall, attended an Indian subscription school at Old Prospect in 1877. Indians built the schools and paid the teachers, all funded through a fee of fifty cents that was charged each month for each student attending the school. The Lumbees responded to the adversity of this period with a determination to gain their own school system and establish a legal and political identity for the Indian people of Robeson County. The Lumbees realized that education and identity were essential for developing feelings of pride and dignity. After fifty years of discrimination, the Lumbees were ready to change the pattern and to ensure that the lives of their children were richer in every way than the lives of previous generations.

FIGURE 1.2. *Hamilton McMillan. Member of the state House of Representatives (1885–1888) from Red Springs who sponsored the legislation establishing Croatan Normal School in 1887.*

Because of animosity on the part of the Democratic Party, the party of white supremacy, the Lumbees generally voted Republican after they regained the vote under the constitution of 1868. In the mid-1880s, a legislator from Robeson County and an advocate of the Indian people, the Honorable Hamilton McMillan, saw an opportunity to help both the Lumbees and his Democratic Party. McMillan and other conservative Democrats realized that their "interpretations" of the origins of Robeson County's Indians "had become a political liability." Evans suggested, "By recognizing them as Indians, the conservative Democrats were offering them a middle legal status: they would have more rights than the blacks but not so many as the whites." Lumbee response to these "conciliatory gestures" marked a "period of accommodation" between Lumbees and conservative Democrats; whites needed Indian votes, and Indians desired a middle-class status with the benefits of a legal identity and separate schools. In 1885 McMillan introduced legislation in the General Assembly giving the Indians of Robeson County a legal identity and schools of their own, which they also controlled.

McMillan was born August 29, 1837, at "Ardlussa House" in Cumberland County and educated at the Trinity School in Hartford, Connecticut, and the University of North Carolina at Chapel Hill. McMillan was a Civil War veteran, an educator, a lawyer, a politician, and a gentleman historian of multitudinous interests. Among the subjects he studied were Scottish history, folklore, the Revolutionary War, and Indian history and culture. Around 1873 McMillan and his wife, Lizzie, settled in Red Springs, a dozen miles northwest of the main Indian community. When McMillan died on February 27, 1916, in Red Springs, county residents memorialized him as one of the county's "most honored men, and certainly there was no better type of Carolinian anywhere in the State. Colonel McMillan was scholar, sage, and exemplar, and he was a powerful force in his community and county in his day of activity." In addition, McMillan "was the type of man who would leave his impress upon any community." Indians took note of the mark he left on their community, as O. H. Lowrey remarked, "We, the true and tried are glad and do appreciate what has been done for us." McMillan's legacy and impression on Robeson County and southeastern North Carolina, like that of the institution's founders and first Board of Trustees, remains today, memorialized in UNC Pembroke.

The murder of three Lumbee youths at the end of the Civil War by a member of the local Home Guard sparked McMillan's interest in the Lumbee. James Brantley Harris (1826–1865), a white merchant and bootlegger from Randolph County, North Carolina, settled and married among the Indians. Remembered as the "meanest man in Robeson

County" who was sometimes "too familiar with the wives and daughters of his customers," Harris, tellingly, was disliked by Indians and whites. At the onset of the Civil War, Harris became an officer in the local Home Guard and was responsible for policing Scuffletown, a term used by whites to designate the Lumbee settlement. In late 1864 Harris murdered brothers Jarman, and later, Wesley and Allen Lowrie, in separate but related incidents. The brothers were sons of George Lowrie, who was the brother of Allen Lowrie, the father of Henry Berry Lowrie. These murders made Harris an enemy of the Lowrie family, putting his life in great peril. Harris "had sown seeds of anger which would ultimately yield a harvest of blood and hate." At an inquest into the deaths of his sons, George Lowrie gave a "dramatic and moving speech"—heard by McMillan—that described how Lumbees had always been friends with whites, the origins of Robeson County Indians, and the lack of justice for the murder of his sons. Although Harris never stood trial for the murders, he met a bloody, bullet-riddled end at the hands of the Lowrie gang on January 15, 1865.

In 1885 McMillan was elected to the first of two consecutive terms in the North Carolina House of Representatives. At the time, there was considerable mystery and controversy surrounding the historical origins of the Lumbees. By 1885, after investigating the origins of the Indians for political, scholarly, and humanitarian reasons, McMillan had concluded that they were descendants of John White's 1587 "Lost Colony" and friendly coastal Croatan Indians who inhabited a place called Croatoan along North Carolina's Outer Banks. Marshaling his evidence, which was later accepted by Stephen Weeks, a nationally prominent historian, McMillan wrote a pamphlet titled *Sir Walter Raleigh's Lost Colony*. Convinced of his findings, McMillan had the Robeson Indians designated as Croatans in House Bill 206, ratified on February 10, 1885. The two major provisions of the act were Section 1—"That the said Indians and their descendants shall hereafter be designated and known as the Croatan Indians"—and Section 2—"That said Indians and their descendants shall have separate schools for their children, school communities of their own race and color and shall be allowed to select teachers of their own choice...." Schools of their own meant opportunity and support for their claims to Indian identity; the struggle for tribal identity is a central issue in much of Lumbee history. Explaining the Lumbees' awkward relationship with Jim Crow, Lumbee historian Malinda Maynor Lowery wrote, "Democrats had portrayed support for education as a limited resource doled out in exchange for votes, and Indians acquiesced, eager to maintain the educational, economic, and political benefits they possessed." As an expression of their appreciation for McMillan's actions on their behalf, many Indians began to vote for Democrats beginning in the 1886 election. Fred A. Olds, director of the North Carolina Hall of History, the predecessor to the North Carolina Museum of History, would later write of McMillan's relations with the Lumbees, "You know them better than any white man on earth. They love you and I refer to you as their discoverer and sincerest friend...." Even if overstated, McMillan was certainly an important figure in Lumbee history.

While the 1885 law gave the Lumbees their own public schools, there is no evidence that any were immediately established. Because no schools had been open to them since 1835, except for occasional subscription schools of poor quality and uncertain operation, the illiteracy rate among the Lumbees was extremely high. Limited funding from the state and a paucity of qualified teachers meant that the education crisis continued. For the 1886 school year, $749.25 was allotted for the operation of the Croatan schools, which enrolled 1,006 students. Whether the schools actually operated as intended is questionable. It was also difficult to find Indians qualified to teach in the newly established system. Following the leadership of Rev. W. L. Moore and others such as Preston Locklear, the Indian community quickly concluded that what was really needed in order to make educational progress was a centralized institution offering "normal" (teacher training) studies. On February 2, 1887, the North

Carolina House of Representatives received a petition from sixty-seven Indians and six whites, stating, "We the undersigned Croatan Indians of Robeson County in North Carolina, do respectfully ask, that you establish for us, a Normal School in Robeson County, for our race...." On February 10, 1887, Hamilton McMillan introduced House Bill 725, "a bill to establish a normal school in Robeson County." On March 7, 1887, the bill was enacted, signaling the beginning of the institution that would eventually grow into the University of North Carolina at Pembroke.

Initially, legislative support was conditional for two years; it was clearly the intent of the General Assembly to see if the Indians would seriously support and use the institution. The 1887 act created a corporation under the control of a board of trustees, composed originally of the Reverend W. L. Moore, Preston Locklear, James "Big Jim" Oxendine, James E. Dial Sr., J. J. (John J.) Oxendine, Isaac Brayboy, and Olin Oxendine. The seven-man board was charged with maintaining a school of "high grade for teachers of the Croatan race in North Carolina." Students who attended the school had to be at least fifteen years of age and obligate themselves "to teach the youth of the Croatan race for a stated period." While the legislature appropriated five hundred dollars for the school, that money could only be used to pay teachers at the institution and for no other purpose. No funds were allocated for acquiring land or constructing a building; it was left up to the Indian community to provide both. The Indian community reacted to this law with ambivalence. McMillan reported that the law produced "much excitement" among the people, prompting one Lumbee to say, "Mon, white men at last are trying to do us justice." But many Lumbees were suspicious of the act simply because there had been so many past injustices. They found it difficult to believe that the whites would do something for their advancement. Consequently, when Moore called a meeting to carry out the provisions of the law, there was considerable opposition and apathy.

Fortunately for the school and the community, the progressive thinking of a few changed the educational future of a people and a region.

The seven members of the Board of Trustees were religious, political, and educational leaders in the Lumbee community and had the political and financial capital, as well as influence among Indians—and whites—to make the school a reality. Among the intergenerational group, "Big Jim" was the elder at age sixty-six, and Moore, the youngest, was twenty-eight. Their shared bond—based in kinship ties, connection to place, church, and interest in the school—influenced the early development of the institution. They were all Indian, but Moore was the only non-Lumbee. The trustees had kinship ties to the influential Oxendine and Lowry families. Three of the seven trustees were Oxendines: Big Jim and J.J. Oxendine were brothers, and Olin was the son of Big Jim. Moore's wife was the niece of Big Jim and J.J. The wife of Big Jim, the mother of Brayboy's wife, and the grandfather of Locklear's wife were all Lowrys. Furthermore, all the trustees lived within just a few miles of the campus, with the exception of Dial, who grew up near the campus but settled in the Saddletree community northwest of Lumberton. The progressive-minded seven drove the transformation of Indian education in Robeson County and the community's acceptance of the normal school.

FIGURE 1.3. *W. L. Moore. Founder, member of first Board of Trustees, and first principal and teacher of Croatan Normal School.*

FIGURE 1.4. *Preston Locklear. Prominent Lumbee leader, and member of the first Board of Trustees of Croatan Normal School.*

FIGURE 1.5. *Olin Oxendine. Member of the first Board of Trustees of Croatan Normal School.*

Rev. W.L. (William Luther) Moore was an outstanding leader of great determination. Born October 12, 1859, Moore was a Waccamaw Siouan Indian from Columbus County, North Carolina, who received a better education as a youth than most of his contemporaries, an education that included four years of normal training. He began teaching school in Columbus County in 1874 and taught there for five years. Moore came to Robeson County as a traveling Bible salesman. During a visit to the county in 1879 he was introduced to Big Jim Oxendine. Both remained friends until Oxendine's death in 1896. Oxendine introduced Moore to his first cousin Mary Catherine Oxendine (March 25, 1854–January 7, 1928); they married that same year and settled in the Prospect community. She was the first Indian female teacher in Robeson County. Moore, an ordained Methodist minister, teacher, administrator, and farmer, was an idealistic man who believed firmly in the uplifting effects of education. Indeed, he came from a family that stressed the importance of character, Christianity, and education, words that describe his importance to the Indian people. During his life he tended the educational needs of the Lumbees for thirty-seven years and their spiritual needs for fifty years. He was later memorialized as a man "devoted to making the world a better place to live in." Given his character he was unwilling to allow the normal school to be stillborn. He quit his job as a teacher, headed a subscription drive to which he donated two hundred dollars of his own money, and got the normal school started—a monument to his commitment to education and his love for his people. Moore is appropriately known in the history of this institution as "Founder, Erector, Teacher." At the time of his death on December 22, 1930, Moore was described as "a man ... without an equal for the uplift of humanity, the education of a devastated people and the pioneer church worker of the Indian race of the state." Moore's "magnanimity was unexcelled" as he "was wide awake to the people's needs ..." UNC Pembroke's Moore Hall, built in 1951, is named in his honor.

Preston Locklear (March 16, 1839–January 21, 1916), a neighbor of Moore's and a native of the Prospect community, was a wealthy farmer and woods rider, and, like the other founders of the institution, an influential and respected member of the community. Prior to serving on the Board of Trustees, Locklear was a trustee for a local subscription school. He was one of the first to make the move for separate Indian schools in Robeson County. Locklear was an honorary member of the Order of the Redmen, an Indian fraternal organization, known locally as the Redman's Lodge, which comprised Lumbee men who advocated for issues affecting the Indian community.

James E. Dial Sr., born in 1855 near Harpers Ferry Baptist Church, south of Pembroke, was a wealthy, progressive farmer who married and settled in the Saddletree community. He served as a trustee for thirty-five years and was a charter member of Mount Olive Baptist Church, also in Saddletree. Piney Grove School in Saddletree was once known locally as the James Dial School in his honor. After Dial passed away on November 8, 1933, Rev. J. E. Sawyer, superintendent of The Cherokee Indian Normal School of Robeson County, described Dial "as a man of public affairs all his life—one who had given his time and thought towards enhancing the educational privileges of the Indian people." Clifton Oxendine '24, a member of the institution's faculty, challenged others to live by Dial's example when he said, "The memory of Mr. Dial's untiring efforts and zeal for improved educational conditions for the Indian race will test our fidelity to his example; recollections of the public-mindedness of him in behalf of mankind will spur us on to a nobler human service."

The member of the original Board of Trustees with the most political clout and financial means for supporting Indian education was James "Big Jim" Oxendine. Born in 1821 Oxendine was a prosperous merchant and farmer who resided in the Prospect community. He was the first Lumbee elected as a Robeson County commissioner, in 1868, serving for eight years. Oxendine was chosen by his peers as the first chair of

the Board of Trustees. He passed away December 16, 1896. Trustees
Olin Oxendine (January 7, 1853–July 6, 1932) and J.J. (John J.) Oxendine
(1826–November 28, 1903), the son and brother of Big Jim, respectively,
were both farmers who lived in the Red Banks community southwest
of Pembroke.

Isaac Brayboy (January 21, 1836–February 3, 1919) was a resident
of the Bear Swamp community, north of Pembroke between the St.
Annah and Union Chapel communities. Brayboy, a farmer and turpen-
tine laborer, was an active supporter of Indian education, the Methodist
Church, and the Robeson County Democratic Party. After the southern
Methodist Episcopal Church "separated out" nonwhite members
in 1870, Union Chapel Methodist was placed under the direction of
Brayboy and Ismael Chavis. In 1906 Brayboy was chosen as an alternate
delegate to the Robeson County Democratic Convention for the Burnt
Swamp district. According to a family oral tradition shared by Barbara
Braveboy-Locklear '90 in an email to Lawrence T. Locklear on March
15, 2010, lumber used in the construction of Old Main was supplied by
his grandson Tecumseh's sawmill located near the community of Buie,
north of Pembroke.

The trustees' dynamic leadership and influence in the community set
into motion the establishment of the campus. The enabling legislation
specified that the school be located in Robeson County between Bear
Swamp and Lumber River. The trustees selected a site in the railroad
community of Pates, located almost one and a half miles west of the
current campus. The town of Pembroke would not be established until
later in 1895. Pates was a natural choice for a number of reasons. It
was a center of commerce, social, and religious activity, located in the
heart of the Lumbee community, and near the railroad. Two major
thoroughfares—Lowry Road and Eureka Road—intersected at Pates.
Lowry Road, today N.C. Highway 710, stretched from the northern and
southern borders of Robeson County. Eureka Road, now St. Anna Road,
ran northeast toward the Indian community of Union Chapel.

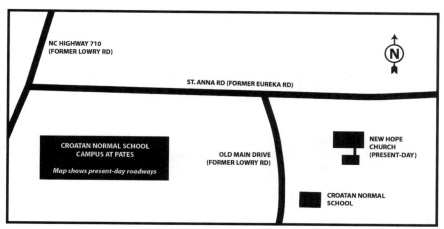

MAP I.I. *Croatan Normal School campus at Pates.*

Land selected for the site of the campus was located immediately south of present-day New Hope Church. The parcel—one quarter of an acre in size—was purchased January 2, 1888, by Croatan Normal trustees Moore, "Big Jim" Oxendine, Dial, and Locklear from Reverend William Jacobs, a farmer, and his second wife, Mary E., both Lumbee, for five dollars. The property was located along Lowry Road. The first written histories of the institution say the school was erected on a one-acre site purchased from the Jacobs for eight dollars. However, Clifton Oxendine '24, who attended school at the Pates campus in 1907, verified the building was located immediately south of the church. By 1908 a second Indian school was situated to the rear of the normal school and east of the church on one acre of land purchased from Rev. Jacobs and his wife on August 15, 1882, for seven dollars by the Robeson County Public School Committee No. 24, made up of "Big Jim" and John J. Oxendine along with Reiley Oxendine, son of "Big Jim."

Early histories of the institution also say the school opened its doors in the fall of 1887; however, evidence supports the school opening in the spring of 1888. According to the 1887 legislation, monies for the school were not appropriated until January 1888. Consequently, the land deed was dated January 2, 1888. According to the 1889 state auditor's report, the school received a one-half appropriation (January–July) for the 1887-1888 fiscal year. The Croatan Normal School opened its doors in the spring of 1888 with an enrollment of fifteen students, which included Anderson Locklear and O.R. Sampson, both major figures in the school's history, and Governor Worth Locklear (1870–1921), later the first Indian physician in Robeson County, and son of trustee Preston

FIGURE 1.6. *Dr. Clifton Oxendine '24, pointing to the original location of Croatan Normal School, located south of New Hope Church in the Pates community. He attended the campus at Pates in 1907.*

Locklear. The first building was a two-story clapboard structure that would have cost one thousand dollars to build had the Lumbee people not provided the material and labor for its construction. Moore's first term as principal and teacher for the school coincided with the first two years of its operation.

The establishment of the Croatan Normal School was both a political and humanitarian gesture. As noted, the Democrats and McMillan wanted to draw the Indians away from the Republican Party in the late nineteenth century; they also, at the time, wanted to minimize growing farmer discontent. Because the Lumbees were farmers as well as voters, the establishment of the normal school was an act of conciliation. Still, it is also clear that McMillan was at least equally concerned with the issue of justice, and that he genuinely wished to assist the Indians in gaining educational facilities for their own benefit. Throughout his long life, he remained an advocate of the Indian people and a staunch supporter of the normal school.

Croatan Normal School operated at the same time as the federal Indian boarding school system, a key component of the federal government's agenda to destroy Indian cultural communities and assimilate

FIGURE 1.7. *Croatan Normal School. Opened in 1888, with one teacher and fifteen students.*

Indians by "kill[ing] the Indian to save the man." In contrast to the federal Indian boarding school system, the normal school arose through the advocacy of Indian peoples themselves and educated Indians in their community as a way to strengthen familial and cultural ties.

Although established with the support of the community, the early years of the Croatan Normal School were years of frustration, struggle, and dissension because of the paucity of resources and contentious political climate. Until 1904 the school remained a one-man operation, with only occasional volunteer help. Additionally, factionalism kept the Indian community divided. Not all Indians were prepared to sever their ties to the Republicans, and a great struggle was occurring between rival Methodist groups concerning the issue of self-determination. The struggle stemmed from the 1870 "separating out" of nonwhite members by southern Methodist Episcopal churches. Because no members of his church at Prospect had been separated out, Moore led those Methodist churches that wished to maintain their ties to the southern Methodist branch. Initially joining the northern Methodists, the Reverend Henry H. Lowry became frustrated with the division within the Methodist Church and led a group of Lumbees, which included Union Chapel Church where Trustee Isaac Brayboy attended, out of the Methodist Church in order to form a conference of all-Indian churches. Rev. Lowry, a grandson of Allen Lowrie, wanted a conference in which the Indian membership made the decisions from top to bottom, including the appointment of Indian pastors, bishops, and superintendents, because, according to Maynor Lowery, he "believed the path to progress required Indian leaders." Rev. Moore, on the other hand, saw no particular advantage to an all-Indian conference and so continued to work with the southern branch because, as Maynor Lowery argues, he "saw nothing amiss in aligning with whites and working with white leadership to promote Indian progress. That progress...enhanced the educational and religious institutions of Indians and thus helped to maintain Indian identity." On October 26, 1900, Rev. Lowry guided the formation of the all-Indian Lumbee River Conference of the Holiness Methodist Church. The name of the conference was changed during the 1950s from "Lumbee River" to "Lumber River." Conference offices are located on Prospect Road, a short distance north of the present-day campus. Indian Methodists to this day are divided between the so-called white conference, now the United Methodist Church, and the Lumbee Conference. This dispute enveloped the normal school because Moore was in the vanguard of its establishment and its first head.

On July 12, 1889, McMillan wrote S.M. Finger, superintendent of public instruction, "There is a disaffected portion of the Croatans which clings to Radicalism and they are agents of certain parties desirous of breaking up the Normal School." He went on to charge that the "disaffected" element had burned two churches and a schoolhouse belonging to the Moore group, "thinking thereby to influence the Legislature then in session against any appropriation for benefit of the Normal School." Curiously, Moore and Lowry were lifelong friends, and the struggle was precipitated by perceptions of what was the best policy for the Lumbees, not the issue of personal power.

In his biennial report, Superintendent Finger stated his reaction to this development by noting, "These people seem to be [so] much divided...that the school is not as effective as it ought to be. I respectfully suggest that, inasmuch as the appropriation of $500 is annual, the Assembly pass an act allowing the State Board of Education to exercise their discretion as to future expenditures for this school." Finger was not at all certain that the school was going to succeed, and he was concerned that state funds were being wasted in its support. While this suggestion was not adopted, its proposal clearly reflects the precarious existence of the institution in its formative years.

Factional strife continued to have impact on the normal school for several more years. In 1889 McMillan again wrote Finger that a campaign was under way to discredit Moore, and he reluctantly recommended that Moore be replaced as principal and teacher. McMillan said it was the intention of the trustees to employ "a wide awake white man, if only for one session, to give the school a new start." As a result of this dispute, Ezra Bauder was hired for the fall term of 1889 and served the institution through the completion of the fall 1890 term. Moore, however, continued to serve on the Board of Trustees.

FIGURE 1.8. *Ezra Bauder. Second principal and teacher of Croatan Normal School from 1889 to 1890.* The National Cyclopaedia of American Biography *(1898).*

Bauder was the first of numerous itinerant teachers who would lead the institution during its first decades. Many, like Moore, were ministers and men of deep religious faith, mostly Baptist or Methodist. Their professional and religious backgrounds set the tone for the educational, religious, and social atmosphere of the campus. Although no evidence has been discovered that details how vacancies at the institution were advertised, a multistate network of religious leaders and church associations in the Carolinas and Virginia might have passed along information about vacancies at the school. During the first four decades, men from central Virginia, all regions of North Carolina, and upstate South Carolina would lead the institution.

As a distinguished citizen of Virginia, Bauder brought to Croatan Normal a wealth of life experiences and knowledge as a teacher and principal. Born at Indian Castle in Herkimer County, New York, on April 6, 1824, Bauder was educated at Kingsboro Academy in New York, the Pennsylvania College, and matriculated at Union College in Schenectady, New York, where he received an AM degree in 1847. He was inducted into the Phi Beta Kappa honor society while at Union College. After completing his AM in 1847 Bauder served briefly as an engineer, tutor to families in Virginia and Maryland, and principal and teacher in Virginia and Michigan. In 1879 Bauder established Brentsville Academy, a boarding and day school, in Brentsville, Virginia, where he resided. He taught engineering and college preparatory courses for several years. The death of his wife in March 1888 compelled Bauder to give up the boarding school. The Culpeper *Observer* on July 3, 1874, described Bauder's success as a teacher: "Prof. Bauder has a peculiar faculty of imparting instruction to his pupils .... Where he has taught, all who have had pupils under his charge have expressed the opinion that he has no superior in the state as an accomplished and successful instructor."

The employment of Bauder, however, did not resolve the crisis. In a letter to Superintendent Finger, dated March 29, 1890, Bauder stated, "I cannot say now whether I will have charge of the school any longer. The Croatans are divided into two parties, mostly on the religious question." He further noted that the Board of Trustees was not united in what it wanted, except to oppose the Lowry faction. He stressed that the dispute had caused many to withdraw their patronage of the institution.

Apparently the growing concerns of state officials, combined with the disruptive effects of local factionalism, caused the Lumbee leaders to reassess the situation and to decide that the institution was more important than their differences—that to continue squabbling might cost them the normal school. While the religious groups continued to pursue separate courses, the normal school was now divorced from the fight. In their report of October 12, 1890, the Board of Trustees stated that the school had not been in operation since July and that the building was still incomplete, but that they had been neither indifferent nor remiss in their efforts "to procure competent instructors and in every way to promote the best interests and secure the highest degree of success to the Institution...." The situation definitely stabilized in this period because, in his 1891–1892 report, Superintendent Finger said, "The Normal Schools for the colored people and the Croatans have been so successful that I have no recommendation to make as to any changes."

One of the major problems of the school in its early years was underfunding. According to the biennial reports of the superintendents, the institution received $500 annually until 1907, when the appropriation was increased to $1,250. Until the early twentieth century, the principal-teacher received a salary of $62.50 per month, pro-rated if he worked less than a full pay period. During the first twenty years of its operation, the school's enrollment varied tremendously, ranging from 15 to 143. Attendance was influenced by many factors, including the labor demands of an agricultural economy; the proximity of students to the institution, because it had no on-campus housing; prevailing attitudes; and the occasional fear of epidemic diseases, such as the smallpox scare of 1904. In its first years of operation, no work was attempted above the eighth-grade level, and the school's curriculum was nonstandard and nontraditional. In 1905 D. F. Lowry received the first diploma issued by the Croatan Normal School for completing a "Scientific Course" of Latin, English, science, mathematics, and history. Recalling his student days many years later, Rev. Lowry observed that students were allowed to study "anything they could handle."

Recognizing as early as 1888 that limited funds were a serious hand-icap, Lumbee leaders sought additional aid from the federal government. This marked the Lumbees first efforts to gain federal Indian services. Fifty-four Indians signed a petition to Congress, asking for "such aid as you may see fit to extend...the amount to be appropriated to be used for the sole and exclusive purpose of assisting your petitioners and other Croatans...to educate their children and fit them for the duties of American citizenship." They emphasized that there were 1,165 school-age children among them. The petitioners concluded by asking that any aid granted be given to the trustees of the normal school "to complete the normal-school building, and that the residue be applied for the purpose of training teachers among the Croatan race who may attend said school." This appeal was supported by Moore in a letter to the Office of Indian Affairs in 1890. "The people for which I am officially interested," wrote Moore, "have a general thing grown up without so much as the rudi-ments of education, yet the youth who have had (to some degree) better opportunities for educating themselves show that the moral, intellectual, and social aptitudes in them are real. Can not something be obtained to assist them in a normal school for them?" This effort was also supported by McMillan, who wrote the government concerning the financial needs of the Indians. On August 11, 1890, T. J. Morgan, commissioner of Indian affairs, finally replied with the government's position. "While I regret exceedingly that the provisions made by the State of North Carolina seem to be entirely inadequate," he wrote, "I find it quite impracticable to render any assistance at this time. The Government is responsible for the education of something like 36,000 Indian children and has provisions for less than half this number. So long as the immediate wards of the Government are so insufficiently provided for, I do not see how I can consistently render any assistance to the Croatans or any other civilized tribes." A shortage of money plagued the institution for years to come.

Bauder's tenure ended in the fall of 1890. He passed away on February 4,

1896, in Brentsville, Virginia. In January 1891 Moore, after again assuming leadership of the institution, opened the spring term of the school and served until March 17, 1891; he was succeeded that month by Charles Stewart, who remained as principal and teacher until 1894. Stewart was born November 2, 1848, in Harnett County, North Carolina. Prior to his appointment, Stewart taught in the Robeson County schools throughout the 1880s. During Stewart's tenure the minimum age for attending the institution was dropped from fifteen to thirteen, with eleven- and twelve-year-olds eligible upon passing an entrance exam. It was reported in this period that the school was "doing good work, and much needed by the people for whose benefit it was established." After leaving the normal school, Stewart continued to teach in Robeson County. He returned to the institution to teach, albeit briefly, in the spring of 1918. He passed away October 15, 1920, while living in Harnett County.

In 1894 the Reverend D.B. (David Balharrie) Simpson took charge of the institution. Simpson was born in Scotland in 1858 and attended the United Free Church of Scotland Training College Normal School and the University of Edinburgh, both in Edinburgh, Scotland, receiving a BA degree, and the Liverpool School of Science and the London University Institute, both in England. He served as principal of St. Andrew's High Grade School in Liverpool, England, and a pupil teacher for five years in Forfar, Scotland, before immigrating to the United States around 1887. Before coming to Croatan Normal in 1894 Simpson served as the principal of high schools in Loudon and Morganton, Tennessee. He was also a Presbyterian minister. Simpson has been described as one of the ablest teachers the school ever had. Under Principal Simpson's direction, academic standards were raised and the school began to acquire a reputation for scholarship. Not long after leaving Croatan Normal in 1895 Simpson continued his career in education. He served as the principal of Reidville Female College in Reidville, and Greer High School in Greer, both in South Carolina, and again as principal of Loudon High School and superintendent of Loudon County schools in East Tennessee. Simpson moved to Cumberland, New Mexico, where he served as principal of Cumberland College. From 1911 to 1912 he was an instructor at East Tennessee State Normal School, now East Tennessee State University. Simpson passed away in Dexter, New Mexico, on March 18, 1912.

For the remainder of the nineteenth century, the school was headed by a succession of short-term principals who were white: Isaac W. Lanner (1895–1896), P.B. Hiden (1896–1898), and G.W. Jones (1898–1899). The *Centennial History* of the university noted that a J. Lamb served as principal from 1895 to 1896. However, state records show that Lanner and Hiden served during that time. The surnames Lanner and Lamb sound very similar. Since records are fragmentary, the full identity of the head of the institution from 1895 to 1986 may never be known. Following Lanner was P.B. (Philip Barbour) Hiden. Born May 22, 1842, in Orange County, Virginia, Hiden descended from elite Virginia families. His father was a state legislator, and of his mother's two uncles, one was a governor of Virginia, U.S. senator, U.S. secretary of war, and U.S. minister to the United Kingdom, while the other was Speaker of the U.S. House of Representatives. Hiden was a private in the Montpelier Guard, Company A, Thirteenth Virginia Infantry, that was ordered to Charles Town, Virginia, now in West Virginia, during abolitionist John Brown's 1859 raid at Harpers Ferry. Although the company did not participate in Brown's capture, it did serve as Brown's escort to his execution. Hiden enlisted in the Confederate Army and served throughout 1861. The following January, Hiden enrolled at the Virginia Military Institute, graduating in 1865. While a student at VMI he fought in the battle at New Market. Hiden studied law at the University of Virginia and Washington College, today Washington and Lee University, receiving a BL degree from Washington College in 1867. Interestingly, Hiden's diploma from Washington College was signed by former Confederate gen. Robert E. Lee, head of the institution and later its namesake. Hiden practiced law in Orange County during the 1870s and 1880s. Prior to leading Croatan Normal from 1896 to 1898 Hiden served as a principal at schools in Fluvanna and Nelson Counties in Virginia during the late 1880s. After leaving Croatan Normal, Hiden farmed and served as a teacher with the Commission of Indian Affairs' Indian School Service in Arizona at Tuba City School, a government Navajo training school, between 1902 and 1904. One year later, he was a teacher in Newport News, Virginia. Between 1905 and 1915, while living in Washington, DC, Hiden was a clerk with the General Land Office and a Freemason. Hiden died from pneumonia on January 7, 1915, while visiting his son in Newport News.

FIGURE 1.9. *O. R. Sampson.*
A pioneer in Lumbee educa-
tion who served as principal
of Croatan Normal School
in 1899 and on the Board
of Trustees for thirty years.
Namesake of Sampson
Academic Building.

In 1899, one of the major figures in the school's history, the Reverend Oscar R. Sampson, had to complete the term of Principal G. W. Jones. The establishment and survival of the institution owed a great deal to determined leaders like Rev. W. L. Moore, the first Board of Trustees, and Hamilton McMillan. While these leaders can appropriately be called the Founders of the school, they were greatly aided by men like Sampson, a devoted member of the normal school's Board of Trustees. Although born January 17, 1866, Sampson attended the first session of the normal school in 1888 at the age of twenty-one and would continue his pursuit of education for the rest of his life. He was appointed a member of the school's Board of Trustees in 1896 and remained on it for the next thirty-two years, thirty of them as chairman.

FIGURE 1.10. *T. C. Henderson.*
Principal of Croatan Normal
School (1900–1904) and
superintendent of The Cherokee
Indian Normal School of
Robeson County (1918–1922).

Under his guidance, the institution grew from a one-teacher school whose physical plant was worth $1,000 to a two-year normal school whose combined primary, secondary, and normal classes totaled over five hundred students, employed twenty-four teachers, and had a value of $250,000. But the physical growth of the school was only one area of his contribution; he also gave the school his labor, time, money, and prayers. Sampson was himself a teacher for forty years, a farmer, and a Baptist minister. He unexpectedly died on January 9, 1928. His death caused N.C. Newbold of the State Department of Public Instruction to write that Sampson was "not only a good Indian, but as far as my judgment goes, one of the best men I have ever known of any race." In later years, after the institution had become a college, his name adorned three buildings—an administrative building, a library, and a classroom building—at different times.

In February 1900 another key figure, Professor T.C. (Thomas Calhoun) Henderson became the principal, and the institution began to make real progress. Born October 9, 1871, in Macon County, North Carolina, Henderson was a graduate of Cullowhee Academy, known today as Western Carolina University, in 1897 and Peabody Normal School, later the Peabody College of Vanderbilt University. Henderson was a resident of Brevard in Transylvania County, North Carolina. His teaching career began in 1897 in the small one-room cabin schools in Transylvania County. Henderson was a dedicated teacher and active church member who stressed both "moral culture" and "mental development." While at Pates, Henderson was an active member in the all-Indian Burnt Swamp Baptist Association. He was the kind of individual who used his own money to purchase books for the use of the students. The trustees, in their annual report to the state superintendent, said that Henderson "has been earnestly endeavoring to raise the standard of work in our Normal, and has spared neither effort nor money in trying to carry out his plans." They later reported that his "Whole life seemed to be wrapped up in the work, and he continues to grow in favor with our people." Henderson escaped a terrible fate on the night of January 16, 1902, when fire engulfed

FIGURE I.II. *First building of Croatan Normal School. The structure, built in 1888 by the Lumbee people, was located in the Pates community, one and a half miles west of Pembroke.*

the home of Henry Biggs in the Pates community. Henderson, a boarder, lost clothing and books valued at thirty dollars. No one was injured in the fire. It was also during Henderson's initial administration that the state superintendent's office created the subordinate position of super-intendent of the State Colored Normal Schools and Croatan Normal School. This official became the immediate supervisor of the Indian institution, an arrangement that existed through the 1920s. It reflected the segregationist attitudes and policies that continued to prevail in state government. Henderson resigned in 1904 to accept the position of super-intendent of schools for Transylvania County, where he served until 1918.

In 1905 M.E. Clark, a native of Cherokee County, North Caro-lina, assumed the headship of the normal school, serving into the fall of 1905, when D.F. Lowry completed his term. Lowry opened the fall term on October 23, 1905, and served until the end of the spring 1906 term. Born January 8, 1881, in the Elrod community, south of Pembroke, Lowry holds a venerable place in the history of the institution as its first graduate and in the Lumbee community as a minister and political leader. He served on the Board of Trustees for a number of years and continued in the Methodist ministry, helping organize many churches, including the First Methodist Church of Pembroke, before retiring from the ministry at age seventy-two. Rev. Lowry, a nephew of Lumbee hero Henry Berry Lowrie, tirelessly advocated for federal recognition of the Indians of Robeson County; he led a movement to adopt "Lumbee"—a name used by Indians for the river—as the official tribal name in 1952.

FIGURE 1.12. *D. F. Lowry. First graduate of Croatan Normal School in 1905 and namesake for D. F. Lowry Building.*

Prior to his death on August 13, 1977, Lowry helped establish the outdoor drama *Strike at the Wind!*, which told the story of Henry Berry Lowrie. The D.F. Lowry Building, which served as the student center between 1965 and 1987, is named in his honor.

Lowry was then followed by T.M. (Thomas Moore) Seawell, who led the institution from 1906 to 1907. He was born December 8, 1885, in Carthage, North Carolina. Seawell had served as principal of Ashpole Institute, a college preparatory school in Fairmont, North Carolina, since August 1905. He benefitted from the increase in the state appropriation to $1,250 and was able to hire Miss M.E. Sharpe as the first full-time assistant teacher. By this point the school had ninety-seven students enrolled in the public school courses it offered and forty-six students taking classes in the Normal Department, though there was still no normal certificate being awarded. The 1907 Summer Institute at Croatan Normal, attended by Indian teachers, proved to be such a huge success that an Indian Teachers' Association was established. The association met annually on the normal school campus for subsequent decades.

By this time, the school had outgrown its original building, and the center of activity had shifted to Pembroke. Consequently, the decision was made to move the institution to its present location in the town of Pembroke, where a new classroom building and dormitory would be constructed. In the early twentieth century, Pembroke, which was chartered in 1895, was becoming the trade center for the Indian community, replacing earlier centers at Pates and Moss Neck. Pembroke developed at the junction of major north-south and east-west rail lines, a distinction it still has. A new site in Pembroke was desirable because of its proximity to the town and train depot. The Indians began a fund-raising campaign to support the move. At the June 28, 1907, Commencement, refreshments were sold by students. On August 2, 1907, trustee James E. Dial Sr. held a dinner with entertainment near his home in the Saddletree community. On October 31, 1907, the Board of Trustees purchased ten acres of land from E.L. (Erastus Lincoln) Odum (1860–1938) and his wife, Elizabeth "Lizzie" (1863–1940), for five hundred dollars. The ten acres now constitute the southeast corner of campus. Odum Street, which forms the eastern border of campus, is named for the Odums. Soon after donating land in 1917 for the Odum Baptist Home for Children, also located adjacent to the eastern edge of campus, the Odums relocated to Georgia.

In October 1907 an institute "designed to encourage the education of [Croatan] children" was held on the campus. Among the hundreds who attended were special guests John Duckett, superintendent of State Colored Normal Schools and Croatan Normal School, and state auditor B.F. Dixon. They were both "delighted with the progress that is being made by the Croatans, industrially, morally, and educationally." Also in attendance was an iconic figure in Lumbee history: Rhoda (Strong) Lowrie, the wife of Henry Berry Lowrie. She lived within walking distance of the campus; Lowrie's presence demonstrated that she was "much interested in Croatan education."

After his resignation from Croatan Normal at the end of the fall 1907 term, Seawell's career took a variety of twists and turns throughout

FIGURE 1.13. *H. L. Edens. Principal and teacher of Croatan Normal School (1908–1911)*
and The Indian Normal School of Robeson County (1911–1912). Seated in front of campus
building with students during a visit to Pates campus by Fred A. Olds in 1908.
COURTESY OF NORTH CAROLINA MUSEUM OF HISTORY.

the southeastern United States. He served as the business manager for
the *Gainesville Sun* in Florida and editor for newspapers in Winnsboro,
South Carolina and Fayetteville, North Carolina. Seawell served as an
insurance executive in Waynesville, North Carolina, before passing away
February 11, 1949, in Clarke, Georgia.

The vacancy at Croatan Normal prompted Superintendent Duckett
to ask Robeson County resident H.L. (Henry Luther) Edens to meet
with the Board of Trustees about the job opening. Duckett considered
Edens a "satisfactory principal." After meeting with Edens to consider
areas of improvement at the school, the trustees elected him as principal
in December 1907. Edens opened the session that following January.
Born in 1857 in Marlboro County, South Carolina, near Bennettsville, he
earned a two-year normal degree from Wofford College in Spartanburg,
South Carolina. Professor Edens's educational career spanned fifty-six
years and included stops at many schools in Marlboro County and

Anson, Carteret, Hoke, Martin, and Robeson Counties in North Carolina. In Robeson County, he taught and served as headmaster of schools
in Red Springs, Barkers, and Marietta. A "champion of education" with
a zeal for causes such as Indian education, Edens led the institution until
the conclusion of the spring 1912 term.

Fred A. Olds, a well-known North Carolina personality, visited
the campus on May 22, 1908 to attend Commencement ceremonies.
Director of the North Carolina Hall of History, the predecessor of the
North Carolina Museum of History, Olds was a collector of antiquities
and possessed an interest in the Indians of Robeson County. Two extant
photos of campus—one of the building and another of Professor Edens
seated in front of the structure with students in the background—were
taken that day. The building photo and an account of Olds's visit were
published one year later in Mary C. Norment's fourth edition of *The
Lowrie History*, her account of the Lowrie War. Olds briefly described
the campus, its students, and his guide, Preston Locklear, a member of
the Board of Trustees.

At the conclusion of the spring 1908 term, Superintendent Duckett
demanded that the Board of Trustees extend the length of contracts for
the principal and assistant teacher from five months to a full year. Prior
to this, contracts were renewed at the end of each term, which periodi-
cally resulted in midyear changes in the school's administration. On the
average, between 1888 and 1908, principal tenures averaged less than two
years. After the Board of Trustees adopted Buckett's demand, tenures
for Edens and his four successors almost doubled to an averaged three
and a half years. This change brought stability in the school's leadership, resulting in less frequent turnover. As a result, Edens and the newly
hired Belle Armstrong, a native of Washington, Pennsylvania, were given
one-year contracts for the 1908–1909 term.

In the 1908–1910 biennial report of the superintendent of public
instruction, J.A. Bivins, superintendent of the State Colored Normal
Schools and Croatan Normal School, wrote concerning the Indians,

"These people are thoroughly interested in their school, and the school has had a marked influence on them for good." As evidence, the Board of Trustees renewed efforts to secure a state appropriation for the new building at Pembroke. The Board met in 1909 and directed Edens to make a special trip to Raleigh, the state capital, to lobby for the appropriation. Edens, along with O. R. Sampson, chairman of the Board of Trustees, and five female students, traveled to Raleigh to address a joint delegation representing the House, Senate, and state school officials. According to Edens, the Croatan Normal delegation "evidently made a favorable impression" on the legislators, who responded with a three-thousand-dollar appropriation toward the new building. Afterward, a state official complemented Sampson's remarks by calling him "the finest speaker I've ever heard from Robeson." Edens was "delighted" with the

FIGURE 1.14. *Classroom Building. First building constructed on the Pembroke campus. Completed in 1909; removed in 1924. Located on site of present-day Herbert G. Oxendine Science Building.*

possibilities "for … enlarged and more efficient educational prospects" but was not content to stop "the wheels of progress there." He told James Y. Joyner, the state superintendent of public instruction, Bivins, and others that "black and white races had college privileges while the Indians had none within their native state[,] and[,] in fairness to a larger segment of industrious citizens[,] this injustice ought to be remedied." Following the triumph of the Croatan Normal delegation, the Indians continued fund-raising efforts.

The final Commencement at the Pates campus was held May 24, 1909. Although special efforts were made to complete the new class-room building in time for the fall term, the new school year opened on October 4 at Pates. A "great day," though, was had that following November 13 when hundreds gathered in the auditorium of the new building at Pembroke to celebrate Indian education and the pending completion of the structure, and to raise the final funds to pay for its completion. All local subscriptions were due that day, and to ensure that the people turned out, entertainment was provided by "the Croatan brass band" and selected speakers. *The Robesonian*, the county's major newspaper, reported the willingness of elder Indians to donate funds for the cause. The reporter wrote, "Many of the old Croatans, gray headed, stooped and tottering with age, who have never had the opportunity of spending a day in school, could be seen pushing their way through the crowd to hand over their hard-earned money in order that their children may have the advantage of an education." Thanks to their donations and those of others in attendance, nearly the entire requisite amount was raised at the rally. All monies had to be in hand before the building could be turned over to the Board of Trustees. The Indians' determina-tion to raise funds for the new building mirrored similar efforts in 1887, again demonstrating their dedication to the normal school and Indian education in Robeson County. The new two-story clapboard building, "handsome in appearance" and one of which the Indians "may justly feel proud," had several classrooms and an auditorium that accommodated nearly five hundred people. It was erected on the site of the present-day Herbert G. Oxendine Science Building. With the state appropriation, plus eight hundred dollars raised locally, the school was moved after the completion of the new building to its present site with minimal disruption in November 1909.

The physical transfer of the institution was an important development, but even more significant was the symbolic importance of the change. The first two decades had been years of turmoil for the school—years of funding problems, internal factionalism, trying to establish a sound education base, and seeking and finally getting strong community support and leadership. The Indian people were aware of the school and of its potential, and by the early twentieth century, it had become a viable part of the Lumbee community, along with their struggle for a separate Indian identity and equal opportunity. While many problems would continue to arise for the institution, by 1909 it was firmly established on a solid foundation. The move to the Pembroke area signaled a break with the tumultuous problems of the school's start. It symbolically represented a new beginning, though one built on the achievements and experiences of the past. The institution had stabilized and now entered an era of growth and expansion.

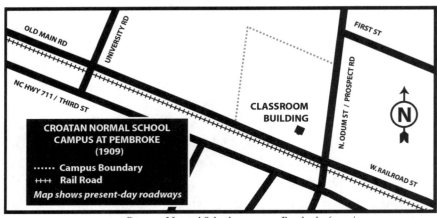

MAP 1.2. *Croatan Normal School campus at Pembroke (1909)*.

TIMELINE OF NOTABLE INSTITUTIONAL EVENTS (1887–1909)

1887
- Petition to establish a normal school for Indians in Robeson County submitted to the North Carolina General Assembly.
- Croatan Normal School established by General Assembly after enacting legislation sponsored by Representative Hamilton McMillan.

1888
- W.L. (William Luther) Moore selected as first principal and teacher; Croatan Normal School opened at Pates with one teacher and fifteen students.

1889
- Ezra Bauder selected as principal.

1891
- W.L. Moore opened spring term as principal.
- Charles Stewart selected as principal.

1894
- D.B. (David Balharrie) Simpson selected as principal.

1895
- Isaac W. Lanner selected as principal.

1896
- P.B. (Philip Barbour) Hiden selected as principal.

1898
- G.W. Jones selected as principal.

1899
- O. (Oscar) R. Sampson selected as principal to complete term of Jones.

1900
- T.C. (Thomas Calhoun) Henderson selected as principal.

1905
- M.E. Clark selected as principal.
- D.F. Lowry became the first graduate of Croatan Normal School after completing a "Scientific Course."
- D.F. Lowry selected as principal to complete term of Clark.

1906
- T.M. (Thomas Moore) Seawell selected as principal.

1907
- Board of Trustees purchased ten acres of land from E.L. and Lizzie Odum for new campus in Pembroke.
- Rhonda (Strong) Lowrie, wife of Henry Berry Lowrie, attended an "institute" at Croatan Normal School.

1908
- H.L. (Henry Luther) Edens, selected the previous December as principal, opened the spring term.
- Length of contract for principal and teacher extended to one year.

1909
- Appropriation received from General Assembly for new classroom building in Pembroke.
- Final Commencement exercises held at Pates campus.
- Croatan Normal School moved to Pembroke.

Chapter Two

1910–1929
THE NORMAL SCHOOL COMES OF AGE

*Students were graduated . . . every year [after 1924], and there in
turn spread the gospel of education among the [Lumbee] people.*

G. G. Maughon Sr., superintendent,
The Cherokee Indian Normal School of
Robeson County, semicentennial history
in *The Robesonian* (November 29, 1937)

The years from 1910 to 1929 represented a period of adjustment,
consolidation, and growth for the normal school. During this
period, the institution slowly but steadily improved in the quality and
quantity of its educational outcomes.

There were, at the beginning of the period, several important legal
changes that affected both the Indians and the school. By 1911, because
many whites had turned the name "Croatan" into a racial slur—refer-
ring to the people as "Cros," associating the term with "blackness," and
thereby questioning their Indianness—a movement was started to gain a
new name with no derogatory connotations. On March 8 of that year, the
General Assembly was sympathetic and, indicative of the relationship
between the Indians and the school, changed the name of the people to

the "Indians of Robeson County" and, at the same time, renamed the
school The Indian Normal School of Robeson County. That same day,
the General Assembly enacted legislation giving the Board of Trustees
the authority to transfer, by deed, the property of the normal school
to the State Board of Education and give that agency the authority
to appoint the institution's Board of Trustees. The General Assembly's
actions were precipitated by Principal Edens's suspicions about the institution's "status" with the state. After further investigation and a meeting
with the Board of Trustees, James E. Dial Sr., a trustee, suggested that
Edens travel immediately to Raleigh to further investigate his suspicions. While in Raleigh, Edens shared his view with James Y. Joyner, the
state superintendent of public instruction, who said Edens was mistaken.
To convince Edens of the error in his thinking, Joyner had Edens visit
state attorney general Thomas Bickett. The attorney general agreed with
Edens's surprising conclusion: due to vagueness in the language in the
1887 legislation, whether intentional on the part of McMillan or by pure
accident, the Indian Normal School was not the property of the state of
North Carolina but the Indian Normal's Board of Trustees and, indi-
rectly, the Indians of Robeson County. As a result, the state had neither
obligation nor legal authority to make supporting appropriations. Sent
to Raleigh by the trustees to "remedy anything that...[he] might find
wrong," Edens consulted with Bickett, who said that for the normal
school to become a legal state institution, each member of the Board of
Trustees had to sign a deed transferring the property to the state. Bickett
drew up a deed to make the transfer from tribal property to state ownership. On June 16, 1911, each of the seven trustees affixed their signature or
mark to the deed transferring ownership of the normal school from the
Board of Trustees to the state Board of Education.

In 1913, new efforts arose to rename the tribe. The 1911 tribal name
change, as one Lumbee scholar noted, "pleased nobody and settled
nothing." Proponents of the 1913 name change included Indian leaders

such as Rev. D. F. Lowry, and Angus W. McLean (1870–1935), an influential white Democrat from Lumberton and a future governor of North Carolina from 1925 to 1929. McLean argued that the Indians of Robeson County were descendants of Cherokees who fought with Colonel John Barnwell's South Carolina militia during the Tuscarora War (1711–1715) and settled in Robeson County at the conclusion of the conflict. At their insistence, on March 11, 1913, the Indians were given the name "Cherokee Indians of Robeson County," with the institution becoming The Cherokee Indian Normal School of Robeson County. The institution retained the Cherokee name until 1941; the people kept the name until 1952.

Although the 1911 clarification of the school's status with the state diminished local control over the institution, it secured future funding for the school. One day following the school's second name change, the General Assembly, on March 12, 1913, increased its annual appropriation to $2,250, making it possible for the school to hire more teachers and offer a wider variety of courses. A measure of the growth of the school can be seen in the fact that in 1910 the school employed a principal and two teachers, but by 1918 it was employing a principal and seven teachers. Early teacher Belle Armstrong stands out for having started a model school program at the institution that was designed to incorporate agricultural education in the curriculum of rural schools. This proved a useful step given the agrarian environment of Robeson County, seen even in the seasonally adjusted school terms, which ran from October through December and January through May.

In 1912, with the support of North Carolina's U.S. senator Furnifold Simmons, the Indians made another effort to get federal assistance to improve their educational opportunities. Simmons introduced and got passed in the Senate a bill "To acquire a Site and Erect Buildings for a School for the Indians of Robeson County, N.C. and for Other Purposes." The intent of the bill was to provide fifty thousand dollars to establish an industrial school for the Lumbees. The bill further provided for an annual appropriation of ten thousand dollars for its support. Such an institution would be under the supervision of the Secretary of the Interior, and such a development would have implicitly given the Lumbees federal recognition as Indians.

Upon passage by the Senate, the measure was then taken up by the House of Representatives in 1913, which referred it to the House Committee on Indian Affairs. This committee, chaired by John H. Stephens of Texas, held a public hearing. Among the advocates of the bill at the hearing were Senator Simmons; Rep. Hannibal L. Godwin, a Democratic lawyer from Harnett County, North Carolina; Angus W. McLean; and Preston Locklear, now seventy-five years old but still a supporter of Indian education. During the course of the hearing, Simmons and the delegation stressed that North Carolina had three separate school systems, and that the Indians had far fewer educational opportunities than the other two races. When Chairman Stephens asked whether it would not be better to give funds to the existing schools, such as the normal school, the delegation pointed out that the Lumbees could get "academic training" but could not get industrial training. Godwin then argued that there was "ample precedent for this bill to be reported favorably" because the U.S. government had established other nonreservation schools at places such as Haskell, Kansas, "without respect to any particular tribe of Indians" in other parts of the country. This prompted the committee to inquire as to whether the Lumbees could attend other existing Indian schools. The committee was told that a few Lumbees had gone off to school but that most were too poor and the distances too great for this to be a solution. It was further emphasized that the normal school only partially met their educational needs. Senator Simmons then bluntly stated that "they have absolutely no opportunity for agricultural or mechanical or industrial training under the system that obtains in North Carolina....There is no college in the State where the higher branches are taught that is open to the Indians. It is for the purpose of giving them these facilities that we are asking the Government to establish this school." In conclusion, he said of the Lumbees, "I do not think that there is any class of our people in recent years that have shown more interest in trying to educate their children than they have."

Although the committee was interested in the Lumbees, their history, and their problems, it was not very sympathetic to the idea that the federal government should give them an industrial college. In the final analysis the committee decided against giving this bill a favorable report for a variety of reasons. It felt that the Lumbees could attend any of the twenty-two nonreservation schools supported by the government, that the expenditure of requested funds was unwarranted, and that the government should not extend recognition to the Lumbees. Chairman Stephens said at one point that "these Indians have never been under the control of the United States and have never been recognized as wards of the Government, and this is the first effort ever made to take jurisdiction of these Indians since I have been on this committee." Rep. Charles H. Burke, a Republican real estate developer from South Dakota who served on the committee, argued that the Lumbees were not of comparable status to other Indians who attended nonreservation schools, and he frankly stated his opposition when he remarked, "It is my belief that these Indians have no right to enter any Indian school because they are not full-blood Indians."

Though the effort to get a federally funded industrial school for the Lumbees ended in failure, it did have the effect of more thoroughly drawing them to the attention of the federal authorities, indicating future directions of development for the normal school, and further helping to explain why the normal school has always been of major importance to the Lumbee people. Quite simply, historical developments, sometimes by default, made it the educational, cultural, and social center of the Indian community.

In 1914 Senator Simmons introduced a resolution in the Senate calling for an investigation into the status and condition of the Indians of southeastern North Carolina; this resolution was passed, and in the summer of 1914 the Indian Office sent Special Agent O.M. McPherson to conduct an investigation and write a report. He met on several occasions with the leaders of the Indian community, and on August 11, 1914, he attended a mass meeting at the normal school called by the Order of the Redmen, a select group of Indian leaders in a fraternal organization known locally as the Redman's Lodge. McPherson recommended that the federal government fund an industrial school for the Indian people, but nothing came of it. However, the "McPherson Report" continues to be a primary source of information on Lumbee history to this day. The failure to gain an industrial college no doubt benefitted the normal school, for it caused the Lumbees to focus their attention and energy on the one educational asset they did have.

Despite all the political activity of the time, the work of the normal school continued. Earlier in 1912, during the institution's twenty-fifth year, John A.B. Lowry (1890–1958), son of Rev. Henry H. Lowry and nephew of Rev. D.F. Lowry, of the Elrod community, became the first high school graduate and second graduate of the institution; he later received a doctor of medicine degree from the University of Maryland School of Medicine and became a physician in Crewe, Virginia. Lowry was also a veteran of World War I. As the spring 1912 term drew to a close, Professor Edens learned that the Indians wished for a change in principalship. In response, he made contact with State Superintendent of Public Instruction Joyner, who expressed his pleasure with Edens's tenure as principal. Edens, however, made a decision that surely surprised Joyner yet simultaneously supported the self-governance and self-determination of the Indians of Robeson County. He obliged the request of the Indians, because, according to Edens, "The Indians are not to be deprived of their inherent right to a voice in their own progress, [and] ... the sympathetic support of the Trustees could only be secured by their choice of a principal." The conclusion of Edens's tenure, however, did not end his interest in the Indian Normal School or his advocacy for Indian education in

Robeson County. After leaving the institution, Edens continued to teach in Robeson County, including a stint at East Lumberton School. In 1937 he was given the official title of "Pioneer Educator" by Robeson County. Less than one year before he passed away on September 13, 1941, in Lumberton, Edens shared memories of time spent at the normal school in a letter dated November 22, 1940, to former Croatan Normal student and Board of Trustee member Martin Luther Lowry Sr. One memory, in particular, convinced Edens of Hamilton McMillan's claim that the Indians of Robeson County were descendants of coastal tribes and the Lost Colony. While the school was still at Pates, Edens asked a group of children, not pupils, "Where are your fathers?" They replied, "Des up dere at de housen." Edens took "their peculiar tone" and use of the old English plural *en* as evidence of the Indians' European ancestry. Edens also rejoiced "that some of those patient, Christian, patriotic Trustees are still living to see the fruits of their past labors crowned with a glorious success—a triumphal present college for their youth's higher education."

The fall 1912 session began under the leadership of Principal O.V. (Otto Vetas) Hamrick Sr. A native of Shelby, North Carolina, Hamrick was born on September 30, 1887. He received a BA degree from Wake Forest College, now Wake Forest University. During his tenure, Winnie Lee (Bell) Jenkins (1898–1992) and Ruth (Sampson) Locklear (1897–1929) received their high school diplomas in 1914, becoming the first female and third and fourth graduates of the institution. Together they went to Carson-Newman College—today Carson-Newman University—in Tennessee;

FIGURE 2.1. *O. V. Hamrick Sr. Principal of The Indian Normal School of Robeson County (1912–1913) and The Cherokee Indian Normal School of Robeson County (1913–1914).*
COURTESY OF WAKE FOREST UNIVERSITY, *THE HOWLER* (1910).

FIGURE 2.2. *H. A. Neal. Principal of The Cherokee Indian Normal School of Robeson County from 1914 to 1918. Pictured (center) with students in front of Girls' Dormitory circa 1916.*
COURTESY OF DOROTHY L. BLUE '55.

received BA degrees in 1920 and 1919, respectively; and became success-ful teachers. They taught in Florida for a number of years. Jenkins taught mathematics and science after settling in Iron Mountain, Michigan. Locklear returned to teach at Cherokee Normal during the early 1920s. After leaving the institution at the conclusion of the 1914 spring session, Hamrick continued his career as an educator, including a stop as the prin-cipal of a high school in Goldsboro, North Carolina. Hamrick died Octo-ber 25, 1960, while living in Shelby.

H.A. (Henry Augustus) Neal led Cherokee Normal from 1914 to 1918. A native of Durham, North Carolina, Neal was born on March 6, 1881. He received a BA degree from Trinity College, now Duke Univer-sity, in 1906. As the normal school's enrollment increased, the need for on-campus housing became increasingly apparent, and the institution's first dormitory, for female students, was completed in 1915. The total value of the school, including land, buildings, and fixtures, was determined to be $8,950 in 1916. During this same period, Principal Neal was paid $1,070 for twelve months' service, and the teachers were paid, depending upon how long they had worked for the school, between $440 and $540 for eight months' service.

In his reports to the state superintendent of public instruction, Principal Neal provided a clear picture of the school and its operation during his administration. In his 1916 report, Neal described the ten-acre institution. "On this piece of land," he wrote, "there are two buildings. One is a dormitory recently erected at a cost of about $3,700 and containing 12 bedrooms, a linen room, a dining-room and a cookroom. The other building is used as a school building, and contains three recitation rooms and an auditorium." According to his report, the auditorium was filled with "home-made seats" and contained one Stieff piano, "paid for by the patrons of the School." Heat was provided by cast-iron heaters. The school also had a library "worth about $50." Both two-story clapboard buildings, the dormitory was located at the southern end of the present-day Quad, while the classroom building was located on the present-day site of the Herbert G. Oxendine Science Building. In 1916 the institution employed one principal and three female assistants, all of whom were white. One teacher was responsible for the first three grades, the second for the next three, and the principal and third teacher for the seventh through tenth grades. He noted that "domestic science" had been added to the curriculum and that it was a great success. "The parents say their girls are interested in house-work as never before, are cooking better than they once did, and are making the family clothes that were hired made before. They are able to see the benefit and do not fail to say so. It is unfortunate that we cannot give more time to this phase of the work." Neal also took this opportunity to stress the need of the school for more money. He pointed out that the dormitory needed furnishings, the classroom building needed repairs, and the school needed more space

FIGURE 2.3. *Classroom Building and Girls' Dormitory. First two buildings on the
Pembroke campus, constructed in 1909 and 1915, respectively. The Girls' Dormitory, the first
housing provided for female students on the campus, was moved from the south end of the
Quad to west of Faculty Row in 1952. Later known as Britt Dorm. Razed in 1965.*

and teachers to meet the demand for enrollment. He concluded this
report by stressing that the Indians needed "one good school that will
fit [prepare] their boys and girls to teach their schools and give those
who want it a preparation that will enable them to enter college. The
education we will give them will make better citizens and better farmers
of them, and the State of North Carolina will be benefitted."

Two years later, as he was leaving the institution, Neal sent his last
report to the state superintendent. This report was more pessimistic than
the first. He noted that because most of the people were farmers, he did
not believe that the school was "reaching the people as it should do." He
favored more emphasis on vocational education and home economics.
"In my opinion," he wrote, "the thing that is needed at the Cherokee
Normal is something on the order of one of our Farm-life schools. If we
can teach the Indian boys how to farm and care for livestock they will
be better farmers and make more money. If you will teach the girls how

to cook, how to sew, and how to select their clothes, they will all live better and be more contented." Interestingly, in the future, the institution did develop both agricultural and home economics departments, though both would be phased out as the school evolved into a university.

In his closing remarks, Neal commented on the character of the Indian people. "The Indian," he observed, "is not like the Negro. The Negro takes what we give him and pretends to be thankful whether he is or not, because he knows that is the best thing for him to do. The Indian will not do it.... Ninety percent of the Indians believe the State is not doing its duty by them so far as a school is concerned. They resent it and harbor their resentment because it is the nature of the Indian to do so. But if the State will do a small part of what it should and furnish them a school they will respect, they will patronize it, be benefitted by it and benefit us in return." Neal left the institution in the summer of 1918; he passed away on January 15, 1956, in Durham.

After Neal called attention to the institution's potential and problems, the school experienced a real surge of progress under the leadership of T.C. (Thomas Calhoun) Henderson, who served a second term as principal from 1918 to 1922. Since leaving Croatan Normal in 1904, Henderson served for a second time as superintendent of the Transylvania County, North Carolina, schools. During that time, the schools made

FIGURE 2.4. *L. R. Varser. State senator (1921–1924) from Lumberton who sponsored legislation that secured the seventy-five-thousand-dollar appropriation for the construction of Old Main.*

tremendous progress, and Henderson was dubbed a "pioneer in education" in Transylvania County. As a consequence of Henderson's energetic policies, Cherokee Normal's enrollment grew from 70 to 192; the faculty increased to seven; new high school courses were offered and vocational courses introduced as the agriculture and home economics departments were added; and, a regular six-week summer school program, for raising and/or renewing teaching certificates, replaced a two-week summer institute in 1918. The title of the head of the institution was changed from "principal" to "superintendent"—a reflection of the school's expansion. In addition, appropriations from the state for maintenance increased from $2,250 to $7,200, and from the county, $300 to $2,190. In his reports to the state superintendent, Henderson, like Neal, was outspoken concerning the importance of the institution to the Lumbee people. On one occasion he wrote, "The State has never provided the room nor the equipment necessary for effective teaching, notwithstanding the fact that this is the only place provided for Indian teachers for the Indian public schools. Practically all of the Indian teachers have received at this school what little preparation and training they have for their work." Henderson went on to say that an additional building was "essential to the future work and growth of the school." The state responded favorably during Henderson's administration, largely because the school found an advocate in Sen. L. (Lycurgus) R. Varser (1878–1959). From Robeson County, Varser served in the state senate from 1921 to 1924 and was appointed as an associate justice of the North Carolina Supreme Court in 1925 by Governor Angus W. McLean, of Lumberton. In 1921 the General Assembly appropriated seventy-five thousand dollars for a modern building, to include a dozen classrooms, administrative offices, four toilets, and a seven-hundred-seat auditorium. The structure, with its towering, stately white columns, was completed in 1923 and became known as Old Main after 1949. The first brick structure on campus, Old Main came to symbolize the Indian origins of the school. Old Main would be the sole classroom building and center of campus activities for the next twenty-five years. Decades later it became the focus of the greatest controversy in the history of the institution. In 1923, however, its completion was an occasion for great rejoicing in the Indian community, and it was used for the spring Commencement exercises of that year. W.L. Moore and O.R. Sampson were speakers during the May 21, 1923, Commencement. Sampson, the chair of the

FIGURE 2.5. *Old Main. The oldest brick building on UNC Pembroke's campus. Erected in 1923, destroyed by fire in 1973, and restored in 1979. Listed on the National Register of Historic Places.*

Board of Trustees, proclaimed the progress of the school and the new structure when he said, "Since 1887, when the Normal was established, till the music of the hammers heralded the erection of the splendid new building we now enjoy, the Indian race has been making progress."

Ironically, the funding of Old Main almost resulted in another new location for the normal school. Because Senator Varser was the key figure in gaining the appropriation for the building and because he wanted it to have great educational impact, he consulted with a close Lumbee friend, Calvin "Fent" Lowry (1860–1933), about where it would have the greatest effect. Lowry suggested that it be built at Union Chapel in the Burnt Swamp Township, which was, in the 1920s, a center of political, social, religious, and economic activity. Lowry, a prominent member of the Union Chapel community, was chairman of the Board of Trustees for Laurel Institute, the Indian school at Union Chapel. When the news got out that there was a proposal to move the normal school to Union Chapel, about four miles northeast of Pembroke, Henderson; O.R.

Sampson, chairman of the Board of Trustees; and Lumbee educator Anderson N. Locklear took the train to Raleigh where they stayed until they had persuaded Senator Varser and the State Board of Education not to relocate the normal school again. Their most convincing arguments were that another move would be disruptive since the school was already well established and that Pembroke was a better location because it was served by two railroads and the best highway in the area, making it more readily accessible. After this abortive attempt in 1921, there have been no further efforts to move the institution.

A final major development of Henderson's important administration involved the issue of local control of the Indian public schools. He reported to the state superintendent in 1920 that three Sappony Indians from Person County and two Coharie Indians from Sampson County were enrolled in Cherokee Normal. Having experienced exclusion from other institutions and fearful of losing control over the public schools created for their benefit if they became general Indian schools, the Lumbees took steps to assure that this would not happen. In 1921 they convinced the state legislature to adopt Chapter 426, a law that created a committee of five Indians "who are residents of Robeson County," and that stated "that all questions affecting the race of those applying for admission into the public schools of Robeson County for the Indian race only shall be referred to the committee," which was given "original, exclusive jurisdiction to hear and determine all questions affecting the race of any person or persons attending the public schools of Robeson County for the Indian race only…" The committee's decisions were final unless reversed by the Superior Court of Robeson County or the Supreme Court of North Carolina. Because Cherokee Normal was under the State Board of Education and considered an Indian public school, the committee's jurisdiction was extended in 1929 to include it. This committee came to be known locally as the "Blood Committee." The General Assembly's actions confirmed the Indians' authority to

FIGURE 2.6. *The Cherokee Indian Normal School of Robeson County campus (circa 1924). From left: Dining Hall, Girls' Dormitory, Old Main, and Classroom Building.*

decide enrollment in its schools. The Lumbees, therefore, saw the law as protective of their interests, rather than exclusionary toward other people. The members of the original "Blood Committee" were Ralph H. Lowry, chair; J.E. Woodell, secretary; James B. Oxendine; William Wilkins; and Calvin Locklear. Lowry (1874–1938), a prominent farmer and proprietor from Pembroke, would later serve as a member of the Board of Trustees at Cherokee Normal during the late 1920s and 1930s, including eight years as chair, until 1937. Lowry's funeral was held in the auditorium at Old Main.

On June 27, 1922, Superintendent Henderson submitted his resignation to N.C. Newbold and the Board of Trustees, effective at the end of the month. He cited the condition of his ailing mother's health, which required him to be away from work for extended periods of time, as the reason for his resignation. Henderson had cared for his sickly parents for the past two decades. The trustees expressed their appreciation of the "valuable service" rendered during his tenure and voiced "sincere regrets" for his resignation. After returning to his home in Western North Carolina, Henderson shared his desires for the future of the institution with *The Robesonian* newspaper. He hoped the General Assembly would appropriate sufficient funds to meet the increased needs of the institution so that it would "become an institution of which the community and the State may be justly proud." Henderson was again elected superintendent of Transylvania County schools. After six years, he then served as a teacher and principal until his retirement at age seventy. Henderson was described as "a lover of young people, and always sought to bridge the chasms and pitfalls that lay in their paths so they might leave the world better than they found it." In recognition of his contributions to education in Transylvania County, T.C. Henderson Elementary School in Lake Toxaway is named in his honor. Henderson died June 17, 1956, in the town of Quebec in Transylvania County. Upon Henderson's resignation, the Board of Trustees turned its attention to finding his replacement; the board would select another native of Transylvania County to lead the institution.

The progressive policies of Henderson were continued by his successor, A.B. (Andrew Beckett) Riley. A math teacher on the Cherokee Normal faculty, Riley served as head of the school from 1922 to 1926. Riley, born April 18, 1869, in South Carolina, was a resident of Brevard, North Carolina. He held an AB degree. Riley became acquainted with his predecessor, T.C. Henderson, long before coming to Pembroke; Riley was employed as a teacher in Transylvania County schools during the first decade of the twentieth century, when Henderson was the superintendent of the county's school system. Along with teaching in Brevard, Riley was a columnist and onetime assistant editor for the *Sylvan Valley News* in Brevard. Under Superintendent Riley, the size of the campus doubled in 1923 to twenty acres with the addition of five acres to the north and to the west of the original ten-acre tract. By 1924 a dining hall had been constructed behind or immediately north of the girls' dorm in the Quad,

FIGURE 2.7. *Boys' Dormitory. The first housing provided for male students on the campus. Later known as McMillan Dorm. Completed in 1925; razed in 1966.*

FIGURE 2.8. *Faculty Row (1953).*

and the first classroom building constructed on the Pembroke campus had been razed. With continued assistance from Senator Varser, a thirty-thousand-dollar building program in 1925 added a second dormitory, for male students, on the site of the Pembroke campus's first building, razed the year earlier, and four cottages—for the superintendent, agriculture teacher, principal, and teachers—along present-day Faculty Row. The cottage for teachers was a two-story building. In addition, the summer school was enlarged; the Board of Trustees was placed under the control of the governor; vocational work was promoted, particularly in agriculture; and in 1924 the high school was accredited by the State Board of Education. Between 1905 and 1922 there were just five graduates of the institution, with four being from the high school. In 1922 Lucy Amanda (Oxendine) Smith (1903–1985) was the lone high school graduate. The high school class of 1924 changed this as they were the first in a line of regular graduating classes from Cherokee Normal. Members of the class were Redmond Cummings, Nettie (Sampson) Locklear, Earl C. Lowry, Clifton Oxendine, Elizabeth (Oxendine) Maynor, Maggie Lee (Oxendine) Maynor, and Stanley Sampson. Administrative changes, reflecting the growth of the campus, were also made at the institution. Beginning in 1923 the school had a superintendent, who was head of the institution, and a principal, S.T. Liles, who supervised the high school.

One of the most colorful and popular teachers at the school during Riley's administration was A.F. (Arthur Foster) Corbin, the vocational education instructor. A native of New York State, Corbin was born on August 25, 1867. He created an interest in both better farming and violin music. He was apparently a generous man who took his students to county and regional activities, helping to break down social and racial barriers. During the summer he traveled about the area in an old Ford truck, checking on the farm projects of his students and teaching many of them how to drive. Corbin organized a farm improvement corporation with the agricultural students as stockholders, the purpose of which was to teach the students more about scientific agriculture. Each share of stock in the organization cost ten dollars. With part of the money, the group bought a pure-bred bull—"Duke Johnson"—which was to be used for the selective breeding of livestock. Corbin and his students entered the bull in area fairs, and they generally won blue ribbons because of the quality of his line and huge size. In fact, they found it difficult to house or transport Duke because of his size and strength. Nobody wanted to board him because he was always breaking out, and they could almost never get him to stay on the back of a truck. As a result, they usually had to walk him to the fairs, which sometimes meant several miles. Professor Corbin was a dedicated and respected teacher. On June 4, 1925, Corbin married Adelaide Bulgin (1884–1951), also a member at Cherokee Normal faculty, at Pembroke's First Methodist Church. A

FIGURE 2.9. *Students taking a ride on the farm truck (1921).*

native of Franklin, North Carolina, she received training at Peabody Normal School, later the Peabody College of Vanderbilt University. Corbin died March 24, 1940, in Diamond, Missouri.

Corbin also penned one of the first school songs, titled "Indian Normal School," which was fondly remembered by Howard Oxendine '35. Although the tune is now lost to memory, the lyrics are as follows:

We are the I.N.S. of the old N.C. of the U.S.A. so grand.
So hurrah for our School, hurrah for our state, and hurrah for our native land.

Today we honor the men of old and the mothers of old.
We praise the maidens and youth, the fair, the bold that lived in the olden days.

But we turn to the future and we see a much nobler and
greater race—for we're molding and training here each day
in our dear old I.N.S.

We are the I.N.S. of the old N.C. of the U.S.A. so grand.
So hurrah for our School, hurrah for our state, and hurrah
for our native land.

Our blood runs red like a crimson stream from the foun-
tains of long ago—where our fathers roamed as free as the
wind and feared not any foe.

But we turn to the future, and we see a much nobler and
greater race—for we are molding and training here each day
in our dear old I.N.S.

We are the I.N.S. of the old N.C. of the U.S.A. so grand.
So hurrah for our School, hurrah for our state, and hurrah
for our native land.

———————

The Riley administration also saw several local Indians question the
legality of the normal school's tuition fee, which at the time was four
dollars. The issue of whether it was legal was raised because the institution received money from both the state and county governments, and
some local people felt they had paid for their children to attend the school
with their taxes. This resulted in an exchange of letters between various
educational officials and the state's assistant attorney general. It was
finally ruled that the tuition charge was legal because the state provided
the bulk of the school's monies and because its Board of Trustees was
appointed by the governor.

After resigning as superintendent in 1926 Riley continued on the faculty of Cherokee Normal until July 1929. After a year in Brevard, Riley returned to Robeson County in 1930, teaching in the county's Indian schools until the late 1930s. He was a teacher and principal at Prospect and Union Chapel schools and later taught at Fairmont Indian High School. Throughout his time in Robeson County, Riley continued to spend his summers in Brevard, where he died on December 25, 1949.

With Riley's resignation in 1926, the trustees elected S.B. (Sherman Bryan) Smithey on May 20, 1926, to take charge of the institution. A native of Wilkesboro, North Carolina, Smithey was born on April 10, 1891. He earned a BA degree in 1917 from the University of North Carolina at Chapel Hill, where he had also completed residence requirements for a master's degree. When hired, Smithey was the principal of the high school at Jennings, North Carolina. He had experience

FIGURE 2.10. *S. B. Smithey.
Superintendent of The Cherokee
Indian Normal School of Robeson
County from 1926 to 1929.*
COURTESY OF UNC–CHAPEL HILL, *YACKETY YACK* (1917).

teaching at UNC–Chapel Hill, had been the principal of high schools in Wilkes and Iredell Counties, and was a former principal of the public schools in Ronda in Wilkes County. At the time of his election, Smithey's services were in high demand. Even though his salary as principal at the Jennings high school was increased and he was simultaneously selected as superintendent of the public schools of Ronda, Smithey chose to accept the position at Cherokee Normal. He was recommended for the position by former superintendent A.B. Riley. Smithey taught during summer school at Cherokee Normal in 1925 and "was well thought of by the Indian teachers" who earned credits toward raising their teacher certification.

Smithey proved a controversial figure, having devoted supporters and bitter detractors. Clifton Oxendine '24, early scholar of the school's history, argued that Smithey "gave the Indians the best school they ever had. He reduced the situation in the school itself to order; discipline of a genuine type was put into effect. More than any other man he was responsible for standardizing the normal school." John L. Carter Sr. '26, '29, '43, a Lumbee, agreed with Oxendine. Carter described Smithey as "a very able leader" who "took great interest and pride in trying to improve the status of the institution." Smithey's greatest accomplishment was the implementation of the two-year normal curriculum.

On August 13, 1926, the Board of Trustees approved the addition of a two-year normal degree to the curriculum—to be implemented over the next two years. At the same time, the elementary coursework was phased out. Pembroke Graded School, a component of the institution, opened earlier in 1923 in a separate structure on the north side of campus on the present site of the James B. Chavis University Center. By 1928 Cherokee Normal was offering only high school and normal studies. Consequently, the Normal and High School departments were organized. The Normal Department facilitated the teacher-training curriculum while the aim of the High School Department "was to give a solid secondary educa-tion." Rev. J. (James) R. Lowry (1889–1959) was named the first dean of students. A native of Elrod and nephew of D. F. Lowry, he gradu-ated from Lynchburg College in Lynchburg, Virginia. Lowry joined the Cherokee Normal faculty in 1927. He later became principal of the institution's high school and the first principal of Pembroke High School in 1939. At the forty-first Commencement of the school on June 1, 1928, Smithey was able to announce that the institution had been accredited as a "Standard Normal School," and to award diplomas to the first ten graduates of the two-year normal program: James K. Braboy, Alton B. Brayboy, Marvin Carter, Marguerite (Jones) Holmes, Rev. L. W. Jacobs, Elizabeth (Oxendine) Maynor, Lacy Maynor, Theodore Maynor, Lonnie

FIGURE 2.11. *The Cherokee Indian Normal School of Robeson County girls' basketball team (1928). Posing on the front steps of Old Main. From left to right: front row—Nettie Locklear, Quida Lowry, Agnes Chavis, Ella M. Jones, Lucy Jane Sanderson, Lucy Sampson, Flowers Locklear, and Gladys Woodell; back row—Edna (Queener) Proffitt (teacher and coach) and Louise Templeton.*
COURTESY OF BRUCE BARTON '86.

H. Oxendine, and William Gaston Revels. Interestingly, Jacobs was a member of the Board of Trustees at the time of his graduation.

By 1928 the environment at Cherokee Normal was becoming more academic in nature. By that year, the institution could boast of four literary societies. All of the students in the normal program belonged to the Lyceum Society, while the high school males belonged to either the Lumbee or the Philomathean societies, and the high school females joined the Excelsior Society. These societies were considered an important part of the school curriculum, and students' grades were tied to their participation in various programs. The Cherokee Normal *Catalog* for 1928 stressed that "Failure in this phase of school work will bring the student under the censure of the Faculty and Board of Trustees." It further noted that student response to this requirement had been "gratifying." Additionally, all students were required to engage in ten minutes of exercise daily. This was considered important for the health of the students, for teaching them sportsmanship, and for giving them some "relief from the dry, indoor, and often boring subject matter courses ..." Outdoor facilities were provided for football, basketball, baseball, tennis, and volleyball. Exercise, frequent chapel talks, and personal student conferences also aided in the "problem of discipline." Rules on social behavior restricted the congregation of male and female students in hallways or meeting rooms for the purpose of "conversation" and walking together on campus. The school had a "moving picture machine of the best make" with a nightly show three times per week. Revenue generated from admission was used to supplement the institution's operating budget. Broadly, the school wanted to develop sound minds as well as sound bodies. The educational programs were supported by a library that had grown to two thousand volumes. These types of developments and activities reflect some of the changes occurring at the school.

FIGURE 2.12. *Ruth (Sampson) Locklear '14. The first Indian with a four-year degree to teach at The Cherokee Indian Normal School of Robeson County. Daughter of O. R. Sampson, and wife of W. R. Locklear.*
COURTESY OF RUTH L. DIAL.

Two notable teachers from this period with ties to the local community were Ruth (Sampson) Locklear, one of the first high school graduates of the institution, and Dr. Earl C. Lowry. The daughter of Rev. O.R. Sampson, chair of the Board of Trustees, she was born June 19, 1897, near Pembroke. After receiving a BA degree in 1919 from Carson-Newman College, now Carson-Newman University,

Locklear taught high school in Florida for three years. In 1922 she was hired by Superintendent Riley, becoming the first Indian with a four-year degree to teach at the institution. She was a member of the faculty from 1922 to 1927, and served as the matron of the girls' dorm and manager of the dining hall for two years afterward. Sadly, Locklear, who was popular with students and the faculty, died January 22, 1929 at age thirty-one; she developed pneumonia a few weeks after giving birth to her second child. Sampson's funeral, like that of her father the year before, was held in Old Main's auditorium. William R. "Bill" Locklear (1898–1969), her husband, was the institution's first superintendent of buildings; he planted many of the oldest trees on campus today. In 1934 William married Mary Herring (1900–1990), a white member of the Cherokee Normal faculty; they passed away in Mount Airy, North Carolina.

FIGURE 2.13. *William R. "Bill" Locklear. First superintendent of grounds. Husband of faculty members Ruth (Sampson) Locklear '14 and Mary (Herring) Locklear.* COURTESY OF RUTH L. DIAL.

Earl C. Lowry, born in 1907 and the son of D.F. Lowry, finished high school at Cherokee Normal in 1924. He enrolled at McKendree College but transferred after the first year to the University of Chattanooga, now the University of Tennessee at Chattanooga. After graduating in 1927 he taught science at Cherokee Normal from 1927 to 1929. Lowry received a medical degree at Vanderbilt University in 1933. Dr. Lowry entered the U.S.

FIGURE 2.14. *Dr. Earl C. Lowry '24. Distinguished physician who served as the personal physician to Generals Dwight D. Eisenhower and George C. Patton during World War II.*

Army Medical Corps in 1937. He graduated from the Army Medical School in Washington, DC, and the Army Field Service School, then in Carlisle, Pennsylvania. Dr. Lowry had a distinguished medical career that spanned more than three decades. During World War II, Dr. Lowry was chief of the Professional Services Division and chief consultant in surgery, Office of the Chief Surgeon in Europe. He treated many notable figures from the war, including President Franklin D. Roosevelt; Generals Dwight D. Eisenhower, Omar Bradley, and George C. Marshall; British field marshal Bernard Montgomery; and Charles DeGaulle. He was the physician attending General George Patton when he died as a result of a broken neck from an automobile accident in 1945. During the Nuremberg war crimes trials at the conclusion of the war, Dr. Lowry was responsible for examining twenty-two high-ranking Germans weekly to ensure that each was physically and mentally capable of standing trial. They included Herman Goering and Rudolph Hess. He achieved the rank of colonel in the U.S. Army. Dr. Lowry later served as the assistant executive director of the Office for Dependents Medical Care, a program that served as the model for Medicaid. Prior to his death in Tennessee in 2002 Dr. Lowry was awarded an honorary doctor of laws degree by Pembroke State University on May 7, 1994.

Superintendent Smithey also promoted improvements in the aesthetics of the campus. In December 1927 the school leased the right-of-way property between the school grounds and the railroad, making numerous improvements. One was the construction of a driveway in front of Old Main to give an unobstructed view while entering the highway from the school. The area around the driveway was cleaned up to improve the appearance of the entrance to campus. Two flagpoles were erected in front of Old Main. Smithey also made plans to erect a "sign...showing that the Indian normal is a state school." Sometime afterward, the name of the institution was painted on the façade of Old Main, above its iconic columns. Initially the building read "Indian State Normal College," never

FIGURE 2.15. *Old Main. Soon after December 1927 the name of the institution was painted on the façade of Old Main. Although Indian State Normal College was not the name of the school, it denoted the school's relationships with the state and its curriculum. The building's façade carried the subsequent names of the school.*

the actual name of the school but more a denotation of the school's relationship with the state and its curriculum. The building's façade would prominently carry the subsequent names of the institution.

While Smithey promoted many positive educational policies, his administration was often crisis-ridden. In the spring term of 1927 he became embroiled in a dispute with one of the teachers in the normal program, Fannie J. Caldwell, and discharged her from her position. Caldwell then demanded and eventually received a hearing before the State Board of Education. In the course of the dispute, Smithey charged that she was dismissed "because she failed to cooperate and failed to perform her duty as a teacher in the classroom." Smithey also noted that Caldwell "let her imagination run away with her" to the extent that she believed "she was appointed in some mysterious way to run the whole works down here" and that "she talked of a number of conspiracies in the school that never existed, except in her imagination." Caldwell defended herself with a fourteen-point petition. To summarize the key points, she claimed that there were problems at the school because of the principal's "autonomy"; that he interfered with her keeping her contract and misrepresented her to the Board of Trustees, the state board, and the county superintendent; that he was "neglectful of his duties" and failed to cooperate when asked for help; that he was more concerned with his image as a leader than with the school; and, finally, "that a thorough investigation of conditions at the school would be beneficial to the school and no doubt the state." The evidence suggests a conflict of personalities between two strong-willed, somewhat eccentric individuals. This particular incident was resolved by compromise. Though the Board of Trustees dismissed Caldwell on January 31, 1927, the state board ruled that she should be permitted to resign as of April 10, 1927, and that she should be given back pay up to that date. Both sides then let the matter rest.

In late 1927 the normal school became involved in a controversy with the Coharie Indians of Sampson County, North Carolina. In December 1927 the Coharie sent a delegation to Raleigh to meet with A.T. Allen, state superintendent of public instruction, concerning the issue of their eligibility to attend the normal school. They informed Allen that some of their young people had attended the school for a number of years but were excluded in 1927 by the Blood Committee established earlier in 1921. It was Allen's opinion that the 1921 law was unfair. "It seems to me," he wrote in a letter to N.C. Newbold, director of the Colored Normal Schools and the Cherokee Indian Normal School, "that an Indian who can show that he belongs to that tribe should be admitted to a school maintained by the State whether he shall have been so fortunate as to have been born in Robeson County or not." He went on to say, "I do not know anything that can be done about it at this time, but I do think that the law ought to be changed so that the people from other counties, and even from South Carolina, could come to this institution on some kind of terms if they can show that they are Indians." Technically, the decision on eligibility to attend the institution remained with the Blood Committee until 1953, when admission was opened to white students and the Board of Trustees was given final approval on the admission of students.

The dispute over eligibility was followed in September 1928 by an academic and racial dispute involving the North Carolina College for Women (NCCW) in Greensboro, known today at the University of North Carolina at Greensboro. Marguerite (Jones) Holmes (1906–2002), a 1925 graduate of the Cherokee Normal high school and a member of the first class to receive a normal degree in 1928, had taught the first-grade class at the normal school the year prior. She applied for admission to NCCW in order to continue her education. She was informed by letter that her application had been rejected because she had graduated from a "nonaccredited school." Jones eventually gave the letter to Smithey, who promptly contacted state education officials. He was the first in a long line of the institution's leaders to advocate for the quality of the school's instruction when the admission

FIGURE 2.16. *Marguerite (Jones) Holmes '25, '28, '49*

of its students into other state institutions of higher education was called into doubt. "As you will readily understand," Smithey wrote, "a letter of this nature would cause considerable misunderstanding and nervousness among the students and prospective students of the Normal. I do not think it has caused more than one student to fail to register, but those who have registered feel somewhat depressed. I have written to the Registrar at NCCW and hope to have an explanation in a few days." In his letter to the registrar, Smithey stressed that the State Board of Education had accredited Cherokee Normal and that he was "at a loss" to understand why Jones had been denied admission. He also stated that the letter from NCCW had been "promiscuously read and scattered over this section of the country and I am sure you can readily imagine the effect it has had on the students and prospective students of this school." He urged the registrar to look into this matter and to let him know of her findings. N.C. Newbold suggested in a letter to State Superintendent Allen, "It is possible that the College declined to accept Miss Marguerite Jones because she is an Indian, and didn't know just the best way to go about it. The method selected, as you will note, has had the most unfortunate effect among the Indians. Some of them, on account of bad advice given by a few white teachers, are already suspicious of the Standard of the Normal School." Superintendent Allen had the last word on this matter. In a letter to Newbold on October 16, 1928, he questioned whether Jones, under existing state law, had any right to attend NCCW since it had been established "for white girls only." Obviously becoming suspicious of this whole episode, he asked, "Has Mr. Smithey, in your opinion, ever been in sympathy with the normal school idea or does he desire a college?" While the evidence on this matter is limited, it appears that Jones sincerely wished to continue her education and that she was denied admission on racial grounds. But it is also possible that Smithey, accused by his enemies of great ambition, tried to use an unfortunate development to his and the school's advantage. Certainly, there was a growing desire after this incident to provide the Indians with a college of their own, particularly since they were excluded from all other state institutions of higher education. Despite the denial of admission to NCCW, Holmes earned a BS degree from Pembroke State College for Indians in 1949.

While Smithey clearly deserves credit for promoting higher academic standards at the normal school and for trying to create an academic environment, his administration ended in confusion, dissension, and near disaster. By 1929 the faculty, trustees, and community had divided into opposing factions concerning his leadership. He became the subject of vitriolic attacks that questioned his competence and his character. One critic wrote that his administration "was the most magnificent display of ignorance, inefficiency, incompetency, and bigotry I have ever seen: a disgrace to the Educational Department of N.C. and a waste of public money." It was also charged that he was controlled and manipulated by N.C. Newbold, director of the Colored Normal Schools and the Cherokee Normal School. His supporters, on the other hand, continued to insist that he was extremely capable. They argued that while he was not as open as he might be, he "did not hurt the institution in the least" and was one of the "best" heads the school ever had. Because of this internal dissension, Smithey was dismissed as principal of the school on April 25, 1929. Less than two weeks before his dismissal, on April 14, Smithey and his family narrowly escaped serious injury in an automobile accident between Monroe and Charlotte. Their car was damaged after it collided with another vehicle that pulled into their path. Although the car's radius rod—a part of the suspension system that controls the movement of the wheels—was damaged, they continued on to Charlotte. After going into a sharp curve, Smithey apparently lost control of the vehicle before it went over an embankment and flipped. The family only suffered minor injuries. That summer, Smithey was named the principal of Old Fort High School in McDowell County in Western North Carolina. He died on November 29, 1948, in Wilkesboro.

The Board of Trustees then split over Smithey's successor, some favoring a former head, A.B. Riley, while others supported C.E. Snoddy, an English teacher at the institution. Snoddy was eventually chosen by a simple majority of the trustees. His selection was forwarded to Newbold, who refused to accept it and convinced the state board to back his decision. After numerous charges and countercharges, J.E. Sawyer was chosen to become the new superintendent of Cherokee Normal. Sawyer took over in the summer of 1929, thus ending the chaos that had surrounded the Smithey administration in its last days.

That S.B. Smithey made significant contributions to the normal school is indisputable; however, it is also indisputable that the divisive forces unleashed by the fight over his leadership plagued the institution for the next decade. While progress continued, it was measurably slowed by internal disunity and the coming of the Great Depression, the most severe economic disaster in this nation's history. Fortunately, the solid foundation of the school helped it weather the difficulties that lay ahead.

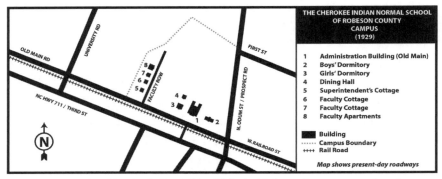

MAP 2.1. *The Cherokee Indian Normal School of Robeson County campus (1929).*

TIMELINE OF NOTABLE INSTITUTIONAL EVENTS (1910–1929)

1911
- Name changed to The Indian Normal School of Robeson County.
- Status with the state clarified; Board of Trustees transferred property to the State Board of Education.

1912
- O.V. (Otto Vetas) Hamrick Sr. named principal.
- John A.B. Lowry, first high school graduate and second graduate from institution.

1913
- Name changed to The Cherokee Indian Normal School of Robeson County.

1914
- Winnie Lee (Bell) Jenkins and Ruth (Sampson) Locklear received high school diplomas; first female graduates and third and fourth high school graduates.
- H.A. (Henry Augustus) Neal named principal.

1915
- First dormitory, for girls, constructed.

1918
- First summer school session held; replaced two-week summer institute held for a few years.
- T.C. (Thomas Calhoun) Henderson named principal and later superintendent.

1922
- Lucy Amanda (Oxendine) Smith becomes fourth high school graduate and fifth graduate of the institution.
- A.B. (Andrew Beckett) Riley named superintendent.

1923
- New administration building, renamed Old Main after 1949, opened; Commencement held in Old Main for first time.
- Campus doubled in size to twenty acres.

1924
- Dining Hall, behind girls' dormitory, erected by this time.
- First classroom building on Pembroke campus razed.
- High school accredited by the State Board of Education.

1925
- Four cottages for the superintendent, agriculture teacher, principal, and faculty constructed along Faculty Row.
- Boys' dormitory constructed.

1926
- S.B. (Sherman Bryan) Smithey named superintendent.
- Two-year normal degree added to the curriculum; elementary instruction phased out by 1928.

1928   · First two-year normal degree awarded to ten graduates.
        · Normal school accredited as a "standard normal school."
1929   · J.E. (John Ephraim) Sawyer named superintendent.
        · Blood Committee jurisdiction expanded to include Cherokee Normal.

Chapter Three

1929–1962
A GENERATION OF GROWTH AND CHANGE

The Indian head on the front of this great stone arrowhead, has become a symbol of the spirit of P.S.C.

If this INDIANHEAD could only speak, how many stories it could weave of the fascinating history of our college—the stirring dreams, growing inspirations, high ambitions, huge endeavors, varied social activities, many campus changes, rapid expansions, insatiable thirst for knowledge, yes, and even golden romance—all these and more, the INDIANHEAD could relate.

Indianhead (1959)

While the onset of the Great Depression adversely affected the progress of the Pembroke institution, coping with adversity was nothing new for the school and its supporters. Rev. J. E. (John Ephraim) Sawyer was selected in the summer of 1929 to serve as superintendent of Cherokee Normal. Born January 26, 1886, Sawyer was a native of Florence, North Carolina, in Pamlico County. A graduate of Ayden Seminary, founded by the Original Free Will Baptists and located in Ayden, North Carolina, he also received an AB degree from Guilford College in 1910 and an MA degree from the University of North Carolina at Chapel Hill in 1929. Sawyer was the principal of Ayden Seminary from 1910 to 1917 and served on the Board of Directors for the Free Will Baptist Press. As superintendent of Cherokee Normal from 1929 to 1935 Sawyer proved a diligent, capable head.

Despite having to operate with reduced operating funds and lowered salaries, the institution still managed to grow. To make way for the additional growth in the physical plant, ten acres were added along the western edge of campus in 1930. An athletic field with a grandstand, a new home economics building, a new agricultural building, and a larger water tank were erected. The athletic field, grandstand, and home economics building were located along Faculty Row on the present site of the Education Center and Business Administration Building, while the water tower was located between Old Main and present-day Moore Hall. By 1931 the Indians had a "well-equipped Normal School valued at over $250,000." Sawyer's tenure also saw the addition of an iconic campus landmark. Known today as simply the Arrowhead, the stone and mortar monument was erected, most likely in April 1933, by J. (Joseph) Hampton Rich (1874–1949), a native of Davie County, North Carolina, who served as director of the Boone Trail Highway and Memorial Association. Rich erected 358 monuments across the United States between 1913 and 1938 to bring public sentiment to bear on state legislators to improve the quality of roads. He would convince town leaders that what the town needed was a monument. Money would be raised, Rich would build the monument, and off he would go to the next town. Rich also raised monuments to other American heroes, including Davy Crockett, Abraham Lincoln, and Cherokee chief Sequoia. Pembroke's monument has a "Sequoia tablet" on the south face and a buffalo trail marker on the north face. According to Everett Gary Marshall, Rich's biographer, "The Buffalo Trail marker is supposedly there to identify original buffalo traces that were then used by Native Americans and early colonists, that eventually became routes for modern highways." Marshall registered Pembroke's monument as no. 136. He has registered 144 original sites, of which approximately 50 still survive with a monument or marker. A similar monument erected by Rich in April 1933 stood near downtown Lumberton on the grounds of the administrative offices for the former city schools. Although destroyed by a runaway car in a 2006 accident, a metal tablet from the monument was adhered to a marble stone, in a similar shape to Pembroke's Arrowhead, and placed on the grounds of the county courthouse in Lumberton. Pembroke's monument has been rebuilt since it was first constructed. Originally erected in the southeast corner of the Quad, the Arrowhead was moved in November 1985 to its present location directly in front of Old Main, after a suggestion by Greg Cummings '74. According to the 1959 *Indianhead*, the Arrowhead "has become a symbol of the spirit" of the university.

Equally important to the physical plant additions, the level of normal work was raised, and the superintendent and trustees implemented the process of phasing in the first two years of a college curriculum in 1933. Establishment of the junior college provided an alternative to a normal degree for students who did not want to teach. More importantly, it was a cheaper, in-state option for

FIGURE 3.1. *J. E. Sawyer. Superintendent of The Cherokee Indian Normal School of Robeson County from 1929 to 1935.*
COURTESY OF THE FREE WILL BAPTIST HISTORICAL COLLECTION, MOUNT OLIVE COLLEGE.

FIGURE 3.2. *G. G. Maughon Sr. Superintendent of The Cherokee Indian Normal School from 1935 to 1940.*
ROBESONIAN (LUMBERTON, NC), NOVEMBER 29, 1937.

Indians who could not afford to attend more expensive out-of-state institutions. Indians were not allowed to attend white institutions of higher
education in North Carolina during this time. Prior to this, the "McKendree Connection" was one way that Lumbees could get a four-year degree,
albeit out of state. McKendree College, a small four-year liberal arts college in Lebanon, Illinois, about twenty miles north of St. Louis, Missouri,
was founded by the United Methodist Church and offered admission to
anyone, regardless of race. The Lumbee connection with the Methodist Church facilitated their attendance at the school. Nine Lumbee men
attended or graduated from the institution during the 1920s and 1930s.
The McKendree Lumbees went on to distinguished careers after returning to Robeson County; Earl C. Lowry '24, Elmer T. Lowry '27, and Clifton Oxendine '24, who finished high school at Cherokee Normal, along
with Herbert G. Oxendine, and James Thomas Sampson returned to
teach at the institution in Pembroke. Frank Epps served on the Board of
Trustees. The first two-year college class graduated from Cherokee Normal with four students in 1935: Herbert Marvin Howington, Louis Curtis Moore, Dorothy Oxendine, and Grover Ernest Sampson. That same
year, Sawyer was reelected by the Board of Trustees but resigned, effective
August 1. He accepted the position of superintendent at Bell Consolidated School in Apex, North Carolina. Sawyer passed away May 15, 1962,
in Greensboro, North Carolina, while living with his daughter.

With the resignation of Sawyer in 1935, the Board of Trustees elected
G.G. (Grover Gaines) Maughon Sr. to be superintendent on July 15, 1935.
Maughon had served as the principal of Lumberton High School in
Lumberton since 1934. Prior to this, Maughon was superintendent of
the Hartwell Public Schools for six years and Tennille Public Schools,
both in Georgia. Born March 29, 1888, in Georgia, Maughon received
an AB degree from Mercer University and an MA degree from the
University of Georgia in 1932. He did additional work in education at
Columbia University. Like Smithey earlier, he was a man of ability, but

not of sociability; he tended to be obstinate and, at times, somewhat condescending. As a result of his personality, he quickly alienated some faculty and community members, a development that augured poorly for Maughon's future at the school. Still, numerous positive accomplishments took place during his tenure.

Most notably, the final two years of the normal and college curriculum were phased in; accreditation from the North Carolina Department of Public Instruction, which was required for all institutions of higher education in the state, was sought and received; and the high school, long an integral part of the institution, was separated from the college in 1939 and moved to a new, off-campus site. With these developments, the school had finally evolved from a normal school offering all levels of instruction to an institution of higher learning. As a result, from 1939 to 1953, Pembroke was the only state-supported, four-year college for Indians in the nation.

Changes in state requirements for "A" grade teacher certification necessitated the addition of the final two years of the normal and college curriculum. New teachers after 1937 would be required to have at least three years of college training. Holders of "B" certificates, beginning in 1929, had to have a degree from a four-year college to raise their certificates to an "A" rating. In order to keep pace with the advanced requirements of a four-year college, the head of a department would be required to have a doctorate. To meet these requirements at Cherokee Normal, the third year of the normal and college programs was added to the curriculum in 1936. The last two-year degrees were awarded the following year. In 1938 the first three-year normal and college class graduated with twelve students. The normal graduates were Venus Brooks, Nettie Mae (Woodell) Godwin, Carlee Gordon Hunt, Purcell Locklear, Vivian Lowry, Prebble (Lowry) Oxendine, and Evelyn (Bell) Stone, while the college graduates were Wade H. Lowry, Marjorie Moore, Hubert Oxendine, Millard Smith, and James Swett.

The accrediting report, issued in spring 1940, was revealing both about how far the school had come and how far it had to go. It was reported that the state appropriated $31,898 for the operation of the institution, that the library contained 2,754 volumes and subscribed to thirty-four magazines, that the school enrolled 63 males and 66 females for a total of 129 students, that 192 quarter hours were required for graduation, and that the highest faculty salary was $1,860 and the lowest $1,000. While the Department of Public Instruction took the position that the school did not meet "specific principles for a standard senior college with respect to salaries, number of volumes in the library, adequacy of lab equipment, and physical facilities," it recognized that those deficiencies could only be corrected with increased state funding. Therefore, the agency recommended that "the institution be given a conditional Senior College rating for the session 1939–1940 with the privilege of conferring degrees, and that its continued rating for 1940–1941 be contingent upon some progress having been made in one or more of those principles that the institution does not now meet."

With the conditional rating, the Board of Trustees approved the addition of year four of the normal and college curriculum on April 27, 1939. Coinciding with the addition of the fourth year, high school coursework at the institution concluded, and the high school separated from the institution at the end of the 1938–1939 school year. Earlier, in 1936, school and state officials recognized the biggest obstacle to adding the final two years of the curriculum was a lack of space; the institution was bursting at the seams and had outgrown Old Main, its sole classroom building. By 1936 Old Main housed the institution's four departments: normal, college, high school, and deaf. Lack of space coupled with a student enrollment of three hundred prompted Superintendent Maughon to deem Old Main "inadequate." As a result, school officials requested a new high school building in 1936. After settling a dispute between the county school system and the State Board of Education over who should pay for the new structure, the county, using funding from President Franklin Roosevelt's Public Works Administration (PWA) program, constructed a separate facility for the institution's high school on property adjacent to the southwestern edge of the campus. As a result of the addition of the final two years of the curriculum, many alumni, who held a two-year degree, returned to complete the third and fourth years. For example, John L. Carter finished high school at Cherokee Normal in 1926, received a two-year normal degree in 1929, and completed the last two years in 1943. Today, the campus of Pembroke High School houses the offices of Indian Education for the Public Schools of Robeson County, a charter school, and a prekindergarten school.

Accreditation was extremely important because it validated the legitimacy of the institution's degrees in relation to other colleges and verified the quality of the school's programs. After gaining state accreditation the school began to seek regional accreditation from the Southern Association of Colleges and Schools (SACS); it finally gained full accreditation as a four-year liberal arts college from the Southern Association in December 1951. Today the institution is accredited by or belongs to ten different higher education associations.

The celebration of Cherokee Normal's semicentennial in 1937 marked a milestone during an era of great institutional change and expansion. The observance was held June 4, 1937, in conjunction with Commencement exercises. The guiding theme for the celebration was "Tracing the History of Indian Education in Robeson County, Reminding Ourselves of the Mental and Moral Qualifications of Teachers, and Planning for the Future." Former state senator L. R. Varser presided over the event which featured the presentation of class memorials and remarks by Rev. D. F. Lowry, its first graduate; Rev. Stephen A. Hammond, who completed studies at the school in 1896, and Rev. L. W. Jacobs '25, '28, both members of the Board of Trustees; Dean J. (James) R. Lowry; Congressman J. Bayard Clark; and Dr. James Hillman, state supervisor of the normal school. Speakers remarked about the school's progress in its first fifty years. Congressman Clark declared, "The influence of this institution, in lifting the lives of the young people of your race to an even higher plane, cannot be estimated." Rev. Jacobs noted the difficulties the institution experienced to reach this point when he described the school as "the product of suffering and hardship and struggle among the early founders of education." The Alumni Association, formed by alumni one year earlier, placed a stone marker in the façade of Old Main to commemorate the occasion.

To share news about the progress of the campus and the county's Indian community with the broader citizens of Robeson County, Dr. John B. May, a professor of education and psychology at Cherokee Normal, first published a newspaper titled the *Odako* on December 14, 1937. According to the publication, "odako" was an Indian term that meant "friendship." The newspaper apparently fell on hard times; after one issue, it appeared each Friday from January through May 1938 as a community correspondence in *The Robesonian*. It featured happenings on campus, profiles of prominent Indians, and news from Robeson County's Indian communities and schools. Carlee Gordon Hunt '38 was listed as the associate editor. The column ended with Dr. May's departure from the campus in 1938. During the early 1940s, other community correspondences titled "News Letter from Pembroke State College for Indians" and "Pembroke State College News," ran in *The Robesonian*; they provided a wealth of information about campus activities during the period.

Other noteworthy developments under Maughon included the hiring of a full-time librarian who was charged with supervising the expanding facility and with organizing the collection according to the Dewey Decimal System; the employment of a business teacher; a growing emphasis on spiritual development and self-discipline; and the establishment of a department for teaching the deaf in the fall of 1935. The program for the instruction of the deaf was short-lived, because it proved expensive to maintain and because of the difficulty of securing trained teachers. It was discontinued in 1939. Maughon helped stabilize the faculty by adopting a policy of hiring, when possible, married male professors with advanced degrees; this tended to reduce the problem of an overly mobile, short-service faculty. Among the faculty of the institution in the 1930s were four with community ties who provided dedicated service for many years: Clifton Oxendine '24; Ira Pate Lowry '29 and his wife, Reba (Millsaps) Lowry; and James A. Jacobs '27, '29.

Clifton Oxendine (1900–1987) was an early historian of the university, administrator, and longtime history professor. The nephew of Mary Catherine (Oxendine) Moore, the wife of Rev. W.L. Moore, Oxendine finished high school at Cherokee Normal in 1924. He received an AB degree from McKendree College, today McKendree University, in 1928 and an MA degree from George Peabody College, later the Peabody College of Vanderbilt University. Oxendine first taught at Cherokee Normal from 1928 to 1932. Between 1932 and 1939 he served as principal at Pembroke Graded School and Prospect High School. In 1939 Oxendine returned to Cherokee Normal, serving as dean and professor of history until 1957. He then taught full-time in the History Department. Upon his retirement in 1970 Oxendine was named professor emeritus. Oxendine became the second recipient of an honorary doctorate—doctor of humane letters—from Pembroke State University on September 3, 1986. Dr. Oxendine passed away in 1987 just a few months after the institution celebrated its Centennial. In December 1988 the second-floor lecture auditorium in the Adolph L. Dial Humanities Building was named Dr. Clifton Oxendine Memorial Lecture Hall in his honor.

Ira Pate Lowry (1906–1992) was a native of the Elrod community south of Pembroke. He finished high school at Cherokee Normal in 1929, received a BS degree from Dakota Wesleyan University and an MA degree from Ohio State University. Lowry also studied voice and piano at the Julliard School of Music. He served as principal of Piney Grove

FIGURE 3.3. *Dr. Clifton Oxendine '24.
Served as professor of history and dean for
thirty-five years.*

FIGURE 3.4. *Ira Pate Lowry '29. Organized and served as head of the Music
Department from 1935 to 1957.*

FIGURE 3.6. *James A. Jacobs '27, '29.
Registrar and professor of mathematics for
thirty-two years.*

FIGURE 3.5. *Reba (Millsaps) Lowry.
Professor in the Department of Foreign
Languages from 1935 to 1975. The Lowrys
coauthored "Hail to UNCP," the university's alma mater, and are the namesakes
for the Lowry Bell Tower.*

High School from 1933 to 1935. Between 1935 and 1957 Lowry organized and served as chair of the Music Department and director of the institution's first pep and marching bands. From 1957 to 1971 he taught music at Pembroke High School. Ira Pate and Reba were married in 1936, a year after they joined the faculty. Reba (Millsaps) Lowry (1906–1980) was born near Maryville, Tennessee. She received an AB degree from Maryville College, today Maryville University, and an MA degree from the University of Tennessee. Lowry also completed requirements for a doctorate, with the exception of the dissertation, from Ohio State University. During her forty years with the institution, Lowry was an instructor and chair of the Foreign Language Department, first dean of women in 1937, adviser to the *Indianhead* from 1952 to 1963, director of the Pembroke Players, women's basketball coach for five years, and organizer of the first student exchange program in 1969. Lowry was also the first woman to join the Chancellor's Club. Upon her retirement in 1975 she was named professor emeritus. The Lowrys, who provided sixty-two combined years of service to the institution, were recipients of the Alumni Association's Distinguished Service Award, Reba in 1975 and Ira Pate in 1981.

James A. (Arnold) Jacobs (1909–1994), a native of Pembroke, finished high school and received a two-year normal degree, both from Cherokee Normal, in 1927 and 1929, respectively. He received a BS degree from Murray State Teachers College, now Murray State University, and an MEd degree from Duke University. He taught in the public schools of Robeson County, serving as principal of Prospect High School, before coming to Cherokee Normal. Jacobs served from 1939 to 1942 as the institution's registrar and chair of the Mathematics Department. After serving in World War II he returned to the college in 1945 and resumed his duties as chair, serving until 1970. Jacobs was named professor emeritus upon his retirement in 1974.

The campus, during Maughon's superintendency, consisted of thirty acres containing eleven buildings. A state audit in 1936 determined that the school's capital assets were worth $184,000. Old Main was the heart of the campus, containing the administrative offices, the library, laboratories, twelve classrooms, and an auditorium, which seated seven hundred. The school had a dining hall where the students could eat for four dollars per week; a large, frame women's dormitory, which housed both female students (second floor) and single female faculty members (first floor); a small men's dormitory, capable of housing twenty-four students; four cottages for the superintendent and faculty; a home economics building; and an agricultural building. It was considered more important that the female students all be housed on campus where they could be given better supervision. For the recreation of faculty and students, there were tennis courts, a baseball field, and basketball courts. The athletic facilities were open to the community, bolstering ties between the campus and the town. The whole operation was conducted by twenty-one faculty and staff—sixteen faculty members, one librarian, the superintendent, a building and grounds supervisor, a book-keeper, and a night watchman. While this pales in comparison with the nearly $81 million operation in 2013, it signified tremendous growth over the situation back in 1888 when one person, with occasional part-time help, ran the school as teacher and principal.

FIGURE 3.7. *College gymnasium. Erected in 1939; razed in 1988.*

The expansion of the physical plant included the addition of a modern gymnasium, completed in 1939. The structure would serve the institution's academic and athletic needs, as well as host numerous community functions, until it was razed in 1988. Almost half of the forty-five-thousand-dollar cost for the building's construction was funded through the Public Works Administration (PWA) program. The gymnasium had a seating capacity of one thousand, with fold-up bleachers on the main floor, permanent seating in the balcony, and dressing rooms with showers and lockers. W.W. Chaffin, resident engineer-inspector of the PWA, spoke at the building's dedication on May 31, 1940. He remarked, "Pembroke has reason to be proud of itself, proud of its citizens, and proud of its new gymnasium, and let me assure you that the Public Works Administration, for which I speak, is proud of you." Cherokee Normal held its first game in the new venue on December 10, 1939, versus Wingate Junior College, now Wingate University. The new gym also hosted the annual Robeson County Indian high school basketball tournament. The first tournament began play on March 14, 1940, in the new gym. It featured boys' and girls' teams from Indian high schools in Robeson, and later, Cumberland and Hoke Counties. Because of segregated schools, the Indian high schools competed in an all-Indian athletic conference. The Cherokee Normal gym was selected because it provided many of the amenities necessary to host the tournament. None of the high schools had gyms at this time; games were played outside on dirt courts. For many of the athletes, the gym's niceties provided their first experience with an indoor shower. The annual tournament was a huge social gathering that featured competition among the county's Indian high schools and their respective communities. The winning schools and communities held the all-important bragging rights until next year's tournament. Among the Lumbee, the popularity of the tournament was only surpassed, decades later, by Lumbee Homecoming. According to Tim Brayboy '64 and Bruce Barton '86 in *Playing Before an Overflow Crowd*, which recounts the story of

FIGURE 3.8. *Class of 1940. First graduates to receive four-year baccalaureate degrees.*
From left to right: Conrad Oxendine, Joseph Sampson, Eteska (Locklear) Hunt,
Dorsey Lowry Sr., and Charles W. Maynor. Not pictured: Inez (Hunt) Bell.
COURTESY OF WOODY HUNT.

Indian basketball in Robeson and surrounding counties from 1939 to
1967, "Sellout crowds were the order of the day, and Indian basketball
players, fans, and coaches looked forward each year to 'tournament time'
when excitement filled the air."

Certainly the high point of Maughon's administration came in the
spring of 1940, when the first four-year bachelor of arts degrees were
awarded to the members of the graduating class: Inez (Hunt) Bell,
Eteska (Locklear) Hunt, Dorsey Lowry Sr., Charles W. Maynor, Conrad
Oxendine, and Joseph Sampson. Maynor is recognized as the first four-
year graduate because he finished his degree requirements one semester
early. Their diploma featured the first seal adopted by the institution.
It included an open book and the year 1887, encircled by the name of
the school and the town. During the early years of the institution,
Commencement spanned four or more days and was a huge campus

and community event. The celebration typically included a baccalaureate ceremony; declamation, recitation, and oratorical contests led by student literary societies; award presentations; a baseball game; student drama productions; and separate graduation ceremonies for the high school and normal/college graduates.

By 1940 Maughon had angered a sizable part of the local community. He seemed to have little understanding of the area and its people, and apparently made little effort to learn. Consequently, as early as 1938, there were calls for his resignation or dismissal. On April 23, 1940, the Board of Trustees declined to reelect Maughon, resulting in a conflict with the State Board of Education, which later overrode the decision of the trustees. By that summer, local opposition to his remaining as head of the institution was intense. On the night of August 29, 1940, the superintendent's cottage on Faculty Row was spattered with five bursts of gunshot, apparently from a passing automobile. No one was injured in the shooting, an apparent "expression of resentment" over Maughon's reappointment. Maughon submitted his resignation a few days later on September 3, 1940, to Clyde A. Erwin, state superintendent of public instruction, effective at the end of the month. Erwin responded, "At no time during a similar period has the institution made as much progress as during your administration. I regret, therefore, exceedingly to lose your services." Maughon died September 1, 1966, in Valdosta, Georgia.

With the hasty departure of Maughon one week before the start of classes, the Board of Trustees picked Dr. O.H. (Owens Hand) Browne as acting superintendent of the institution on September 3, 1940. Dr. Browne, a member of the faculty since July 30, 1937, taught chemistry, math, and biology. He was born on December 2, 1899, in Illinois, and in 1921 received a BS degree from North Carolina State College, now North Carolina State

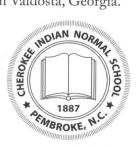

FIGURE 3.9. *Seal of The Cherokee Indian Normal School of Robeson County*

University, where his father was the first chair of the Department of Electrical Engineering; Browne also received a PhD in chemistry from Johns Hopkins University in 1926. His tenure as a caretaker administrator began September 30, 1940, continuing for the next two years while the school sought a permanent replacement.

There were, however, several important happenings and developments during the Browne administration. First, Ella Cara Deloria, an anthropologist of Yankton Dakota descent and an aunt of Vine Deloria Jr., a leading Indian intellectual in America, wrote, produced, and directed a drama titled *The Life Story of a People*. It was performed on the nights of December 5, 6, and 7, 1940, in the college gymnasium. Opening night was a great social occasion, with even the governor of North Carolina, Clyde R. Hoey, in attendance. According to the program, this was "a pageant showing the development of the Indians of Robeson County from earliest times until

FIGURE 3.10. *Dr. O. H. Browne. Acting superintendent of The Cherokee Indian Normal School of Robeson County (1940–1941) and acting president of Pembroke State College for Indians (1941–1942).*
COURTESY OF LENOIR-RHYNE UNIVERSITY, *HACAWA* (1943).

now." It was produced under the sponsorship of the college as well as the Farm Security Administration (FSA) and the Bureau of Indian Affairs (BIA), both in Washington, DC. Deloria, an employee of the FSA and BIA, came to Robeson County at the behest of John Collier, commissioner for the BIA, to shed light on anthropologist John Swanton's theory of Siouan ancestry for the Indians of Robeson County. The pageant, with an all-Indian cast of over three hundred, emphasized the major influences and concerns of the Lumbees—the importance of the church and education, the dominance of agriculture, and their great concern for social justice—and it noted new influences emerging in the community, such as the American Legion and the

Boy Scouts. The finale consisted of expressions of Indian loyalty to one's home and family, to the nation, and to God. Repeated the next year, with performances on December 5, 8, and 10, 1941, the pageant was a patriotic and historical drama, remembered for decades by many of the older citizens of the Indian community.

FIGURE 3.11. *Seal of Pembroke State College for Indians.*

The next significant event of the Browne years came on March 15, 1941, when the General Assembly recognized that the school had truly become an institution of higher learning and changed its name from The Cherokee Indian Normal School of Robeson County to Pembroke State College for Indians. The purpose of the name change was to improve the institution's chances for securing additional state appropriations, particularly for much-needed additions to the physical plant, such as new buildings for home economics, agriculture, the library, and music. The legislation also changed the title of the institution's head from superintendent to president. Consequently, Dr. Browne became the acting president. Interestingly, the Lumbees asked that the school be named Pembroke State College, but Gov. Melville Broughton interceded and added the phrase "for Indians" to distinguish it from other state institutions.

In 1941 the United States became a combatant in World War II against the Axis powers of Germany, Japan, and Italy. Pembroke State students and alumni certainly did their part in that conflict, with 130 serving in Europe and the Pacific; 4 were killed in action: Marvin Chavis; James Swett '37, '38; Wade H. Lowry '37, '38; and Verl Thompson. Lowry was the first Lumbee killed in action during the war. The Veterans of Foreign Wars post in Pembroke is named the Locklear-Lowry Memorial Post No. 2843 in honor of Lowry and the first Lumbee killed in World War I. During the institution's Diamond Jubilee Celebration in 1963, the auditorium in Old Main was designated "Memorial Auditorium" in honor of students and faculty who had served in World War I, World War II, and the Korean War.

The early years of the war presented the campus with numerous challenges. By the end of the 1941–1942 school year, enrollment had dropped to 90 students. The year before, enrollment was 135. There was fear of the possibility that the school might close. But, to keep the institution open, Dr. Browne and faculty member Ira Pate Lowry '29 visited Indian high schools, recruiting students. Lowry, Browne, and student Albert Hunt '43 set up a cooperative meal program so that students could have meals on campus. Because few students could afford the cost of a meal plan, they brought eggs, ham, wheat, and flour, which were credited to their meal account. Students who could not provide food instead did chores to earn their meals. Hunt later remarked, "We ate real good."

Two notable faculty, Mary H. Livermore and Ida Ten Eeyck O'Keeffe, were hired by Dr. Browne on September 16, 1941. Livermore (1883–1965), a native of the Pates community, was a retired missionary. She received

FIGURE 3.12. *Mary H. Livermore. Dean of women and teacher of the Bible at Pembroke State College from 1941 to 1951. Namesake for the Mary Livermore Library.*

an AB degree from Adelphi College and taught previously at the Baptist University for Women, later Meredith College; Flora MacDonald College in Red Springs; and Thomasville Orphanage. She also did home service work in New York, Virginia, and Tennessee. She was the daughter of Russell W. Livermore and brother of Russell H. Livermore, local influential farmers, land owners, and merchants. Already well known to the faculty and students, she was hired as the dean of women and teacher of the Bible. Livermore would become the first professor of the Religious Education Department. She retired in 1951, at which time the Board of Trustees thanked Livermore for her "indefatigable energy, her faithful devotion to

Christian ideals, [and] her winsome spirit." The campus library is named in her honor. O'Keeffe (1889–1961) was sister of internationally known artist Georgia O'Keeffe. An artist herself, Ida held an MFA degree from Teachers College, Columbia University. She was hired to head the newly established Fine Arts and Crafts Department, today the Art Department. O'Keeffe had wide experience in teaching drawing and handcrafts. Her hiring filled a "long-felt need" for the creative arts at the institution. O'Keeffe resigned during the fall of 1942 to work with Douglas Aircraft in California. She was replaced by Angelika Reckendorf (1893–1984), who taught art at the college until 1959. A native of Germany who became a naturalized U.S. citizen in 1944, Reckendorf earned BA and MA degrees from the University of North Carolina at Chapel Hill.

FIGURE 3.13. *Ida Ten Eeyck O'Keeffe. Head of the Fine Arts and Crafts Department from 1941 to 1942. Sister of internationally known artist Georgia O'Keeffe.*

On April 22, 1942, the Board of Trustees elected Dr. Browne for another term. His stay at the college, however, was short-lived. Browne and Dr. John Preston Ingle, a member of the faculty, were at odds over alleged "false accusations" that Ingle had made against the administration and the college. At the May 20, 1942, trustees' meeting, Ingle's "connection" with the institution was terminated, effective June 2, 1942. The trustees noted at the same meeting that they were "of the opinion that neither Dr. Ingle nor Dr. Browne can serve the best interest [*sic*] of this institution after the close of this year's work." Dr. Browne apparently caught the hint, submitting his resignation at the next trustees' meeting, on June 2, 1942, effective at the end of the month. He accepted a position teaching physics and chemistry at Lenoir-Rhyne College, now Lenoir-Rhyne University, where he taught for eight years. Dr. Browne then taught at Saint Mary's College, today Saint Mary's School, in Raleigh, for eighteen years before retiring. Before his death on November 3, 1996, in Raleigh, Dr. Browne visited the campus during the 1970s and 1980s, noting its dramatic growth.

On August 18, 1942, Dr. Ralph D. Wellons was selected as the first president of the college. Born on January 28, 1891, in Bloomington, Indiana, Dr. Wellons proved to be an excellent choice. He brought to the position a strong academic background, holding AB and MA degrees from Indiana University and a PhD from Teachers College, Columbia University. Moreover, he was a longtime Methodist minister and missionary to India, where he served from 1931 to 1941 as the president of Lucknow Christian College, an educational institution of the United Methodist Church. Before going to India as a missionary, he taught at a country school for a year, and was superintendent of town schools, both in Indiana, for four years. Dr. Wellons first went to India in 1916 as a professor of English, where he served as a member of the faculty for twenty years. During a furlough in the United States, he was professor of psychology and education at Drury College, today Drury University, and conducted research work for the Board of Missions of the Methodist Church and for the International Missionary Council. From 1926 to 1929 he was a dean at Tusculum College. Soon after his return to India in 1929 he was elected head of Lucknow, a position he held until returning to the United States in 1941. Dr. Wellons worked for the Board of Missions of the Methodist Church between 1941 and 1942. He has been described as "a man of deep scholarship and farsighted leadership, with a broad outlook for the future."

FIGURE 3.14. *Dr. Ralph D. Wellons. President of Pembroke State College for Indians (1942–1949) and Pembroke State College (1949–1956). Namesake for Wellons Hall.*

President Wellons led the college for the next fourteen years. At the start of his administration, he had to deal with the problems caused by the war, such as reduced enrollment. Earlier, in June 1942 the Board of Trustees had offered the college and its facilities to the U.S. government for use in the war efforts. The campus was used for training purposes; both a Civilian Pilot Training Program (CPTP) and a ninety-day ship-building program operated on the campus during the war. Pembroke State was one of over eleven hundred educational institutions to partici-pate in CPTP. The national program was originally started to train civilian pilots but morphed into a military pilot training program at the onset of World War II. Pembroke State students were recruited to participate in the local course in Lumberton, which focused on training Indian navy pilots for service during the war. Participants were John W. Blanks '41, Willie Bowen '37, Otis Burnette '41, Carlton H. Chavis '42, siblings Carlee Gordon Hunt '38 and Fannie Belle (Hunt) Locklear '41, James Q. Locklear '41, and Tom Oxendine '48. Funds for the local course were procured by pilot Horace Barnes, a pioneer aviator in Lumberton and barnstorming pilot in the 1920s who flew with Charles Lindbergh. The terminal at the Lumberton Municipal Airport is named for Barnes. Fannie (1919–2005) was the first Indian female offered a commission as a pilot by the navy. By the time she was offered the commission, her brother Carlee had been shot down by Germans (May 1944) and was a prisoner of war. Although he would later escape, Fannie's mother would not let her "fly over Europe in a metal bull's eye." She served as an educator in Robeson County for thirty-eight years. Oxendine (1922–2010) became the first Indian commissioned as a navy pilot in November 1942. Known locally as "Tom Boy," he would buzz Pembroke during flights over his hometown. Oxendine won a Distinguished Flying Cross during World War II for a daring sea rescue while under fire. After the war, Oxendine finished his education at Pembroke State, where he starred in football, basketball, and baseball. Oxendine served in the Korean and Vietnam Wars before retiring after twenty-nine years in the navy. Oxendine then worked for sixteen years as the chief of public affairs for the Bureau of Indian Affairs in Washington, DC. The last fifteen years of his career

FIGURE 3.15. *Tom Oxendine '48. Shown (left) in 1942 taking flight training at the Naval Air Station in Atlanta, Georgia. He was the first Indian commissioned as a navy pilot in November 1942. With him is Lt. Jr. Grade Ted Mann, public information officer of the station.*

were spent consulting with the EOP Group about Indians and Alaska natives. In 1967 Oxendine was awarded the first Outstanding Alumni Award by the Pembroke State Alumni Association. In 1980 he was a member of the inaugural class inducted into the university's athletic Hall of Fame.

Wellons also had to try to meet the demands of the state accrediting agency for improvements in the quality of the curriculum and facilities. In 1943 the college had a faculty of sixteen, 30 percent of whom had doctorates and three of whom were Indians. While teacher training had been the major emphasis at the institution since 1926, under Dr. Wellons the college began to broaden its academic program, adding the bachelor of science degree in 1943, with the first graduates in 1944. He also took steps to increase library holdings; by 1945 the library had seven thousand volumes.

One of Wellons's strengths as president of the college was his involvement with the community. He was in the forefront of an effort to get a local hospital in 1945, and although the effort failed, it showed his concern for the welfare of the people. He also reached out to the community through the Citizenship Institute, established to bring notable speakers to the area. On March 15, 1946, for example, Gov. R. Gregg Cherry delivered the third lecture in the series, titled "The Citizen and Public Welfare," in Old Main's auditorium. He also appeared in the reviewing stand during the college's Veterans Day celebration parade, which was organized by student veterans. Cherry, who served in World War I, remarked on this occasion that he had never seen a parade "more splendidly conducted" and that he had never been "more cordially received or had more real enjoyment than in the Pembroke community." Starting in 1947 and for several years afterward, in yet another type of outreach effort, Wellons allowed the Robeson County Indian Fair, later the Pembroke County Fair, to be held on campus. Wellons hoped to promote better relations between the town and farmers. Another outreach effort brought Indian grammar and high school students from across the county to the campus. The first countywide Indian Field Day was held in the Quad in 1953. In general, the Wellons administration enjoyed good relations with the surrounding communities.

Early in Wellons's tenure, Dean Clifton Oxendine recognized that Wellons's life experiences and travels in India and the United States had the potential to supplement the educational and cultural development of the college's student body. In 1943, at the request of Oxendine, Wellons began teaching a three-credit course in the principles of philosophy to the senior class during the spring quarter. Wellons used his "wide knowledge of world affairs" to teach students the "current thought to be found in world philosophies." President Wellons taught this course throughout his tenure at the college.

Like all institutions of higher education, Pembroke State welcomed an influx of students following the end of the war in 1945. Indian veterans returned home more conscious than ever of the need for an education in a rapidly changing world, and many took advantage of the Servicemen's Readjustment Act or G.I. Bill to earn a college degree. The returning veterans were also responsible for the baby boom that would have a dramatic impact on higher education in the 1960s. Because there was a tremendous demand in the postwar period for skilled workers in the building industry, the college operated a trade school for several years; this was a cooperative effort with the Veterans Administration.

FIGURE 3.16. *Sampson Hall. Completed in 1949; razed in 1995. Named after*
O. R. Sampson, a longtime chair of the Board of Trustees. It housed administrative
offices and the library before the construction of the Mary Livermore Library.

As the college's enrollment increased, so did the need for an enlarged physical plant to accommodate this growth. During Wellons's tenure, a new administration-library building, two classroom buildings, and a president's residence were constructed. The administrative-library building was completed in 1949 and named Sampson Hall in honor of Rev. Oscar R. Sampson, a major figure in the early history of the school. The building, with its rotunda, was patterned after Monticello, home of President Thomas Jefferson in Charlottesville, Virginia. Of particular importance was the new library, which could seat one hundred and had a capacity of forty-five thousand volumes; at the time, the library actually contained sixteen thousand bound volumes. The movement of administrative offices and the library from Old Main to Sampson Hall prompted Dean Clifton Oxendine to propose the name "Old Main" for the former administration building. He got the idea for the name from an old administration building at McKendree University where he received an AB degree in 1928. Sampson Hall was razed in 1995 to make room for an addition to the Mary Livermore Library.

One of the new classroom buildings served the needs of the Science and Agricultural Departments. It was completed in 1950 and named

Locklear Hall in memory of Anderson N. Locklear, a leader in Indian education in Robeson County and former member of the Board of Trustees. Locklear (1870–1934), a native of the Prospect community, began his education at an Indian subscription school at Old Prospect in 1877. A member of the first class at Croatan Normal, he attended for two years and began teaching in July 1890. Locklear's forty-two-year educational career included serving as a principal or teacher at Barton, Prospect, Union Chapel, New Hope, Angus Locklear, and Pembroke graded schools. Seeking federal assistance for the county's Indian schools, Locklear had an audience with President Theodore Roosevelt in 1907. President Roosevelt shared

FIGURE 3.17. *Anderson N. Locklear. Lumbee educator. Member of the first class at Croatan Normal School in 1888 and the Board of Trustees from 1923 until his death in 1934. Namesake for Locklear Hall.*

his appreciation with Locklear for an invitation to visit North Carolina. The president said the history of the Lumbee Indians had greatly interested him. Locklear served on the Board of Trustees from 1923 until his death in 1934. His funeral was held in the auditorium of Old Main. Today, Locklear Hall houses the Art Department.

The other classroom facility included an auditorium and housed the Music, Dramatics, Art, and Home Economics Departments. Completed in 1951 as the Arts Building, this structure was named Moore Hall in 1963 to honor Rev. W.L. Moore, one of the founders of the college and an outstanding leader among the Lumbee people. Moore Hall is now home to the Music Department. In 1952 the president's house, situated on the southwestern corner of the campus, was constructed, and the girls' dormitory and dining hall, old frame structures located at the front of

FIGURE 3.18. *Berteen (Oxendine) Prine. Executive secretary for forty-seven years, serving five administrations from September 1943 until her retirement in February 1991. Namesake for "Bert's" eatery in the James B. Chavis University Center.*

the campus along present-day Old Main Drive, were moved to new locations west of Faculty Row. The boundaries for the Quad were also defined as a result of the building program. During his presidency, Dr. Wellons also prepared plans for the future physical development of the campus.

Many long-term members of the faculty and staff became campus fixtures during this period. Berteen (Oxendine) Prine (1923–2000) was hired in September 1943 as the executive secretary to President Wellons. A native of Pembroke, she would serve in that capacity for five administrations, before retiring in February 1991. Prine's forty-seven years of service is the longest in the institution's history. In 1986 she was named a recipient of the Pembroke State Alumni Association's Distinguished Service Award. "Bert's" eatery in the present-day James B. Chavis University Center was named for her in 1987. Notable faculty included Frances Stinebring, professor of English, who taught from 1936 to 1953; Mary E. Sharpe, primary critic teacher (1936–1957); Dr. Herbert H. Todd, history (1938–1958); Marjorie Kanable, librarian (1943–1968); and I. Ruth Martin, dean of women and professor of religious education (1953–1985).

As the college grew and produced more graduates, Dr. Wellons became increasingly angry that qualified Indian students were denied admission to graduate programs at white state universities. In 1948 he publicly protested the fact that they were denied admission to the University of North Carolina system strictly on racial grounds. The UNC system at that time consisted of the present-day University of North Carolina at Chapel Hill, North Carolina State University, and the University of North Carolina at Greensboro. He said, "To open the graduate schools of the state university to Indians is the most practical, the most economical and the most sensible thing to do...." The Board of Trustees, during the following year, noted "deep concern" over the issue and the damage done to Pembroke State because of it being perceived as a "dead-end" college since its graduates were not allowed to pursue advanced degrees

FIGURE 3.19. *Marjorie Kanable. Head librarian of Pembroke State College from 1943 until her death in 1968.*

at other public state institutions. In 1950 Dr. Wellons said that, in the past, some Pembroke State students had been admitted to other state institutions through error. He adamantly stated, "We want them to be admitted through the front door instead of the back." Others were also protesting, and in 1951 the UNC system finally began to admit minorities to its graduate, law, and medical schools.

An interesting aspect of the college's history in this period was the proliferation of student activities. Until 1945, there had been some attention given to literary societies and their presentations, to developing a music program, and to sports activities; after 1945 the college experienced an explosion of student organizations, athletics, and activities.

The school's athletic program developed slowly and gathered strength as it evolved from an intramural and high school program to intercollegiate competition by the late 1930s and early 1940s. Athletics had a simple beginning at Cherokee Normal in the 1920s as students were required to perform ten minutes of exercise daily. The 1928–1929 Cherokee Normal *Catalog* noted the value of physical fitness when it stated, "Setting-up

FIGURE 3.20. *Cherokee Indian Normal School of Robeson County men's basketball team (1940). Pictured is Coach John Paul Sampson, standing.*

exercises are very helpful, both for health and for securing that proper coordination of the functions of mind and body so necessary for real education. In addition, they are a real aid in the problem of discipline." The school provided facilities for football, basketball, tennis, and volleyball—for girls and boys. All students were "urged to take part in some form of organized athletics." Edna (Queener) Proffitt, a science teacher, was one of the first coaches at the school, leading the 1927–1928 girls' basketball team. By the 1930s the Intramural Program, which included basketball, softball, volleyball, and baseball, was an integral part of student life as "the classes, societies, and other groups of students organize athletic teams and arrange contests with each other freely."

Cherokee Normal had the only Indian high school in the county until high schools opened in the mid-1920s at Prospect and Union Chapel. The lack of Indian competition, coupled with the absence of an indoor athletic facility, slowed the development of the school's athletic program. However, during the late 1920s and 1930s, a baseball game between the school and a local Indian high school or regional all-star team was held as one of the final events during multiday Commencement exercises. Throughout the 1930s, Cherokee Normal's other teams—football and basketball—also competed against Indian high schools in the county. In the fall of 1931, the football team played two games against Presbyterian Junior College from Maxton, North Carolina. The school employed "an athletic coach who encourages, trains, and directs participation in all the athletic sports, both for girls and boys." In June 1936 John Paul Sampson (1912–2000) was hired as the high school coach and English teacher. Sampson, the son of Rev. Oscar R. Sampson, received a BA degree from McKendree College in 1937 and a master's degree from the University of Illinois in 1941, and completed sixty-four postgraduate hours toward a doctorate. Under his leadership, the school attempted to schedule "as many inter-school contests as possible." The expansion of the school's curriculum coupled with the presence of college-age students prompted the institution to also begin intercollegiate competition in basketball and baseball during the decade. In April 1938 the baseball team competed against Wingate Junior College, now Wingate University.

The following year proved to be a watershed year in the school's athletic history. In 1939 the high school separated from the institution, allowing the institution to focus on intercollegiate competition. As a result of the addition of the final year to the school's curriculum, the school began competition as a four-year college. Sampson was elevated to the full-time coach and became the school's first athletic director. Most notably, the gymnasium opened that fall. Prior to its construction, all athletic competition was held outdoors, and basketball games were played on dirt courts. The absence of such a facility prevented the true development of intercollegiate competition on the campus. The school now had a modern gym that brought immediate benefits, propelling its athletic programs to the next level. The first athletic competition in the new facility was an intercollegiate men's basketball game on December 10, 1939, against Wingate Junior College.

By 1941 the school sponsored basketball teams for men and women and a baseball team. Coach Sampson left the college that year to become the principal at Fairmont Indian High School. He was succeeded by Jerold C. Weissfeld, who served as coach for one year. In 1942 Weissfeld was followed by Harold Kennedy, who served as coach and athletic director until 1946. As athletics prepared to turn a corner in 1941, World War II began. Student enrollment dropped precipitously, particularly among male students, while limited resources were diverted to other needs on the campus. Pembroke State, however, continued to compete during the war, although intermittently. The 1942–1943 baseball squad held a few practices but was disbanded. In 1943 the men's basketball team was "village-bound" because of a shortage of gasoline.

At the beginning of President Wellons's tenure, the college competed against high schools, all-star teams, military institutes, military bases, and junior colleges, mainly from Robeson County and southeastern North Carolina. The end of World War II and the return of military veterans contributed to the college's postwar athletic climb; they formed the nucleus of postwar football, basketball, and baseball teams. After the war, the men's teams dropped high school teams from the schedule, only competing against all-star teams, military institutes, military bases, and junior colleges. In 1945–1946 the women's basketball team scheduled other college teams for the first time. Intercollegiate competition was now the most prominent athletic competition on campus as it brought excitement, school spirit, and regional visibility to the college.

On April 18, 1946, the Board of Trustees approved the creation of an intercollegiate football program and hired James Thomas Sampson (1911–1962) as the first collegiate football coach. Sampson served as a professor of physical education, athletic director, and coach of the football, basketball, and baseball teams from 1946 to 1951. A native of Pembroke and nephew of Rev. Oscar R. Sampson, Sampson was an outstanding high school and college athlete. He finished high school in Griffin, Georgia, where he captained the basketball team and was voted

FIGURE 3.21. *Pembroke State College football team (1950).*

FIGURE 3.22. *Pembroke State College women's basketball team (1957).*

FIGURE 3.23. *Pembroke State College for Indians baseball team (1949).*

the school's "Most Outstanding Athlete." Upon graduation in 1933 he attended McKendree College but earned BS and MA degrees from Fort Hays Kansas State College, now Fort Hays State University. While at Fort Hays State, Sampson was all-conference in football and lettered in basketball, baseball, and track. Sampson completed coursework toward a doctorate at Boston University. While in the navy during World War II, his many duties included serving as chief specialist in the Gene Tunney Welfare and Physical Education Program and head of the physical fitness program for about thirty-four hundred men who were training for Pre-Midshipman School.

From 1946 to 1950 Pembroke State fielded an intercollegiate football team. The 1948 squad played games in Alabama and Georgia for the first time. Ten games were played during the 1949 season, finishing with four wins and six losses, but the 1950 team was the most successful. In games against the Tabor City Red Yams, Pope Airmen from Fort Bragg, and Edwards Military Institute, the team finished with six wins and one tie. The football program was discontinued in 1950 because of the difficulty of finding opponents to play the still all-Indian school and because of the expense of the sport.

When student-athletes left the safe confines of the Pembroke State campus to play at white schools, they were reminded of the harsh realities faced by Indians and persons of color who lived in the South during the period. James C. Dial '54 recalled such an experience. While en route to a game at Newberry College in South Carolina, the football team stopped to get something to eat. From the bus, the athletes could see the "white only" sign on the door. They sent in a member of the team who was more light-skinned than the others. Once they noticed their teammate was able to make purchases, everyone got off the bus and went into the store. A gentleman came from out of the kitchen and talked with the waitress at the counter. He then walked over to Coach Sampson and said he could not serve the team. Coach Sampson told everyone to get back on the bus.

After the war, men's basketball found success against other junior college and all-star teams. In 1948 basketball was the favored sport at Pembroke State. That year's team finished with eight wins and eight losses, but the highlight was the defeat of Presbyterian Junior College in their second meeting by the score of 42-34; Pembroke State lost the first game, 34-29. The 1949 team finished the season 22-10, defeating Edwards Military Institute, Campbell College, the freshman team of Atlantic Christian College, and the 504th of Fort Bragg. The team followed up in 1950 with a 21-6 record. During the 1950–1951 season, the men's basketball team won the school's first athletic championship, defeating Ellerbe in the championship game

FIGURE 3.24. *Belus Van Smawley. Athletic director and basketball and baseball coach from 1951 to 1956. Star of the early National Basketball Association and credited with inventing the turnaround jump shot.*

of the Ellerbe Lions Tourney. From 1952 onward, the men's basketball teams faced only collegiate teams. They opened the 1960s with a win in the 1960 Seafood Fiesta Tournament in New Bedford, Massachusetts.

In 1951 Belus Van Smawley (1918–2003) was hired to replace Sampson. Smawley was a star of the early National Basketball Association (NBA) from 1946 to 1952. He served as the athletic director and coached all teams between 1951 and 1956. A native of Ellenboro, North Carolina, Smawley was an NAIA (National Association of Intercollegiate Athletics) All-American at Appalachian State Teachers College, later Appalachian State University, and one of the first basketball players to regularly use the jump shot. Smawley is credited with inventing the turnaround jump shot or "turnaround jumper." In December 1951 he took a three-month leave of absence from his duties at Pembroke State to finish his playing career with the Baltimore Bullets. In his absence, Vernon Felton, a member of the faculty and former Appalachian State athlete, took the reins of the team. Smawley was inducted into the North Carolina Sports Hall of Fame in 1992.

Throughout the 1940s and 1950s, each baseball game was a community as well as college activity. The first postwar baseball team finished the season with seven wins and one loss. On May 6, 1955, the first home night baseball game was held after lights were installed on the athletic field, located on the site of the present-day Business Administration Building. Like men's basketball, the baseball team, by the 1950s, faced a schedule filled with college teams.

Although the focus of postwar athletics at the college was men's basketball and baseball, women's basketball began intercollegiate competition during the 1945–1946 season. They continued to face high school and junior college teams for the remainder of the 1940s and 1950s. Women's basketball also proved to be a success. The 1947, 1948, and 1949 teams won all but one game each season. During the 1950–1951 season, the women finished second in the Ellerbe Lions Tourney. Women's basketball produced who was probably the first all-star athlete at the college. Janice (Lowery) Bryant '60, a sophomore forward on the 1957–1958 squad, was named as a forward to the North Carolina all-state basketball team by the *News and Observer* in Raleigh. Bryant averaged seventeen points per game over a twelve-game season. The women's basketball team was discontinued after the 1957–1958 season; women's intercollegiate athletics would not return to the college until the early 1970s.

The burgeoning athletic program added men's cross country and outdoor track and field in 1957 and 1959, respectively. In 1958 Pembroke State's athletic program became a member of NAIA District 26; it remained a member until 1992. Per NAIA membership requirements, the college was banned from playing anyone except accredited four-year institutions. The college's athletic program produced many of the first Lumbee athletic role models, promoting them to near legendary status, and provided for continuation of their playing careers at the collegiate level. In later years, as the school continued to grow, additional sports were added to its athletic program. The foundation had been laid for unparalleled success in athletics from the 1960s through the 1980s.

The growth of athletics prompted the establishment of two college traditions. Since at least 1944, the school colors have been black and gold, although the color gold has been associated with the school since the 1920s. For years, fans have turned out to support the Braves, the nickname of the college's athletic teams. Students and faculty selected the nickname in September 1946, coinciding with the establishment of the football program. When football took to the field for the first time against Campbell College on September 26, 1946, it marked the first time the institution's athletic teams competed under the nickname "Braves"—a name reflective of the all-Indian student body and history of the school.

The period welcomed the addition of another campus tradition that would ring sweet to the ears of students and alumni for generations to come. "Hail to PSC," the alma mater, was written in 1954 by professors Ira Pate Lowry '29 and Reba M. Lowry. Ira Pate spearheaded a contest in December 1953 to write the lyrics for a school song. He had written a tune in 1941 and sought lyrics to go with it. Reba, his wife, responded with the lyrics. Her words and his music will "float on forever" as the alma mater is now an integral part of campus ceremonial events. The tune was renamed "Hail to PSU" and, later, "Hail to UNCP" to reflect the institution's name changes. The Lowry Bell Tower, named in their honor, plays the alma mater daily.

The postwar years brought many other activities to the campus besides sports. Returning GIs organized a Veterans Club, which served their educational and social interests. This club faded out in the mid-1950s, several years after the Korean War. Still other campus developments were the establishment in 1946 of the *Indianhead*, the student yearbook, which replaced a paperback publication from 1941 and 1942 called the

FIGURE 3.25. *Aerial view of the campus of Pembroke State College (circa 1953).*

Lumbee Tattler, and the establishment in 1947 of a student newspaper, *P.S.C. News*, renamed *The Pine Needle* in 1953. The Student Council was started in 1948, which, according to the preamble to its constitution, sought to establish "a more perfect community of students, to afford opportunity for training in American citizenship, and to secure progressively the blessings of liberty, learning, and integrity" for the students, all of whom were expected to be involved in the operation of the council as either participants or supporters. This Student Council evolved into the modern Student Government Association. In 1952 Rosa (Dial) Woods '53 was voted May Day queen; she would later be acknowledged as the first Miss Pembroke State College. During the next three decades, students crowned ambassadors for their organizations, including Miss *Indianhead* and Mr. and Mrs. Student Body. Alumni organized the first Homecoming, held May 19, 1954. The gathering featured a concert by the Pope Field Air Force Band; an open house; a barbecue supper; guest speaker Dr. Carlisle Campbell, president of Meredith College; and a social hour. Alumni raised thirty-nine hundred dollars that was used to pay for the installation of lights on the athletic field.

Additionally, the college still had literary societies, the Emeritan and the Pontiac, which existed for men and women who wanted the opportunity to learn more about parliamentary procedures, public speaking, and debating. The literary societies were an important part of the Commencement exercises, which usually spanned four days. Like most colleges in this period, Pembroke State had a glee club and an orchestra; rather uniquely, for several years it also had a whistling chorus. Without question, one of the most active groups on the campus was the Pembroke State College Players; when they were not performing themselves, they sponsored touring companies for the entertainment of citizens and students alike.

Other student societies nurtured interest in local history and recognized academic achievements. The Henry Berry Folklore Society, at a

1943 meeting, asked for the "immediate establishment of a permanent museum" on campus that would feature items related to the history of Robeson County and North Carolina. By the 1950s the college had "The Pembroke Room" which, according to the 1957 *Indianhead*, was "one of the most intriguing places on the campus." Located in Sampson Hall, items on display included books, manuscripts, photographs of Rev. W. L. Moore and Preston Locklear (among others), archaeological artifacts, farm tools, and articles on local history. Phi Epsilon Chi, a scholastic honor society, was chartered in 1952 at Pembroke State to encourage high academic standards among students. Although the charter class comprised alumni from 1948 to 1952, membership was open to current students and faculty. Eligibility was limited to students who made the dean's list each semester.

Throughout its history, the college was concerned about the spiritual health and welfare of its students, a concern partly attributable to the fact that many of the leading Indian educators were also ministers. During the postwar years, there was an active Wesley Foundation and a Baptist Student Union on campus; since the majority of the Lumbee people are either Methodist or Baptist, these two organizations touched most of the students. Because this was before the decisions of the U.S. Supreme Court requiring strict separation of the church and state in public institutions, the college held, as it would for the next twenty-five years, a "Religious Emphasis Week" on campus each spring. The purpose of this occasion was to give the students an opportunity to hear and question knowledgeable religious leaders on important theological and ethical issues. As early as the 1920s the college also had compulsory chapel services each Thursday morning in the auditorium of Old Main. Members of the faculty even worshipped together. President Wellons attended First Methodist Church in Pembroke with librarian Marjorie Kanable and faculty members Angelika Reckendorf, Ira Pate Lowry '29, and Reba M. Lowry.

The influence of religion was readily seen in the early 1940s in the strict policies of the college governing social behavior. Young women could leave campus only in pairs, the women's dormitories were closed to male visitors, all social activities were closely chaperoned, and there could be no open displays of affection between students. Violations of social rules resulted in suspension. All of this reflected the moral and conservative values of the community and of this era in history. Indeed, in the 1940s there was considerable opposition in the community even to dancing. It was felt that dancing led to other potentially sinful activities. To get around the prohibitions against dancing, the college had a "Mum Club," presumably called that from the phrase "Mum's the word," meaning to keep silent. Students would simply say that they were going to attend a meeting of the "Mum Club," and then go off to dance. A popular student hangout during the late 1940s and 1950s was the College Esso station. Operated by Lumbee merchants, it was located across Third Street from Old Main. Commuter and on-campus students could listen to tunes on the jukebox, purchase sandwiches, and even fraternize with GIs from Fort Bragg in Fayetteville, who were invited by fellow Indian soldiers or had just heard about the campus. Some of the soldiers even found spouses. Another popular spot, Ms. Elsie's convenience store, was located next door to the College Esso.

In many ways, this was an age of innocence in higher education, particularly at Pembroke State College. It is difficult to imagine present-day students viewing a Sadie Hawkins' Day event as a social highlight; this was a day when the girls were allowed to be the pursuers, rather than the pursued. It was a day eagerly awaited during the postwar years. It is equally difficult to imagine modern males starting a Lonely Hearts Club, the objectives of which were pristinely pure. There was also an innocence in the events held on the campus that became popular community activities, such as the annual field days, which involved students of all ages and from all levels of education. These kinds of events largely disappeared in the decade of the 1960s, a decade marked by the rapid growth of higher education, the civil rights movement, the Vietnam War, and the student revolution against it. The sixties clearly represented a watershed in higher education, bringing changes that altered the academic environment in significant and permanent ways.

On July 1, 1949, almost as a prelude to future changes, the name of institution was shortened to Pembroke State College, the name it would keep for the next twenty years. From the founding of the school to 1945,

 enrollment was legally limited to Indians from Robeson County or Indians admitted by the Blood Committee. In 1945 the privilege of admission was extended to include "Indians who are duly accredited members of any tribe of Indians whose Indian status is recognized and accepted by the Bureau of Indian Affairs." This action was

FIGURE 3.26. *Seal of Pembroke State College.*

probably prompted by the decline in enrollment due to the war, the need to grow the campus, and the restrictions placed on admission, which was limited to Lumbees. To grow the campus and keep its student body all-Indian, admission was opened to Indians whose heritage was unquestioned due to their recognition by the Bureau of Indian Affairs. By 1949, a small number of non-Lumbees were attending the college, many drawn to the campus and community through their former military service at nearby bases. They included Ray Holy Elk '52, an Oglala Sioux from South Dakota, and Walter M. Scott '53, a Southern Ute from Colorado. Elk married a Lumbee woman and settled in the community.

In 1952 the Board of Trustees believed the campus was equipped to handle an enrollment of 350 students, a far cry from its actual enrollment of less than 150. Apparently, the 1945 legislative action failed to increase enrollment as hoped. On May 2, 1952, the trustees noted, "Large investments by the state for permanent improvement and maintenance ... would yield large returns by the admission of larger number of students." Coupled with their concern that the local Indian population would not be sufficient to "supply this larger student body," and the need for a regional institution of higher education in southeastern North Carolina, the trust-ees requested the General Assembly, during its 1953 session, to "amend the statutes as to provide for the admission of students from the white race, up to a maximum of not more than 40% of the total enrollment." While awaiting action from the General Assembly, admission was granted to Rev. Christian White (1920–2006), who transferred to Pembroke State in the fall of 1952, becoming the first white student to enroll in the col-lege. Rev. White had become the minister at Pembroke's First Method-

ist Church just a few months before. On March 26, 1953, the General Assembly amended the statutes, as requested by the trustees, opening admission to "any other person of the Indian or White race who may be approved by the board of trustees," effectively ceasing the function of the Blood Committee. Rev. White became the first white graduate in 1954; Commencement exercises were paused to recognize this milestone. Three weeks before his graduation, the U.S. Supreme Court, in the landmark decision *Brown v. Board of Education*, decreed an end to school segregation, opening the school

FIGURE 3.27. *Christian White '54. First white student to enroll and graduate from Pembroke State College.*

to all applicants without regard to race, religion, or national origin. Stu-dents later recalled the seamless integration of the campus as Indian stu-dents welcomed white students to the college. Rev. White was one of the most popular students during his two years at the campus. His children attended Indian schools in Pembroke. Other white students followed, including Joyce Antone '57, William Gene Jones '59, and Christine Corn '56 and Joyce Smawley '56—wives of faculty at the college—and Henry Levon Cribb '56 and Joseph Allen Williams Jr., both from Laurel Hill,

North Carolina. Williams became the college's first white athlete when he joined the basketball team during the 1954–1955 season. Over a decade later, Larry Barnes became the first African American student to enroll in the summer of 1967; Sylvia (Baugham) Banks was the second to enroll in the fall of 1967. To its credit, Pembroke State was one of the first southern colleges to take this step and today is recognized as the most diverse institution of higher education in North Carolina and the southeastern United States.

With fourteen years of successful leadership, President Wellons retired in 1956 after reaching the voluntary retirement age of sixty-five. He took over the college at one of its lowest points during World War II and led the small teacher institution into a brave new world that included the addition of multiple campus buildings, the expansion of student activities, the establishment of campus traditions, and the integration of the college. Dr. Wellons moved to Orlando, Florida, where he served as pastor of St. Paul's United Methodist Church. He died on May 22, 1974, at the United Methodist Retirement Home in Durham, North Carolina.

As President Wellons's successor, the Board of Trustees selected Dr. Walter J. Gale on May 16, 1956. He led the institution from July 1, 1956, through September 1962. Gale, a native of Haddonfield, New Jersey, was born July 14, 1914. He earned a BS degree in elementary education from the New Jersey State Teachers College, known today as The College of New Jersey, in 1936, and an MEd and PhD in education from Duke University in 1946 and 1956, respectively. He was a former teacher in New Jersey. After service in the navy during World War II, Dr. Gale taught at Duke University and served as principal of Needham Broughton High School in Raleigh, from 1948 to 1953. He then taught educational psychology at Woman's College of the University of North Carolina, today the University of North Carolina at Greensboro, from 1953 to 1955. Dr. Gale was also a visiting lecturer at the University of North Carolina at Chapel Hill and Duke University from 1955 to 1956. He loved music and enjoyed playing bridge.

President Gale was an energetic man who was determined to publicize the college and its programs. His philosophy was, "Get on the ball and get the job done," and his slogan for the college was, "Quality Education at a Minimum Cost," a slogan that is still applicable. He particularly began to promote the school's teacher education, music, and athletic programs, all of which were high-visibility programs and attracted attention to the institution. At the same time, however, he worked diligently to raise academic standards and to develop a solid program of financial aid. Scholarships were awarded each year to a number of students who showed scholastic ability and promise. A faculty-endowed scholarship was given annually to the entering freshman who ranked highest on the comprehensive exam administered to all new students. There was also a loan fund supported mainly by gifts to the Alumni Association, to aid worthy students enrolled in the college, and there was a work program for those who did not qualify for other aid but still needed help. The

FIGURE 3.28. *Dr. Walter J. Gale. President of Pembroke State College from 1956 to 1962.*

FIGURE 3.29. *John L. Carter Sr. '26, '29, '43. First full-time registrar and member of the Board of Trustees. Served the university for twenty-eight years.*

results of Gale's efforts were dramatic. During the 1958–1959 academic year, Pembroke State College was recognized, for the first of two times in its history, as the fastest-growing college in North Carolina. At the beginning of the fall semester in 1956, the college enrolled 151 students; by the fall semester, 1962, that figure had increased to 758 students. To manage the increase in student courses and records, John L. Carter Sr. (1906–1983) '26, '29, '43, was hired as the institution's first full-time registrar in 1959. A native of Pembroke, Carter was a former teacher and principal in the Robeson County schools and had served eighteen years as a member of the institution's Board of Trustees. He retired in 1975. Another result of this rapid growth was that whites came to outnumber Indians on the campus. Signifying this change, in 1959 four whites from North Carolina were appointed to the formerly all-Indian Board of Trustees: Charles Hostetler of Raeford, Hal Little of Wadesboro, Ashley Murphy of Atkinson, and Edward L. Williamson of Whiteville. Little was the first white elected chair of the trustees in 1968.

While this period of growth was partly due to general trends in higher education and partly due to the opening of the institution to all qualified students at Pembroke State, it was also due to the ability of the college to recruit out-of-state students. During the 1960s, all expenses for a resident student were $306.50 for in-state residents and $406.50 for out-of-state residents. Because of these moderate costs, the college attracted many students from South Carolina, Virginia, New York, and particularly New Jersey and Massachusetts. In this period Gale believed the college could easily grow to fourteen hundred students if it had dormitories, but the state was unwilling to fund the number he requested. Even so, the college received a steady influx of outsiders during these years. While these out-of-state students got an education at low cost, they also brought different ideas and perspectives to the college in a two-way cultural exchange between local and out-of-state students.

With the growth in enrollment came concomitant growth in the physical plant and the size of the faculty. During the six years that Dr.

Gale was president, the campus increased from thirty to thirty-five acres; a new cafeteria opened in 1959; a new L-shaped, two-story men's dormitory was built in 1961; several buildings were renovated; several parking lots were paved; and the faculty was increased from twenty-three to fifty-five in number. The Carolina Inn, a downtown hotel, was leased as temporary male housing from 1959 until the early 1960s to accommodate the recent enrollment growth. Overall, Gale's years as head of the college were years of consolidation, strengthening of the academic program, increased recruitment of students, and preparation for future growth.

Although it never directly became a part of the college's history, an event in 1958, during Gale's administration, brought the Lumbees national and international attention. In that year, the Ku Klux Klan became active in Robeson County, saying that they were going to put the Indians in their place and end race-mixing. To promote their goals, they announced a rally for January 18, 1958, to take place about ten miles outside of Pembroke in Maxton, near Hayes Pond. On the night of the rally, the Lumbees turned out in force and drove the Klansmen away in an embarrassing rout in what is known locally as the "Victory at Hayes Pond." According to several Indian participants, Dr. Gale was involved in planning the Indian action against the Klan, a reflection of his concern for the community and the college. If the Klan had held a successful meeting, there is every reason to believe that they would have eventually turned their attention to the college with its Indian and white student body.

In a surprise move on June 21, 1962, President Gale tendered his resignation to the Board of Trustees, effective June 30 of the following year. His resignation highlighted a rift between himself and the Board of Trustees. In a letter published in *The Robesonian*, he mentioned that he had considered resigning numerous times during his tenure but remained "because of the unique opportunity for service offered." Although he felt the position of president of the college was one of respect, he was being "criticized, attacked and slandered at will," having to "stand alone without support." President Gale suggested he was the "victim of an internal 'struggle for power' among the Lumbee Indians that is vicious to the point of having no conscience." He called attention to trustees who failed to support the college and a "minute minority" of Lumbees who were "interested only in their selfish ends." Rev. L. W. Jacobs '25, '28, chair of the Board of Trustees, said the trustees expressed satisfaction with the advancements made at Pembroke State during President Gale's tenure. Those included the growth of the campus, the lowered cost per pupil to the state, and the increase in enrollment, particularly with out-of-state students. Rev. Jacobs stated that the college had the support of the majority of the trustees and the Lumbee community. Although President Gale expressed his willingness to assist the trustees with the selection of his replacement, he left the college in September 1962 to accept the position of dean of academic affairs at West Chester State College, now West Chester University. A few years later, Dr. Gale served as chief of the Loans Branch Division of Student Financial Aid for the Department of Health, Education, and Welfare in Washington, DC. In 1973 the Pembroke State Alumni Association named Dr. Gale as the recipient of its Distinguished Service Award. He passed away September 9, 1976, in Washington, DC, following his retirement the previous summer.

In September 1962 the Board of Trustees selected English E. Jones, dean of student affairs and assistant to Dr. Gale, to serve as interim president during the 1962–1963 school year.

Between 1929 and 1962, while navigating the challenges of the Great Depression and World War II, the institution evolved from The Cherokee Indian Normal School of Robeson County into Pembroke State College. The curriculum expanded from a two-year normal degree to offer numerous four-year baccalaureate degrees in teaching and nonteaching fields. Student enrollment increased as the campus was opened to all students regardless of race. Additional faculty were added; the campus physical plant was enlarged, and the quality of academic programs improved. The institution earned the nickname "fastest-growing college in the state," and because of its low costs, attracted students from throughout North Carolina and the eastern United States. Pembroke State was now positioned for two decades of unparalleled, rapid growth not seen during the institution's first seventy-five years.

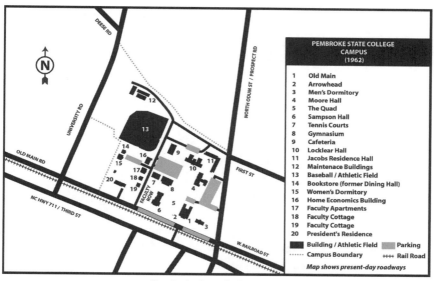

MAP 3.1. *Pembroke State College campus (1962).*

TIMELINE OF NOTABLE INSTITUTIONAL EVENTS (1929–1962)

1929   • Rev. J. E. (John Ephraim) Sawyer named superintendent.

1930   • Ten acres added along western edge of campus.

Early 1930s   • Athletic field with grandstand constructed.

1933   • Arrowhead erected in the Quad by J. Hampton Rich.

               • First two years of college curriculum added.

1935   • Home Economics Building opened; razed mid-1960s.

               • First two-year college class graduated with four students.

               • G. G. (Grover Gaines) Maughon Sr. named superintendent.

               • Department for Teaching the Deaf established; discontinued in 1939.

1936   • Alumni Association established by alumni.

               • Third year of normal and college curriculum added.

1937   • Celebrated semicentennial.

               • Last two-year normal and college degrees awarded.

1938   • First three-year normal and college class graduated with twelve students.

1939   • Received "conditional Senior College Rating."

               • Fourth year of normal and college curriculum added.

               • Last high school class graduated; high school separated from the institution and moved to the new Pembroke High School on property adjacent to campus.

               • College gymnasium built; razed 1988.

Late 1930s   • Men's basketball and baseball began intercollegiate competition.

1939–53   • Only state-supported four-year college for Indians in the United States.

1940   • First four-year bachelor of arts degrees awarded to six students.

               • Dr. O. H. (Owens Hand) Browne named acting superintendent.

               • The pageant *The Life Story of a People* performed in the college gymnasium; held again December 1941.

1941   • Name changed to Pembroke State College for Indians, and title of head of institution changed to president.

               • First yearbook, *Lumbee Tattler*, published; second and final edition published in 1942.

1941–45   • 130 students and alumni serve in World War II; 4 (2 students and 2 alumni) were killed in action, including Wade H. Lowry '37, '38—first Lumbee killed in World War II.

1942	• Dr. Ralph D. Wellons named first president.
1943	• Bachelor of science degree first offered.
By 1944	• Black and gold are school colors.
1944	• First bachelor of science degrees awarded.
1945	• Enrollment opened to "federally recognized" Indians.
	• Women's basketball began intercollegiate competition.
1946	• *Indianhead* yearbook first published.
	• "Braves" nickname adopted for athletic teams.
1946–50	• Fielded intercollegiate football team.
1947	• *P.S.C. News*, the student newspaper, established.
1948	• Student Council established.
1949	• Name shortened to Pembroke State College.
	• Sampson Hall (administration building and library) opened; razed 1995.
1950	• Locklear Hall opened.
1951	• Received full accreditation as a four-year liberal arts college.
	• Moore Hall opened.
1952	• President's residence opened.
	• Christian White, first white student, enrolled.
1953	• *P.S.C. News* renamed *The Pine Needle*.
	• General Assembly amended statutes to provide for the admission of white students.
1954	• "Hail to PSC," the alma mater, written by Ira Pate Lowry '29 and Reba M. Lowry; later renamed "Hail to PSU" and "Hail to UNCP."
	• First Homecoming held.
	• Christian White, first white graduate.
	• Following the Supreme Court's *Brown v. Board of Education* school desegregation decision, college opened to all qualified applicants without regard to race.
1956	• Dr. Walter J. Gale named second president.
1957	• Men's cross country added.
1958	• President Gale supported student involvement in Indian rout of Ku Klux Klan.
	• Women's basketball discontinued.

- Athletic teams became members of National Association of Intercollegiate Athletics (NAIA) District 26; remained members until 1992.

1958–59   • Recognized as fastest-growing college in North Carolina.

1959   • Men's outdoor track and field added.

- First full-time registrar hired.

- Four whites added to former all-Indian Board of Trustees.

- Cafeteria opened.

1960   • Campus increased from thirty to thirty-five acres.

1961   • Jacobs Residence Hall opened; today known as Jacobs Hall.

1962   • English E. Jones, first Lumbee named interim president.

Chapter Four

1962–1979
AN ERA OF PROGRESS AND TUMULT

We feel that this occasion is somewhat symbolic of the Parable of the Mustard Seed which a man took and sowed in his field: Which indeed is the least of all seeds, but when it is grown, it is the greatest among herbs, and becomes a tree.

In the fall of 1887 the first Indian School was opened with one teacher, fifteen students, and a plant valued at less than $500.00. A small beginning yes—but, "a mustard seed still."

Through careful cultivation this little seed has grown into a small tree, "Pembroke State College."

English E. Jones, president,
Pembroke State College, Diamond
Jubilee Celebration Program (1963)

The 1960s and 1970s were the halcyon days of higher education. During these decades, there was unprecedented, virtually unlimited expansion of enrollments, facilities, faculties, and programs. As a result of the phenomenal growth of these years and of generous state funding, Pembroke State College experienced a virtual transformation. In 1969 it was designated a "regional university" by the state legislature and was renamed Pembroke State University; then, in 1971, the General Assembly adopted legislation making all four-year, state-supported institutions of higher education a part of the University of North Carolina system. As a result, Pembroke State became one of the sixteen constituent units of the University of North Carolina, with this change taking effect July 1, 1972. Today, the UNC system comprises seventeen institutions. These changes were symbolic of the dramatic developments occurring in higher education in the 1960s and 1970s. As they pertained to Pembroke State, they were presided over by English E. Jones.

Born in Robeson County on October 22, 1921, Jones, a Lumbee Indian, was the son of tenant farmers. At age four, Jones and his family moved to Dillon County, South Carolina. During a fateful meeting, Jones was plucked out of a cotton field by teacher James K. Braboy '28, '58, also a Lumbee, who enrolled Jones at Leland Grove School, where Braboy taught. In 1970 Braboy was named South Carolina Educator of the Year and runner-up for the national honor. Through Braboy's lifelong friendship and mentoring, Jones became an honor graduate at Pembroke High School in 1942. At the onset of World War II, Jones served four years in the Army Air Force, spending three of them in Europe. He flew sixty-one combat missions over Germany as a tail gunner on B-25 and B-17 bombers. Jones was honorably discharged in 1946 with the rank of first sergeant. With the help of the G.I. Bill, he received a BS degree in science from Western Kentucky State College, today Western Kentucky University, in 1948. Jones was a highly successful agriculture teacher at Pembroke High School from 1948 to 1952, and the assistant Robeson County agricultural agent with the North Carolina Extension Service between 1952 and 1956. He was hired by President Gale in 1956 to teach agricultural science. Jones earned an MS degree in science from North Carolina State College, today North Carolina State University, in 1959. He became the dean of men in 1957, the dean of students in 1958, and, in 1960, dean of student affairs and assistant to the president. Two years later, in September 1962, he was named the interim president of the institution. On June 21, 1963, Jones was appointed the third president of the college, becoming the first Lumbee president in the institution's history. In June 1965 he was awarded an honorary doctor of laws degree by Wake Forest University. Dr. Jones, known as a charismatic leader, was an avid golfer, a great storyteller, and a very active Baptist lay leader who served as a member of the General Board of the North Carolina Baptist Convention. The Jones administration, from 1962 to 1979, was a period of extensive growth and change for the institution. It was an exciting time in higher education and in the history of Pembroke State College.

Notably, the end of Dr. Jones's first year as president coincided with the college's Diamond Jubilee Celebration, held to recognize the first seventy-five years of the institution's history and service. The anniversary marked a time to celebrate the past and talk of the future. The first event of the celebration was held December 1, 1962, in conjunction with Homecoming. At a

FIGURE 4.1. *Dr. English E. Jones. President and chancellor of Pembroke State University from 1962 to 1979.*

luncheon attended by more than three hundred alumni and friends, President Jones shared his plans for the future growth of the campus, which included a presentation on the master plan and state budget requests. The luncheon was followed by class reunions and a basketball game, where the Braves defeated the College of Charleston. During halftime, Judy (Locklear) Lowery '64 was crowned Miss Pembroke State College. Other Diamond Jubilee events followed. On May 9, 1963, Dr. John T. Caldwell, president of North Carolina State College, was the keynote speaker during a ceremony in which three campus buildings were dedicated to individuals who had devoted their lives to the institution. As previously mentioned, the Arts Building, which opened in 1951, was named in honor of the Reverend W.L. Moore, one of the founders of the institution; the library wing of Sampson Hall was dedicated to the memory of Mary H. Livermore, a religious leader in the area for fifty years and a professor and dean of women at the college from 1941 to 1951; and a men's dormitory, which opened in 1961, was named in honor of the Reverend L. (Lonnie) W. Jacobs '25, '28, who ultimately served as chairman of the Board of Trustees for thirty-five years, including from 1937 to 1968. Rev. Jacobs was born in 1893 near Fairmont, North Carolina. A veteran of World War I, he completed high school at Cherokee Normal in 1925 and was a member of the institution's first class to receive a two-year normal degree in 1928. Rev. Jacobs attended two summers at Southeastern Baptist Theological Seminary and served as a Baptist minister for over fifty years. He was a teacher and principal in Robeson County for eighteen years. With the exception of four years, Rev. Jacobs was a member of the Board of Trustees from 1924 until his death in 1968.

FIGURE 4.3. *L. W. Jacobs '25, '28. Chairman of the Board of Trustees for thirty-five years and namesake of Jacobs Hall.*

The auditorium in Old Main was also designated "Memorial Auditorium" in honor of students and faculty who served in World War I, World War II, and the Korean War. The dedication ceremony was followed by a concert in Memorial Auditorium featuring the College Band and the College Mixed Chorus. The following day, May 10, 1963, during the final Diamond

FIGURE 4.2. *Diamond Jubilee logo (1962).*

Jubilee event, North Carolina governor Terry Sanford, recognized as an "Education Governor" in the state's history, delivered the major address, praising the school for its continued progress and development. The celebration was followed by a dramatic production of *The Diary of Anne Frank* by the College Playmakers in Memorial Auditorium, a baseball game versus Erskine College, and a formal ball in the college gymnasium. The Diamond Jubilee Celebration concluded with Commencement exercises, held on June 2–3, 1963. Although the Jones years produced many achievements, he always took great pride in characterizing himself as a brick-and-mortar president. The campus witnessed a building boom during his administration, with twenty facilities or buildings being constructed or renovated, representing 75 percent of the college's physical plant.

The tremendous growth of the institution's physical plant was matched by growth in other areas. Indicative of the changes that were taking place was the increase in faculty members from 55 in 1962 to 112 in 1972, and 134 by 1979. Perhaps more important was the fact that the qualifications of the faculty improved; whereas less than 40 percent held

FIGURE 4.4. *Memorial Auditorium in Old Main (1961).*

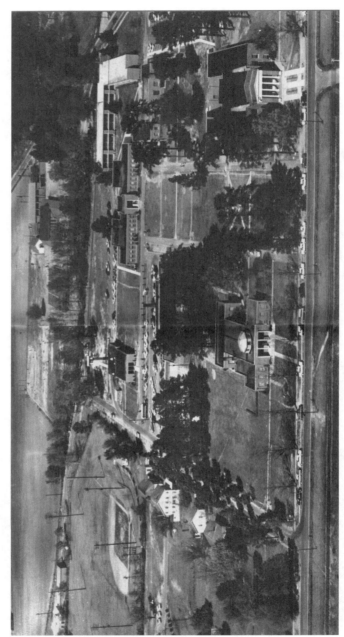

FIGURE 4.5. *Aerial view of the campus of Pembroke State College (circa 1962).*

terminal degrees in 1962, that figure had risen to 57 percent by 1979. A new generation of faculty and staff would provide valuable service to the university for decades to come. One of the more memorable faculty members from the period was Dr. Paul Freiwirth (1929–2006). Dr. Freiwirth, a professor of history, taught at the university from 1962 to 1982. He did undergraduate work in theology at Atlantic Union College and received an MA degree from Potomac University and a PhD from the University of Maryland. According to Dr. Jose D'Arruda, a colleague and physics professor, "Students would say that his lectures were really interesting and when the bell rang to end classes, he would stop his lecture in the middle of a sentence, and then when the next class started, he would begin with the next word in that sentence." Another colleague, Dr. Tom Ross, who taught geography, remembered Dr. Freiwirth as a "brilliant academic" with a "world-class photographic memory." During the 1970s a student came to Dr. Ross seeking permission to withdraw from Dr. Freiwirth's class. Dr. Ross asked why the student wanted to withdraw. "I'm afraid of him," said the strapping student. "Afraid?" Dr. Ross responded, "Why, you are twice as large as he is." The student said, "Oh, it's not that. I'm afraid of his brain. You see, on the first day of class he asked us all our names, and fifteen minutes later he called the roll, from memory. I can't deal with someone that smart. I like people more like you and the other professors here." After retiring, Dr. Freiwirth continued to live in Pembroke. He walked daily, wearing his trademark "cooter shell" hat, to the Livermore Library at 9 a.m. to read newspapers.

There was growth in other areas. The college's support staff increased from 35 to 134. One notable hire was Gene Warren (1929–2009) as the first director of public relations in 1968. He also served as the first sports information director and established what is today University Communications and Marketing. Warren's press releases and columns in *The Robesonian* kept the campus and community abreast of the changes at the college. For the purposes of this text, they also provided invaluable insight into the growth and expansion of the period; one of his first columns touted the affordability of attending Pembroke State. Warren retired in 1994. The size of the campus also increased, expanding from thirty-five to ninety-five acres as the campus grew north along Odum Street/Prospect Road to the site of the present-day Cypress Residence Hall and University Village Apartments. The value of the institution went from $1.5 to $13.5 million. Because university funding is tied to enrollment, little of this growth would have been possible if the college had not been attracting increasing numbers of students. By the early 1960s, the babies of the postwar boom had reached college age; in combination with the increasing need for education to cope with a more complex world, that fact spurred college enrollments enormously. Pembroke State grew from an enrollment of 758 in 1962 to 2,334 in 1979. To assist with student recruitment, Jason B. Lowry '48 (1919–2013), a Lumbee and native of Pembroke, was hired in the summer of 1965 to fill the newly created position of director of admissions. Two years after Lowry's hire, the first African American students enrolled at the college in 1967, Larry Barnes in the summer and Sylvia (Baugham) Banks that fall. Banks, after transferring to Pembroke State, became the first African American graduate in 1969, and Barnes the second in 1971. Summer Commencement exercises were held between 1966 and 1971 to accommodate the growth in graduates.

The August 16, 1973, meeting of the Board of Trustees marked two milestones in the history of the university, both symbolic of the campus's growth during this period. Beth (Dail) Finch and Janie (Maynor) Maynor Locklear '66 were installed as the first female members of the formerly all-male Board of Trustees. Finch (1921–2012) was a member of the Fayetteville City Council. Later, in 1975 she was elected mayor of Fayetteville, making her the first woman to be elected mayor of a major North Carolina city. Maynor Locklear (1945–1992), a Lumbee and native of Pembroke, was a community activist and staff member with the Lumbee Regional Development Association (LRDA), a community action organization founded in 1968 to serve as a voice for the Lumbee people. Soon after being sworn in, Maynor Locklear became the first female officer of the board after being elected secretary. Also during the meeting, the first donation was made to the university's endowment after two thousand dollars was contributed on behalf of McNair Investment Company of Laurinburg, North Carolina. The endowment is managed by the university's Foundation Inc., which was established in 1968. Today, the university's endowment is more than $17 million. It was the "golden age" of expansion and democratization for higher education.

With the influx of students, however, came many changes in campus life. This was partly a product of sheer numbers, but it was also related to the social unrest of American society in the 1960s. Though there were many forces responsible for this development, none was more potent than the Vietnam War. While Pembroke State was touched by student and faculty unrest, it experienced no violence or student takeovers. Many of the institution's students were concerned about national and international events, but most came from conservative backgrounds and were mainly intent on preparing themselves for future employment. Still, the students did organize a "coffeehouse" where they could meet, argue the issues, listen to folk music, and socialize.

FIGURE 4.6. *Larry Barnes '71. First African American student to enroll at Pembroke State College, in 1967.*

FIGURE 4.7. *Sylvia (Baugham) Banks '69. First African American student to graduate from Pembroke State College.*

In the 1968 presidential election, a busload of the college's students went to work in the Eugene McCarthy campaign; U.S. senator McCarthy was a leading opponent of

American involvement in Vietnam and became, for a time, the focus of the antiwar movement. On campus, a small group of students started an underground newspaper called *The Pine Noodle*. They were disenchanted with the student newspaper *The Pine Needle*, which they felt was too conservative and indecisive. They wanted, as they wrote, "to fill a vacuum." According to the first issue, "THE PINE NOODLE exists as: An appeal to students to explode the myth of faculty-administration-student fur-smoothing; An opportunity to become the controller, not the controlled; An expression of student thought and ACTION; A forum for discussion." It was, in part, an antiwar protest, as seen in statements such as "MARINES ARE MURDERERS," but it also sought to stir up the students on issues such as the bookstore, the cafeteria, freedom of speech, and the role of the student government. It is one of the best examples of the limited student activism at Pembroke State. After an initial outburst of enthusiasm that produced several more issues, it succumbed to the general lack of interest on the part of the majority of the students.

The other, even more important example of student activism came in 1970 when a group of students presented the university administration with a list of sixteen demands. The students took the position that they elected people without power to offices without functions; they proclaimed that the student government should assert its rights to govern itself. Many of the demands concerned the social rules of the university related to visitation in the women's residence halls, alcoholic beverages, and privacy. But others involved the honor code and student participation in the governing of the university. Dr. Jones responded to the demands by noting that his administration would listen to any proposals that came from the student government, the duly elected spokespersons for the student body. President Jones stressed that when properly considered proposals were submitted to his office, they would get his attention and "appropriate action." He concluded that his door was always open "to all individuals with information or suggestions which might improve the total institutional program."

This position did not satisfy the protesting students, and they were able to nullify the spring student elections by which student officials were chosen. Under the Student Constitution, a petition signed by 10 percent of the student body could prevent student officers from assuming office. Consequently, by the students' own choice, there was no functioning student government for the academic year 1970–1971. That year, a new constitution was adopted, and the student government resumed operation in the fall semester of 1971. This type of protest was common in the sixties and seventies, resulting in students

FIGURE 4.8. *Serving as an all-Indian school until 1952, UNC Pembroke is today the most diverse institution of higher education in North Carolina. Representatives of the university's diverse student body standing next to the Arrowhead in the Quad (circa 1979).*

across the country gaining a larger role in university governance. At Pembroke State, students were given representation on faculty committees, and the president of the Student Government Association was made an ex officio member of the Board of Trustees. R. Gary Strickland, the 1971–1972 student government president, was the first student member of the Board of Trustees.

While there was some unrest on the part of the Pembroke State faculty in these two decades, it was more generalized than specific. There were periodic concerns over salary appropriations and how they were distributed, and over relations between the faculty and administration, relations that waxed and waned. But for the most part, faculty members were content to be a part of a growing and increasingly progressive university. There were protests from several faculty members who were not reemployed. They maintained that the university's administration was repressive and that it managed all the news that came out of the institution. There is, however, no way to gauge the validity of their claims since a state investigation provided no support for their claims, and no litigation resulted in any legal decisions.

A far more important issue to come out of this period was the "de-Indianization" question, which reflected the concern of the Lumbees that they were losing control of the institution originally created for their benefit. While this had been a nagging worry since the integration of the school in 1954, it was first formally articulated by Lew Barton '56, a noted Lumbee historian and writer, in a letter of November 18, 1971, to *The Robesonian*. This concern was brought to a head by the changes occurring in the state's system of higher education, which highlighted the fact that the school had become predominantly white and which led to charges that relations between the Pembroke community and the university were deteriorating. The issues of change and de-Indianization are intertwined in a rather complicated fashion.

Until 1952 Pembroke State was an all-Indian college. Up to 1955, an addition of new programs and facilities was the prerogative of the individual institution, provided that they could get funding from the legislature or elsewhere. Consequently, the president of the college made direct appeals to the legislature. While this resulted in a strong tie between politics and higher education, it also meant that small colleges such as Pembroke State remained essentially under local control. In 1955 the State Board of Higher Education was established and given responsibility for allotting the "functions and activities" of all public institutions. As it turned out, it was not given authority equal to its responsibilities, and the legislature continued its direct involvement in higher education. Few restraints existed on institutional growth and program proliferation from 1955 to 1969, and local boards of trustees retained considerable control over their institutions. In the midst of this era of expansion in higher education, Pembroke State, like a number of other public senior institutions, sought university status, which it achieved on April 30, 1969, when its name was changed from Pembroke State College to Pembroke State University, and it was designated a "regional university" by the General Assembly. The changes became effective on July 1 of that year. The gaining of university status and designation as a regional university were certainly high points in the institution's history that brought increased prestige to the campus, leading to increased loyalty by alumni and friends of the university. The achievement of this goal was accomplished by students, faculty, administrators, trustees, community citizens, and area legislators all working together. President Jones was in Raleigh when the General Assembly passed the law, and his reaction was one of great elation. Back home, the college community celebrated. In commenting on the act, Dr. Jones noted that "university status will allow us to expand our programs which means expanded services.... I am extremely pleased over the long-range impact it will make." On

FIGURE 4.9. *Seal of Pembroke State University.*

May 2, a celebration, held in the college gymnasium, reflected the excitement and optimism for the future of the university. It was attended by an overflow crowd after classes were dismissed for one hour. The legislation elevating Pembroke State to a regional university did the same for all other public senior colleges in the state.

For a brief period, the regional universities were given virtually unlimited opportunities to continue their expansion. The statute that redesignated public colleges as universities spelled out clearly the purposes of the regional universities. According to the law, "The regional universities shall provide undergraduate and graduate instruction in the liberal arts, fine arts, and sciences, and in the learned professions, including teaching...; and said regional universities shall provide research in the liberal arts and sciences, pure and applied. The regional universities shall provide other undergraduate and graduate programs of instruction as are deemed necessary to meet the needs of their constituencies and of the State." It went on to give the new universities the power to confer all degrees, "including the doctor's degree." In February 1970 Dr. Jones created a University Graduate Council to formulate proposals for graduate programs at Pembroke State. While future changes precluded doctoral degrees being offered by the university, the Graduate Council took the first steps in establishing a graduate program for the institution. A meeting was held on campus on April 1, 1974, to gauge interest in a cooperative graduate program between Pembroke State and Appalachian State University in Boone, North Carolina. An impressive audience of six hundred attended, and the first graduate courses on campus were offered from 1974 to 1976 through the cooperative agreement with Appalachian State. In 1976 another cooperative graduate program with the University of North Carolina at Charlotte followed. Though not accomplished without a struggle, Pembroke State finally received permission from the Board of Governors in 1978 for its own graduate program. In July of that year, Dr. William Howard Dean was hired as the first director of Graduate Studies. The first graduate degrees—master of arts in education—were awarded to fifty-seven students one year later in 1979.

The creation of the regional universities touched off a great debate in North Carolina over higher education; there was concern over rising costs as each institution expanded virtually unchecked, and there was continuing concern over legislative involvement in educational decisions. As a result of this debate, in October 1971 the General Assembly adopted the Higher Education Reorganization Act. This made all public senior institutions part of the University of North Carolina under a General Administration headed by President William C. Friday and ultimately under the overall authority of a Board of Governors. This action was taken to give North Carolina a quality system of higher education with centralized control. In this manner, costs were to be reduced, the duplication of programs was to be minimized, and politics were to be eliminated from the system. The executive head of each of the constituent institutions in the UNC system was designated "chancellor." Thus, President Jones became Chancellor Jones. The Board of Governors, designed to be a central governing and policymaking body for the public senior institutions, began to function on July 1, 1972. Charged with developing a long-range plan, subject to periodic review, for the University of North Carolina and with developing a single unified budget for all of public senior higher education, the Board of Governors in August 1972 declared a moratorium on the establishment of any new degree programs within the system. This effectively stopped the uncontrolled expansion of the state's public institutions.

From the beginning, Chancellor Jones adopted the position that the new organizational structure must be given time to show whether it would work effectively. He insisted that the new Board of Governors would have to think in terms of what was good for the state and not in terms of individual institutions. At the same time he also maintained that local boards of trustees must be left in charge of the "internal affairs" of each constituent institution. As of July 1, 1972, each of the seventeen campuses had a thirteen-member Board of Trustees, with eight elected by the Board of Governors, four appointed by the governor, and the thirteenth being the president of the student government, serving ex officio. Each local board is charged with promoting "the sound development" of its institution and with advising the chancellor and the Board of Governors "on matters pertaining to…the management and development of the institution." The chancellor is "the administrative and executive head of the institution and shall exercise complete executive authority therein, subject to the direction of the [p]resident." Furthermore, the chancellor is "responsible for carrying out policies of the Board of Governors and of the board of trustees." With minor adjustments, the University of North

Carolina system continues to operate as designed by the Higher Education Reorganization Act.

The relative benefits of these changes for the campuses have been
debated since the law was implemented, and the debate will continue
because changes of this magnitude mean losses as well as gains. Some
Lumbees perceived these changes as a loss of local autonomy, something
they feared and fought through the years. That, combined with non-
Indians becoming a majority of the student body, faculty, and administration, raised the issue of de-Indianization, which is still a concern of
part of the Indian community. The issue is difficult to resolve because the
university has been important to the community throughout its existence;
it was the Indian educational, cultural, and social center, symbolizing
opportunity and dreams. In short, it would be difficult, if not impossible,
to overstate the importance of the institution to the Indian community.

Most Lumbees are excited about the progress of the institution. While
they are pleased over its physical growth and broader range of educational
programs, there is a sense of loss in that the school is no longer totally
a part of the Indian community. Many of these feelings became evident
in the Old Main dispute, which occurred in the midst of this period
of rapid change. Notably, this period was also one of national Indian
political activism and militancy driven by the Red Power Movement, an
Indian political and cultural renaissance during the late 1960s and 1970s.
Some of the militancy spilled over into Robeson County. While most of
the Indian people were content to be known as Lumbees, a small faction
insisted that they were Tuscaroras and demanded total control over
their schools. The most radical of the Native American organizations,
the American Indian Movement (AIM), sent several representatives
to Robeson County to support the Tuscaroras, including the nationally
known Dennis Banks. Regardless of the justice or logic of their position,
AIM and the Tuscaroras did introduce a degree of militancy among the
Indian people of Robeson County. As a result, there were confrontations,

marches, caravans, and support for the takeover of the Bureau of Indian Affairs offices in Washington, DC, in November 1972. Whether coincidental or not, there was also a series of more than forty fires in Robeson County during this eventful period, arson being suspected in most cases. Without question, the fire that produced the greatest outrage and concern was the one that consumed Old Main on March 18, 1973.

Back in July 1970, when the university submitted its capital improvement requests to the Advisory Budget Commission, it requested as its priority item an auditorium costing $1.6 million to replace Old Main. By January 1971, that request had been approved and the university's administration announced plans to demolish Old Main and build the new auditorium at that location. At the time, Old Main was a deteriorating, termite-infested structure with dangerous stairs and a leaky roof, but it was also a half-century-old landmark. Unfortunately, the university was landlocked and had no place to put the new auditorium other than on

FIGURE 4.10. *Save Old Main protest.*
COURTESY OF BRUCE BARTON '86.

the same location as Old Main. The realization that Old Main was about to be razed led a growing number of Lumbee and Tuscarora Indians to voice protests. They wanted to preserve the structure as a symbol of the years when the institution served only Indians. As opposition to the destruction of Old Main gained momentum, a Save Old Main movement began. The movement galvanized the Indian community like nothing had since Indians routed the Ku Klux Klan in 1958. The movement had deep roots within the Lumbee Regional Development Association (LRDA) but quickly came to include a majority of the Lumbees, as well as other Indians and many non-Indians. Movement leaders included Lumbees such as Lew Barton '56, Brantly Blue, Dalton Brooks '60, Adolph L. Dial '43, Danford Dial Sr. '47, Janie (Maynor) Maynor Locklear '66, and Lonnie and Ruth (Locklear) Revels '58. Other members included Howard Brooks and Carnell Locklear of the East Carolina Indian Organization. They all supported turning Old Main into an Indian cultural center and museum.

Old Main became an emotional and political issue that attracted local, state, and national attention, particularly from Indian Country. A small number of AIM members relocated to the area to join in the fight to save the historic structure. The Save Old Main movement occurred around the same time as the nationally publicized Indian takeover of the Bureau of Indian Affairs in 1972 and Wounded Knee in South Dakota in early 1973. Other Indians advocated for saving Old Main, including Leo Vocu, executive director of the National Congress of American Indians, who came to Pembroke to speak at a rally, and Louis Bruce, commissioner of the Bureau of Indian Affairs. Bruce commented, "Old Main is a monument to the Indian people throughout this country." Non-Indian national political figures also supported the Save Old Main movement. Shirley Chisholm, the first African American woman elected to Congress and the first woman to run for the Democratic presidential nomination, lauded efforts to save Old Main during a May 4, 1972, campaign stop in Pembroke, when she proclaimed, "Hold on, my Indian brothers. Hold on. Lots of the people are with you."

Once the controversy was under way, Dr. Jones, speaking for the administration and the trustees, stressed that he did not want to lose the new auditorium in order to save Old Main, and that it should be understood that the institution was state property and belonged to all North Carolinians. He concluded that the whole university was a memorial to the early determination of the Indian people. In reality, most Lumbees wanted both the new auditorium and the restoration of Old Main, and those who favored the demolition of the historic structure did so for reasons of practicality.

FIGURE 4.11. *Shirley Chisholm. First African American woman elected to Congress and the first woman to run for the Democratic presidential nomination. Speaking from the steps of Old Main on May 4, 1972, during a presidential campaign rally.*
COURTESY OF BRUCE BARTON '86.

Lew Barton's November 1971 article on the de-Indianization of Pembroke State had galvanized community support for Old Main. By December, over one thousand Indians had signed a petition started by Danford Dial Sr. '47 to spare the building. Dial felt that "if she [Old Main] goes down, she will carry with her the heritage of thousands of Lumbee Indians who saw their community life centered in this old building." To Dial and many other Lumbees, Old Main was a de facto social, cultural, and educational center for the tribe. Dial said Lumbees "went there for entertainment, drama, [and] movies...During election years, political candidates came and spoke to us in Old Main. Many great personalities have stood on that stage." The auditorium also hosted the funerals of prominent Lumbees and was the site of meetings during the 1930s and 1950s when tribal members gathered to discuss federal recognition and changing the tribe's name. Less than one month later, more than seven thousand people had signed the petition. Dial carried a symbolic "STOP" sign during protests to emphatically convey his feelings about razing the historic structure.

In January 1972 Carnell Locklear said, "To destroy this building would be to cut the last tie between the university and its Indian heritage." A poem by Ruth (Locklear) Revels '58 captured the essence of Locklear's comments and also inspired the movement. Titled "I Am Old Main," the widely distributed poem asked pointedly, "Do they have no respect for me as a historical monument to their past?/ Am I a permanent part of their heritage—not worth preserving?" The poem continued, "Destroy me and I tell you, you destroy the very heart of the Lumbee people!/ What else can they point to proudly and say, [']This is the first—or I/ remember when?[']" The poem fanned the flames of discourse over the future of the landmark that sometimes pitted the university against the community.

In the months that followed, the dispute continued unabated with vitriolic, divisive discourse. However, on July 10, 1972, the Board of

FIGURE 4.12. *The burning of Old Main on March 18, 1973.*
COURTESY OF JAMES A. JACOBS JR.

Trustees, in a pivotal decision, approved a recommendation from Chancellor Jones to relocate the new $1.6 million auditorium to a tract of 15.5 acres of land, on the then north side of campus, that was acquired in June 1972 after the state condemned it some years earlier. The vote spared Old Main. Chancellor Jones suggested that Old Main remain on its current site "until those interested in the building can find sufficient funds" for restoring the structure. The community and many alumni were very pleased about the university's change of heart. The leaders of the Save Old Main movement immediately mobilized to raise local, state, and federal funds to restore the structure.

Then, in the early morning hours on a windy Sunday, March 18, 1973, disaster struck as Old Main was gutted by a fire. Hundreds of students and community members watched helplessly as the building burned. Arson was the cause of the fire, and there was wide disagreement over who might have been responsible. In an ironic twist, the arsonist may have given Old Main new life. Like the fabled phoenix, Old Main would fittingly rise from the ashes. On the evening of the fire, newly elected governor James E. Holshouser Jr. came to the university, where he spoke to a gathering of Indians in front of the smoldering building. Holshouser, the first Republican elected governor of North Carolina since 1896, would serve from 1973 to 1977. Janie (Maynor) Maynor Locklear '66 and Lonnie Revels, both Republicans, had strong ties to the governor and surely influenced his decision to come to Pembroke that evening. On this occasion, the governor pledged his help in getting Old Main restored. Four months later, on July 19, 1973, Governor Holshouser appointed the twenty-two-member Old Main Commission, comprising many of the leaders from the Save Old Main movement, to assist with a feasibility study for reconstructing the building. One year later the Board of Trustees approved a reconstruction plan, which had been endorsed earlier by the Old Main Commission.

While seeking funding for the reconstruction, 1976 proved to be another memorable year in the history of Old Main. On May 13, 1976, it became the first and only campus structure to be listed on the National Register of Historic Places. The register is a national list of distinctive properties worthy of preservation because of their historical value. The Lumbee musical icon Willie F. Lowery, who wrote the Lumbee anthem, "Proud to Be a Lumbee Indian," immortalized Old Main in his song "Old Main." The tune urged Lumbees to continue their fight to save the structure. Later that year, in October, Governor Holshouser and Chancellor Jones stood together on the steps of the burned-out Old Main as the governor announced that funds had been secured for the restoration of the college landmark. The cost for the renovations was $1.6 million, ironically the same amount as the new auditorium.

The Old Main issue helped draw the Indian community together behind a common goal, and it clearly revealed the importance of this structure to the Lumbees, as well as to Indians across the nation. The Performing Arts Center was completed in 1975 to house the dramatic arts as well as community and university events. It is an outstanding facility capable of seating sixteen hundred. On July 7, 1978, ground was broken to begin the restoration of Old Main. During the ceremony, Professor Emeritus Reba M. Lowry observed, "If the building could talk, what a number of interesting stories it could tell. It stands for education. The spirit of [the u]niversity lives inside these walls. It is a part of us. Many a person got his start inside this building." Finished the following year, Old Main was completely rebuilt without the auditorium; that area was repurposed for use as the Native American Resource Center. The Museum of the Native American Resource Center offers a rich collection of Indian artifacts and resources about Indian people from all over North America, with an emphasis on the Lumbees. Old Main also houses the Department of American Indian Studies and various other university programs.

As a result of the de-Indianization debate and the Save Old Main movement, a "college without walls" was established in the Indian community. It was called the Henry Berry Lowry College, in honor of the nineteenth-century folk hero of the Lumbees. Its concerns were Indian culture and Indian needs, and the college sought to provide opportunities through minicourses, night and Saturday classes, lectures, and a variety of nontraditional approaches to teach about Indian art, dance, belief systems, and other aspects of Indian culture, as well as provide practical help to those who needed jobs or help in the social sphere. It began a bimonthly publication—*Carolina Indian Voice*—as a means of communication with the Indian community. While the college had only limited success and a short life, some of its goals were later taken over by the Lumbee Regional Development Association, and its journal, under publisher-editor Bruce Barton '86, became a weekly newspaper that served the area until 2005.

While there was obviously a great deal of change and some controversy during the administration of Chancellor Jones, the university made enormous progress. As mentioned, Chancellor Jones's administration was marked by significant expansion of the institution's physical plant. The faculty cottages and Home Economics Building on Faculty Row, along with the boys' dormitory, were razed to make way for the new construction. In addition to those previously noted, other major structures built during the Jones years were D.F. Lowry Student Center (1965); Wellons Residence Hall (1965); West Residence Hall (1965); annex to Moore Hall (1965); a new Home Economics Residence House (1965); a new Mary Livermore Library building (1967); a science building (1967); the Infirmary, known today as Student Health Services (1967); the Business Administration Building (1969); the Environmental Building (1969), behind the science building; South (1970) and North (1972) Halls, both six-story women's residence halls capable of housing two hundred students each; a new health and physical education center (1972); the Performing Arts Center (1975); the Education Center (1976); and a new maintenance building (1977). In the mid-1960s, the baseball field was moved immediately west of its former location to a site occupied today by Oak and Pine residence halls. Around 1976 the baseball field was moved again to its current site. The Classroom North Building, begun during Jones's tenure, opened in 1980, one year after his retirement. A track, constructed on the west side of the health and physical education center prior to its construction, hosted campus academic and athletic events and was open to the community for its use. With the addition of the new residence halls, female students were clustered in North, South, and West Halls, while male students resided in Wellons and Jacobs Halls. Interestingly, North and South Halls were the tallest buildings in Robeson County until the construction of the bed tower at Southeastern Regional Medical Center in Lumberton in 2003. Campus structures Livermore, Student Health Services, and the science and Business Administration buildings, all built between 1967 and 1969, have a similar architectural style, with a brick façade trimmed with stone. Although the buildings have sometimes been described as "shoe boxes," due to their rectangular, nondescript shapes, no one can argue with President Jones's efforts to maximize the square footage of the new structures.

Other buildings were named in honor of individuals who provided years of service to the institution. On May 16, 1965, the D.F. Lowry Student Center and Wellons Residence Hall were dedicated in honor of

FIGURE 4.13. *Dr. Herbert G. Oxendine. Professor and dean of Pembroke State College from 1953 to 1966.*

FIGURE 4.14. *Mary (Irwin) Belk. Namesake for Belk Residence Hall.*

FIGURE 4.15. *Walter J. Pinchbeck. Head of the Maintenance Department for twenty-eight years and namesake for the Walter J. Pinchbeck Facilities Planning and Maintenance Complex.*

Rev. D. F. Lowry '05 and former president Ralph Wellons, both featured speakers at the event. In October 1972 the Board of Trustees voted unanimously to name two of the new buildings on campus in honor of two distinguished Lumbee leaders and educators—one was Dr. Jones and the other was Dr. Herbert G. Oxendine. Dr. Jones was honored for his decade of leadership and his roles as a civic and religious leader. Dr. Oxendine, born on November 7, 1913, in the community of Buie, north of Pembroke, was honored for his educational, civic, and religious contributions, but perhaps most important of all, for the example he set for others. He was the first Lumbee to earn a doctoral degree. After attending one year at McKendree College and two years at Cherokee Normal, Oxendine earned a BS degree from Western Carolina Teachers College, now Western Carolina University, and EdM and EdD degrees from Boston University. A World War II veteran, Dr. Oxendine was dedicated to helping others improve their lives, and he was a tireless worker. He came to the college in 1953 following a teaching career in the Indian public schools of Robeson County. Dr. Oxendine served the college in many capacities, including head of the Education Department and dean of the faculty. Tragically, he died December 14, 1966, at the age of fifty-three. His funeral was held in Memorial Auditorium in Old Main. It was said of Dr. Oxendine that he "will always remain a model of what a man can accomplish with his life if he will only try." An October 15, 1972, editorial in *The Robesonian* summed up the appropriateness of naming campus buildings after these two individuals: "The different talents of these two men have been devoted to Pembroke State, and each has filled a need. In honoring both men, the university links the spectacle of new buildings with the struggle of human beings to bring higher education within reach, and within the means of their fellow citizens." At a public convocation held on January 18, 1973, the English E. Jones Health and Physical Education Center and the Herbert G. Oxendine Science Building were officially dedicated. With William C. Friday, president of the UNC system, giving the major address, it was a memorable occasion for Pembroke State University, the community, alumni, and friends of the institution. The Jones Center replaced the college gymnasium, which opened in 1939. At the time the largest building on campus, it featured two gymnasiums, a natatorium with a swimming pool and diving tank, weightlifting and training rooms, and a lecture hall. Tennis courts were also constructed between the Jones Center and the Performing Arts Center and a few years later north of the Jones Center. With the addition of the Oxendine Science Building, the sciences moved from Locklear Hall into the modern, state-of-the-art facility. The new structure included the first elevator on campus. Both buildings were cornerstones to the continued growth of the campus.

Two other campus buildings were renamed during the late 1970s. South Hall, a women's residence hall, was dedicated October 27, 1976, as Mary (Irwin) Belk Hall. Belk (1882–1968) was a native of Charlotte and the wife of William Henry Belk, the founder of the Belk department stores. The dedication was made possible by a donation from the Belk family to recognize her love and concern for education and her many accomplishments. On October 20, 1978, the Board of Trustees voted to name the new maintenance building, constructed in 1977, the Walter J. Pinchbeck Maintenance Building, in honor of Pinchbeck (1904–1977), who was employed in the Maintenance Department for twenty-eight years, most of that time as superintendent of buildings and grounds. Pinchbeck supposedly painted the Indian head on the Arrowhead in front of Old Main. In 1960 Pinchbeck was the first Pembroke State staff member to whom the *Indianhead* was dedicated. He retired in 1969 but not before May 31 was celebrated as Walter Pinchbeck Day in Pembroke. He had settled and married into the Lumbee community in 1931 after traveling throughout the United States as a transient worker. Pinchbeck was Scoutmaster for Troop 327 in Pembroke from 1939 to 1969. On July 1, 1978, the Walter J. Pinchbeck Boy Scout Hut, located across Third Street from Old Main, was named in his honor. At the time of his death, Pinchbeck, a Cree Indian from Williams Lake, British Columbia, Canada, had guided more

Indian boys into Scouting than any other Indian. He was awarded the Silver Beaver for Distinguished Service to Boyhood and the Wood Badge. Pinchbeck was named Outstanding Indian Scoutmaster of the U.S. and also named one of the Outstanding Civic Leaders of America.

While expansion was the most obvious feature of the Jones administration, there were many other changes also taking place. The university greatly enlarged its intercollegiate athletic program starting in the 1960s, adding soccer (1964), golf (1964), wrestling (1964), tennis (1964–1992), and indoor track and field (1966–1978) for men. Later, women's intercollegiate athletics were reinstated in 1973 when women's basketball returned after being discontinued following the 1957–1958 school year. Other women's teams were added in volleyball (1973), tennis (1974–1992; 1997), and softball (1977, slow pitch; 1990, fast pitch). Also in 1973, the women's teams began competition in the North Carolina Association of Intercollegiate Athletics for Women (NCAIAW), joining the national Association of Intercollegiate Athletics for Women (AIAW) in 1978. The AIAW was founded in 1971 to govern collegiate women's athletics in the United States. Its rapid growth paralleled national growth in women's athletics as a result of the adoption of Title IX. It functioned in a role very similar to the NCAA. The Lady Braves competed in the NCAIAW and AIAW until 1982. On September 1, 1975, the men's teams joined the National Collegiate Athletic Association's (NCAA) Division II, maintaining a dual membership in the NAIA and NCAA until 1992. Most of the nation's major college and universities now belong to the NCAA. It has three divisions: I is for major colleges, II is for small colleges that provide athletic scholarships, and III is for small colleges that do not provide athletic scholarships. Lacey Gane, Pembroke State's athletic director from 1965 to 1983, expressed his delight in joining the NCAA when he said, "Becoming a member of the NCAA means we can compete with many of the major colleges in sports in which some have been reluctant to play us in the past…[because] we were not members of the NCAA." The prestige of joining the NCAA and the possibility of forming a conference with other NCAA Division II teams were cited as

FIGURE 4.16. *Pembroke State University 1978 NAIA Cross Country National Champions.*

other reasons for Pembroke State joining the NCAA. The following year, on September 8, 1976, Pembroke State joined its first athletic conference, the Carolinas Intercollegiate Athletic Conference (CIAC), commonly known as the Carolinas Conference. Pembroke State was already competing with many of the conference's members—Atlantic Christian College, Catawba College, Elon College, Guilford College, High Point College, and Pfeiffer College, all NAIA members hailing from North Carolina.

Intercollegiate athletics reached unprecedented levels of success between 1967 and 1979. Pembroke State won numerous conference and NAIA district championships: baseball—five district; men's basketball—one district and one area; men's golf—one district; softball—one conference; and wrestling—three conference and seven district. The men's baseball team participated in two NAIA World Series, in 1970 and 1973, while the men's basketball squad advanced to the NAIA national tournament in 1973. While the university has fielded some outstanding athletes in most of its sports, its greatest team athletic accomplishment was winning the NAIA National Championship in cross country in 1978 under Coach Ed Crain, the 1978 National Cross Country Coach of the Year. The late 1960s through the early 1980s were the glory days of men's cross country and track and field. Between 1967 and 1979, men's cross country won eleven district championships, finishing as runner-up twice, and four area championships. During the same period, the men's outdoor track and field team won twelve district championships, including eleven in a row, and finished as runner-up once. They also won two conference championships, in 1978 and 1979. The 1979 outdoor track and field team finished third at the NAIA nationals. The men's indoor track and field program won eight district championships between 1967 and 1977. Pembroke State athletes won nine individual national championships in cross country and track and field between 1973 and 1979. They were Jeff Cushing '76, 1,000-yard run (indoor track and field), 1975; Jeffery Moody '79, 1,500 meters, 1979; Dave Phillips '81, high jump (indoor track and field), 1973; and Charles Shipman '78, discus, 1976 and 1977, and shot-put, 1978. The greatest track and cross country runner in the institution's athletic history was Garry Henry '82, a student from Australia, who

FIGURE 4.17. *Garry Henry '82. A native of Australia who won the 1978 individual NAIA Cross Country National Championship and led Pembroke State University to its first team national title.*

was a six-time national champion. He was a member of the 1978 national championship team, and won individual national championships in 1977 and 1980, both for the 5,000 meters and 10,000 meters, in 1978 and 1982, and was a fifteen-time All-American. The athletic program also produced seventy-nine NAIA or NCAA All-Americans during this same period.

As Pembroke State's athletic program grew, so did its operating costs. In 1977 a group of athletic boosters, composed mostly of alumni and

members of the Pembroke Chamber of Commerce, established the Braves
Club to serve as a fund-raising organization for the university's Athletic
Department. Chaired by Bruce Barton '86, members of the organizing
committee included James F. "Buddy" Bell '58; Coach Ed Crain; Arnold
Locklear '65; Theodore Maynor '26, '28, '46; Jim Paul; and Dr. Gerald
Maynor '59 and Walter Oxendine '64, both of Pembroke State. Crain
had served as head of an earlier version of the Braves Club from 1973
to 1976, whose membership was "mostly campus-based." He cited the
widespread community interest in the new club as the main reason for its
success. At its first fund-raiser dinner on November 28, 1977, Braves Club
members and Chancellor Jones could barely contain their excitement
over two recent athletic accomplishments. Garry Henry '82 had just won
the NAIA National Cross Country Championship, and the undefeated
men's basketball team had just swept the Campbell Tip-Off Tournament
championship, beating two NCAA Division I teams in the process.
Chancellor Jones joked, "You organizers of the Braves Club know what
you are doing. First, you form the club; then, our athletes turn in three

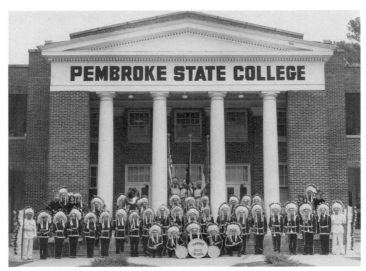

FIGURE 4.18. *Pembroke State College Marching
Band standing on the steps of Old Main.*

superlative performances back-to-back." It was a good omen according to Chancellor Jones. He shared his appreciation for the support of the one hundred charter members of the Braves Club when he remarked, "In my twenty-one years at this university, this is the most significant thing that has been done to support our athletic program."

Rallying the Braves to victory were the cheerleaders and the College Band, both campus fixtures since the late 1940s. The College Band was organized during the 1945–1946 school year. By the 1960s, the small pep band had grown into a concert band and a large marching band that participated in numerous activities on campus, in the surrounding communities, and throughout North Carolina and South Carolina. One of the most recognizable attributes of the marching band during this period was its uniform which featured gold, black, and white headdresses modeled after those worn by Indians from the Great Plains. They were made by Walter J. and Bertha (Lowry) Pinchbeck and Bonnie (Jones) Maynor '34. The band was led by a drum major and a color guard, who carried the symbols of the college, the state, and nation. The majorettes also charmed "crowds with their high-stepping, eye-catching routines."

The 1960s and 1970s saw many changes in terms of student life. The D. F. Lowry Student Center was opened in 1965, providing better recreational facilities than the institution had ever known, although the growing enrollment quickly made it inadequate. In 1972, the area between the student center and the cafeteria, which opened in 1959 and was expanded in 1966, was enclosed, completing the present-day D. F. Lowry Building. The Wagon Wheel, a snack bar in the student center, was a popular student hangout.

Social fraternities and sororities were chartered, as well as many new clubs. Phi Sigma Chi was the first local fraternity on campus, established during the 1964–1965 school year. Theta Kappa Sorority, a local sorority, was established at Pembroke State in 1969. The first national fraternity on campus was Pi Kappa Phi, chartered on March 24, 1973. The first national sorority on campus was Kappa Delta Sorority, founded on May 5, 1973.

The first African American fraternity and sorority were Phi Beta Sigma Fraternity Inc. and Zeta Phi Beta Sorority Inc., chartered on December 7, 1980, and March 4, 1982, respectively. The first Indian sorority was Alpha Pi Omega Native American Sorority Inc., chartered on November 27, 1996. Phi Sigma Nu Native American Fraternity, the first Indian fraternity in the United States, was established at the university on February 13, 1996. Beginning in the 1970s to promote Greek life, certain suites and floors in the residence halls were designated specifically for members of Greek organizations. Later, an external wall of these buildings carried the Greek letters of the fraternity or sorority residing in the facility. This campus tradition was discontinued during the first decade of the next century.

To enhance student life through on-campus entertainment and promote a broader cultural awareness among students, the Lyceum Series featured renowned speakers and artists in the fields of music, drama, dance, and comedy. Beginning in 1967, the series was the most recent incarnation in a long line of campus performing-artist series that began in the 1920s and continued through the 1960s with the Fine Arts Series. Prominent performers included the Wayfarers, folksingers; Kenneth Crawford, a news analyst; Dick Leibert, the Radio City Music Hall organist; guitarist Gene Bertoncini; Buffalo Bob Smith, the creator of *The Howdy Doody Show*; Dick Gregory, social satirist; bluegrass musician Doc Watson; *Tommy*, the rock opera; Buffy Sainte-Marie, a Cree Indian folk singer; comedian Lily Tomlin; the Amazing Kreskin; and the Danish gymnastics team. The 1975 opening of the Performing Arts Center, with sixteen hundred seats and modern amenities, further enhanced the quality of the acts in the series and the audience experience. On September 7, 1976, aspiring singer Pat Benatar, one of the most popular recording artists of the 1980s, performed in the National Theatre Company presentation of *Catch a Rising Star*, which featured New York's newest comedians, musicians, and singers. The series is a source of great community and regional interest.

The improvement of student life has been a difficult problem because of the small number of residential students. In 1975, 65 percent of

Pembroke State students were commuters, earning the campus the label of "suitcase campus"—the campus would empty out on the weekends as students went home. That year's *Indianhead* best described the "Ol' Commuter Blues." It read, "'Ughhh,' is probably the first word uttered by a PSU commuter as he turns off his alarm clock which is set at six. He is up and gone by six-thirty ready to face the fog, rain, trucks, and the many other obstacles which may stand in his way." The train also proved to be a hindrance to getting to class on time. The *Indianhead* continued, "Commuting as viewed by students has its trials and tribulations.... Many of them live within driving distance and so due to a variety of reasons they find it sensible or mandatory to commute." By the beginning of the twenty-first century, the percentage of commuter students had declined as the number of students living on campus or in nearby apartments had increased sharply.

By 1967 the number of alumni had increased dramatically due to the growth of the college. On March 25 of that year, the Alumni Association awarded its inaugural service awards to an outstanding alumnus and friend of the institution for their distinguished service to the campus. The first recipient of the Outstanding Alumni Award was Tom Oxendine '48, while State Rep. David M. Britt of Robeson County was awarded the Distinguished Service Award. Local merchant Russell H. Livermore was also recognized for his distinguished service to the community and the county.

In the academic realm, the curriculum expanded as the number of degree programs offered by the university expanded from fourteen undergraduate degree programs in 1962 to twenty-one undergraduate and three graduate degree programs by 1980. The university, like most institutions of higher education in the seventies, made the decision to follow the trend toward more flexible graduation requirements—to establish a system of Basic Studies requirements, known today as General Education requirements, which gave the students more options. Students were demanding "relevant" courses and a greater responsibility for their academic programs. The changes adopted in this period meant students no longer had to take foreign languages, speech, history, or many other subjects if they felt them to be unnecessary to their goals. It was a popular change with most students, but less so with many of the faculty. To help convince the faculty of the wisdom of these changes and to learn more about new trends in higher education, Pembroke State participated in the Institute for Undergraduate Curricula Reform in the fall of 1972. The purpose of the institute was "to induce curricular revision in order to provide better services to students, and to eliminate obsolescence, repetitiveness, irrelevance, and lack of appreciation of students' needs." Whether the institute was effective or not, the curricula changes of that time radically altered the academic program of the university.

Another important curriculum development was the establishment of an American Indian Studies Department. Because of the unique history of the institution and because of the issue of de-Indianization, it was believed that a strong academic program in American Indian studies would strengthen the university and improve its ties with the

community. After a great deal of work, the department developed an initial program of six courses and was approved to begin in the fall semester of 1972. Adolph Dial '43 was a key figure in the establishment of the department and served as chairman from its inception to 1988. A grandson of Rev. W.L. Moore, Dial was born in the Prospect community in 1922. He received a BA degree from Pembroke State College for Indians. Dial later served in World War II and saw firsthand the horrors of Nazi concentration camps. Upon returning home from the war he served as a teacher and principal in Prospect, Pembroke, and Lumberton from 1947 to 1958. Dial was denied entrance to North

FIGURE 4.19. *Dr. Adolph L. Dial '43. Professor of American Indian studies and history. Namesake for Adolph L. Dial Humanities Building.*

Carolina's graduate schools because he was Indian. However, he earned a master's degree from Boston University and joined the Pembroke State faculty in 1958. At the university, he served as a thirty-year faculty member. Dial coauthored *The Only Land I Know: A History of the Lumbee Indians* with colleague Dr. David Eliades in 1974. On May 7, 1988, Dial was awarded an honorary doctorate—doctor of humane letters—by Pembroke State University. He also received an honorary doctorate from Greensboro College. Although he was wary of the negative effects of dependency on the Bureau of Indian Affairs, Dr. Dial was a major advocate for Lumbee federal

FIGURE 4.20. *Norman MacLeod. Founder and editor of* Pembroke Magazine, *recognized as one of the finest college literary magazines in the nation.*

recognition. After his retirement, Dr. Dial was elected to the State House of Representatives in 1990. At the time of his death in 1995 Dr. Dial was a member of the Board of Trustees. His legacy as a scholar, teacher, and friend to the university lives on through the Adolph L. Dial Humanities Building, named in his honor on February 14, 1997, an endowed scholarship, and faculty awards for scholarship and community service.

Faculty governance was yet another development of the Jones administration. In 1967, partly in response to guidelines from the Southern Association, the major accrediting agency for educational institutions in the Southeast, and partly in response to the growth of the faculty, the Faculty Legislative Assembly was established. This proved a cumbersome operation because all faculty-involved business was conducted in a monthly assembly meeting. Consequently, a special committee was established in 1970 to write a new faculty constitution. Upon completion and acceptance, the assembly was replaced by a Faculty Senate with standing committees to handle most academic matters. The faculty meets

once each semester to approve or reject the actions of the senate. The new
model has proved to be a more efficient faculty governance organization.

Other noteworthy developments of this time were the establishment
of the Upward Bound and College Opportunity Programs, the creation
of *Pembroke Magazine*, and a new emphasis on service to the community.
The Continuing Education Division and a university data processing
center were also founded. Upward Bound, a federally funded program at
the university from 1973 to 2012, provided opportunities for high school
students from low-income households or first-generation college students
to succeed in higher education. Similar to Upward Bound, the College
Opportunity Program was designed to give at-risk students a chance to
show they could handle college-level work. It helps them develop better
study and communication skills, and it lets them test themselves in regular
college courses. Successful students in this program are admitted as regular
students. *Pembroke Magazine* was started in 1969 by Norman MacLeod, a
poet and novelist of national reputation. MacLeod served as editor for ten
years. It quickly came to be recognized as one of the finest college literary
magazines in the nation, a reputation it continues to have under subsequent editors such as Dr. Shelby Stephenson, a North Carolina poet, who
served as editor from 1979 until 2010. In seeking to be of greater service,
the university has opened up its facilities, offered more public programs
like the Lyceum Series, and provided more activities. For example, the
university celebrated the nation's bicentennial in 1976 with a week of public
programs designed to entertain and instruct. The Continuing Education
Division also helped to meet the goal of community service by offering
night classes and other programs aimed specifically at adults. With the
coming of the computer age, the university established a data processing
center to manage student records more efficiently and accurately. These
developments are cited as representative examples of the many objectives
and efforts of the modern university to serve its region and students.

Throughout all the changes during this period, Pembroke State
remained one of the most affordable institutions in the state. In 1978

annual in-state tuition and fees for twelve or more undergraduate hours was $470, and $1,960 for out-of-state students. Room and board was $920 for the year.

On June 30, 1978, Dr. Jones announced his retirement as chancellor of Pembroke State University, effective June 30, 1979. On behalf of the state of North Carolina and the Town of Pembroke, Gov. James B. Hunt jointly proclaimed April 20, 1979, as Dr. English E. Jones Day to honor his service to the university. Lumberton banker and former state senator Hector MacLean said of Chancellor Jones, "An 'English Jones Day' is not only appropriate, it's a must. He deserves great honor on that day. We want people all over this state and the Southeast to know how we feel about him. Dr. Jones has done a marvelous job for Pembroke State University, putting it on a strong and solid foundation and making it a tremendous asset to this area." A parade and appreciation dinner, with more than six hundred attendees, were held in his honor. His tenure of seventeen years was the longest in the history of the institution, and it produced the greatest changes. In announcing his resignation, Chancellor Jones said: "I have accomplished what I came to Pembroke State University to accomplish. During my tenure here I wanted to build a university, both facility-wise and academically, that would be a credit to the University of North Carolina. I feel satisfied that we have accomplished these things. In view of that fact, I believe this is the appropriate time for me to step aside and give someone else with new ideas and new energies—an opportunity to step in, grab the reins and really go with the university." During Commencement ceremonies on May 10, 1981, Chancellor Emeritus Jones was conferred Pembroke State's first honorary doctorate—a doctor of humanities—in recognition of his twenty-three years of service to the university.

Tragically, a debilitating illness prevented Dr. Jones from attending the ceremony and enjoying his retirement. After a prolonged struggle, he died on May 18, 1981, less than two years after leaving office. Upon learning of Jones's death, William C. Friday, president of the UNC system, eulogized him as an outstanding leader who "served the university with uncommon devotion, great energy, and with total personal commitment...He was always inspiring, always helpful, and he shared his friendship with thousands of us." With Jones's careful cultivation, the small seed planted by the founders of this institution grew from a fledgling Pembroke State College into the sturdy Pembroke State University, casting its shadow over the southeastern region of North Carolina.

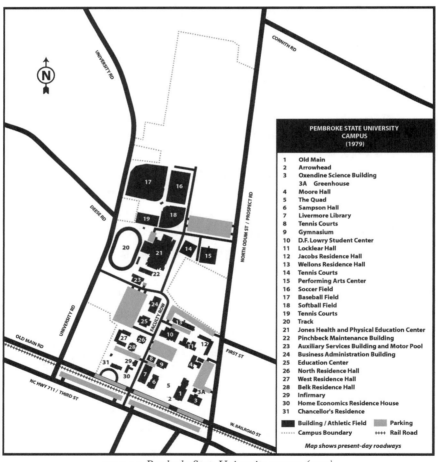

MAP 4.1. *Pembroke State University campus (1979).*

TIMELINE OF NOTABLE INSTITUTIONAL EVENTS (1962–1979)

1962   • English E. Jones, first Lumbee, named interim president.

1962–63   • Celebrated Diamond Jubilee.

1963   • English E. Jones, first Lumbee, named third president.

1964   • Men's soccer, golf, wrestling, and tennis added. Tennis was discontinued in 1992.

       • Phi Sigma Chi, first social fraternity.

1965   • D. F. Lowry Student Center, Wellons Residence Hall, annex to Moore Hall, and West Hall, formerly West Residence Hall, opened.

       • Home Economics Building opened. Known today as Hickory Hall, it was once known as the Admissions and Nursing Building.

1966   • Men's indoor track and field added; discontinued in 1978.

1966–71   • Summer Commencement held.

1967   • Mary Livermore Library, Herbert G. Oxendine Science Building, and Student Health Services, formerly the Infirmary, opened.

       • Faculty Senate established as the Faculty Legislative Assembly.

       • Larry Barnes, first African American student to enroll; graduated in 1971.

1968   • Foundation Inc. established.

1969   • Sylvia (Baugham) Banks, first African American graduate.

       • Renamed Pembroke State University and designated a "regional university."

       • Business Administration Building and the Environmental Building completed.

       • Theta Kappa Sorority, first social sorority.

       • *Pembroke Magazine* established.

1970   • Belk Residence Hall, the former South Hall, opened.

1972   • Became constituent institution of the University of North Carolina system, and title of head of institution changed from "president" to "chancellor." Also, thirteen-member Board of Trustees established with president of the Student Government Association serving as an ex officio member.

       • North Residence Hall opened.

       • English E. Jones Health and Physical Education Center opened.

1973   · Women's basketball reinstated and women's volleyball added. Women's teams began competition in the NCAIAW.

            · Beth (Dail) Finch and Janie (Maynor) Maynor Locklear '66, first female members of Board of Trustees.

            · Old Main gutted by fire.

1974   · Women's tennis added; discontinued in 1992 and returned in 1997.

1974–76   · Cooperative graduate agreement with Appalachian State University.

1975   · Men's athletic teams joined NCAA Division II; dual NAIA and NCAA until 1992.

            · Givens Performing Arts Center opened.

1976   · Men's athletic teams joined the Carolinas Intercollegiate Athletic Conference.

            · The Education Center completed.

1976–78   · Cooperative graduate agreement with the University of North Carolina at Charlotte.

1977   · Braves Club founded.

            · Softball (slow pitch) added; moved to fast pitch in 1990.

            · Walter J. Pinchbeck Maintenance Building completed; renovated and renamed Auxiliary Services Building in 2006 after new Walter J. Pinchbeck Facilities Planning and Maintenance Complex constructed.

1978   · Women's athletic teams began competition in the AIAW.

            · First three graduate programs in Education established.

            · Designated Comprehensive II university.

            · Men's cross country won the NAIA National Championship.

1979   · First graduate degree—master of arts in education—awarded to fifty-seven students.

            · Chancellor English E. Jones retired.

Chapter Five

1979–1989
A GOAL OF EXCELLENCE

While education for subsistence is a basic concern, we must insure that the graduates of this university will develop those habits of inquiry, criticism and creativity that will help them maintain intellectual vitality throughout life.

> Dr. Paul R. Givens, chancellor,
> Pembroke State University,
> Installation Address (1979)

The sturdy oak of Pembroke State University continued to grow outward and soar upward in the pursuit of excellence during the 1980s. Its roots and shadow of influence over southeastern North Carolina were strengthened and extended as the university established a solid foundation for future growth that was marked by the celebration of its Centennial in 1987.

With the announcement that Chancellor English E. Jones was retiring in the summer of 1979, a university search committee was established to screen applicants and nominees for the position, and to make recommendations to the Board of Trustees. After a ten-month search, the board sent four names to William C. Friday, president of the University of North

Carolina system, who would then submit his choice to the Board of Governors. Two of the four candidates were Lumbee—Dr. James B. Chavis '63, vice chancellor for student affairs at Pembroke State, and Dr. Joseph B. Oxendine, a Pembroke native who was a dean and professor at Temple University—while the remaining two were white; one was Dr. Paul

R. Givens of Millikin University. On May 11, 1979, President Friday recommended to the Board of Governors that Dr. Givens be named the new chancellor of Pembroke State University, and the board gave its unanimous approval.

The selection of a non-Indian angered many of the Lumbees, some of whom talked of seeking a federal investigation into "camouflaged inequities" at the university. Most Indians desired to have another Indian leader of the institution; Chancellor Jones led Pembroke State for seventeen years. While a number of Indians complained about the selection of Givens, most

FIGURE 5.1. *Dr. Paul R. Givens. Chancellor of Pembroke State University from 1979 to 1989.*

acknowledged that they were not opposed to him personally. They argued that the issues concerned local control and the fact that there were qualified Indian candidates for the position.

In response to the furor over his selection, Dr. Givens said, "I can appreciate how the Indian people feel. I can understand they might be unhappy with a non-Indian in such a position. But I fully anticipate working with them to develop as strong an institution as we can. And I anticipate they will be wanting to do what is in the best long-range interest of Pembroke State University." He stated that all he wanted was a chance "to show what I can do." Dr. Givens's interpersonal skills soon won him many friends among all races in Robeson County. Consequently, the criticism that arose when Givens was named chancellor quickly dissipated after he proved what he could do "if given a chance." Givens served as head of the institution from 1979 to 1989.

Dr. Givens came to Pembroke State from Millikin University in Decatur, Illinois, where he had served as vice president for academic affairs since 1972. Givens, the descendant of Welsh miners, was born on November 16, 1923, and reared in Wellsburg, West Virginia. During high school, Givens set his sights on a career in the ministry. Since Givens's parents were members of the Reorganized Church of Jesus Christ of Latter Day Saints, known today as Community of Christ, he enrolled in the church's college, Graceland College, now Graceland University, in Lamoni, Iowa, in 1941. Givens was the first of seven children in his family to attend college. After earning an associate of arts degree at Graceland in 1943, Givens entered the U.S. Navy. During this time, Givens changed his mind about joining the ministry, deciding instead to pursue a teaching career with the goal of becoming a public school administrator. He enrolled at George Peabody College for Teachers, now Peabody College of Vanderbilt University, and received a BA degree in psychology, sociology, and biology in 1948, and an MA degree in psychology in 1949. Givens earned a PhD in psychology from Vanderbilt University in 1953.

Prior to coming to Pembroke State, Chancellor Givens had a distinguished career as a professor and scholar. He was an instructor in psychology at Lawrence College, today Lawrence University, from 1949 to 1951; a counselor at Vanderbilt University from 1951 to 1953; chair and associate professor in the Department of Psychology at Birmingham-Southern College from 1953 to 1960; and professor and chair of the Department of Psychology and coordinator of independent studies at the University of South Florida from 1960 to 1967. Givens was also dean of arts and sciences and director of institutional research and planning at Ithaca College from 1967 to 1972. On a personal level, his hobbies included playing golf and listening to light, classical, and country and western music.

Dr. Givens was installed as the second chancellor of Pembroke State University on May 10, 1980. Presiding over the ceremony was President

Friday, who proclaimed that Givens would "build on the strong tradition of Chancellor English Jones." Dr. Givens detailed his goals for the
university. He wished that Pembroke State would "show even greater
leadership in demonstrating that higher education can raise individuals
from the swamps of hesitancy and self-doubt to the hills of wisdom
and confidence." To realize this goal, Givens committed the university
to strengthening its undergraduate and graduate programs. He noted
a need for expansion of the school's graduate program. As a reflection
of his personal religious faith and regard for morality and academic
excellence, Givens argued, "We must turn our attention—our curricular
designs—to the merging of intellectual and moral purposes. From this
perspective," he said, "I see Pembroke State University providing an
education that goes beyond education for vocational preparedness to
education that stirs the individual to consider the moral questions that
confront him and her every day. While education for subsistence is a
basic concern, we must ensure that the graduates of this university will
develop those habits of inquiry, criticism, and creativity that will help
them maintain intellectual vitality throughout life."

At the installation, William A. Johnson, chair of the UNC system
Board of Governors, remarked that Chancellor Givens, in less than one
year, had proven his ability to provide outstanding leadership for the
university. From the start of his administration on July 1, 1979, Chancellor Givens sought to chart a progressive course for the institution, a
course based on the guiding principle of excellence. To achieve that goal,
he urged the university community—faculty, students, and administrators—to establish definite and positive goals, to expect the best from
themselves and from others. He worked to give the university greater
visibility, to get it in the forefront, and to have area citizens think of it
in terms of being "Our University." One of the first groups Dr. Givens
engaged was alumni. During his first year at the helm, alumni chapters
were established in Charlotte, Fayetteville, and Greensboro. Then, an
annual statewide alumni reception was organized; the 1986 reception

was held at the Governor's Mansion in Raleigh. Though not foreseen, an alumna who brought visibility to the campus was Francesca (Adler) Adler-Baeder '83, chosen Miss Pembroke State University in 1981 and Miss North Carolina in 1984. Adler-Baeder, the first of three Miss North Carolinas to hail from the institution, used her titles to publicize the university and its strengths; she was an outstanding spokesperson for the school and represented university alumni at their best. Chancellor Givens also concerned himself with effectively marketing the institution as a quality university that offered personal attention. Consequently, he began a weekly radio program that utilized interviews with faculty and staff to provide the university and its academic programs with additional exposure in the region. To bring additional visibility, the university, in conjunction with the state Department of Transportation, placed signage along U.S. 74 promoting "Pembroke State University" to the thousands of travelers driving to and from local beaches.

Yet another priority of his administration was a major effort to give the university a solid financial base built on private giving. To accomplish this objective, a strong fund-raising program was developed, which included an annual Kickoff Banquet. The event featured popular personalities such as the charismatic Jim Valvano, head men's basketball coach at North Carolina State University; Horace "Bones" McKinney, former head men's basketball coach at Wake Forest University; and Charlie "Choo Choo" Justice, a former University of North Carolina at Chapel Hill football player. Chancellor Givens also placed an emphasis on growing the Chancellor's Club—individuals who pledged one thousand dollars a year to Pembroke State for ten years. Chancellor English Jones founded the club in 1974 as part of a fund-raising campaign to raise $4 million by 1984. During Givens' administration, the club grew from thirteen to almost fifty members. Other fund-raising efforts included direct solicitation through phone-a-thons and benefit golf tournaments. The monies raised were administered by the university's Foundation Inc., which used them for such purposes as scholarships and faculty development.

As part of the effort to take fund-raising at Pembroke State to a new level, Chancellor Givens named Joseph Sandlin, president of Lumberton-based Southern National Bank, as codirector of the Annual Fund campaign. Sandlin joined the university in March 1986 as an executive-in-residence and was instrumental in the university reaching its Centennial giving campaign goal of $1 million, ultimately raising $1.3 million by March 1987. The three-year campaign, begun in 1984 and cochaired by Hector MacLean, CEO of Southern National Bank, had success in corporate giving as well. It secured the then-largest single gift ever in the history of the university. In June 1986, the Belk Foundation Inc. of Charlotte donated one hundred thousand dollars toward establishing a William H. Belk Endowed Chair of Business Management. The donation was made after a matching fund plan was established by the General Assembly to create distinguished professor chairs at each UNC system school.

Corporate relationships cultivated through the Annual Fund campaign benefited the university and the region in other ways. In September 1986 Chancellor Givens was elected as the first president of Robeson County's Committee of 100, which was organized to attract industry to the county. His leadership of the committee influenced the establishment of an Office of Economic Development at the university in September 1987. Proposed and developed by Vice Chancellor for Academic Affairs Charles R. Jenkins, the office was a catalyst for outreach and economic development in the local and regional community. It was the predecessor of the Regional Center for Economic, Community and Professional Development. Chancellor Givens was active in other community organizations, serving on the Board of Trustees for Southeastern General Hospital in Lumberton and the Board of Directors for the Lumberton Chamber of Commerce.

The university's academic program was also strengthened and expanded under Chancellor Givens's leadership. Entrance requirements stiffened, and a concerted effort began to recruit high-achieving students under the Chancellor's Scholars Program. Begun in 1981, eligible students had to meet certain criteria. They must be in the top 10 percent of their graduating class, have high scores on their Scholastic Aptitude Test, be well-rounded students, show strong motivation, and be highly recommended. Program participants were awarded a one-year tuition scholarship, renewable each year depending on meeting grade point average requirements. The Chancellor's Scholars Program replaced an interdisciplinary honors program that did not offer financial assistance. At the same time, the College Opportunity Program continued for less qualified students who demonstrated promise of a successful college career. The recognition of student accomplishments was also important to the new chancellor. Accordingly, the university instituted an annual Awards Day ceremony, beginning at the end of Givens's first year, to recognize student academic and athletic achievements.

Additional areas of study were added as the period was marked by an expansion of the curriculum. While the university continued to offer the traditional undergraduate degrees in the liberal arts, the social sciences, education, and the sciences, it began to offer majors in areas such as computer science, criminal justice, and social work. A development of great interest to the Lumbee community occurred in 1984 when the Department of American Indian Studies was authorized to offer a major. It was and continues to be a unique program offered by few other colleges in the country. In 1981 Pembroke State received a $145,000 grant from the U.S. Department of Commerce to help it equip a public television station. At that time, an advisory committee was created; with the grant, plus additional gifts of equipment and money, the foundation was laid for WPSU-TV, the university's television station. At its inception, the cable-casting facility served Pembroke, Lumberton, Charlotte, Greensboro, Rockingham, Fayetteville, Hope Mills, and Spring Lake. It supported the academic program in broadcasting by providing a working laboratory for practical experience. There was also a rapid expansion of the graduate program. Responding to requests from regional educators and teachers, the university established graduate work in areas such as administration, math education, and English education. In the summer of 1989 the university added a graduate program in administrative studies, known today as the master of public administration. Graduate programs enrolled more than four hundred students. Most were schoolteachers from a thirteen-county radius who drove long distances to attend classes part-time in the evenings and full-time during summer school. At the end of Givens's tenure, the university was seeking additional areas in which to expand its graduate program. The university offered forty-four majors and thirty-six minors at the undergraduate level, and two graduate degree programs with six areas of certification by 1989.

Moreover, the university added several programs to recruit minority students into the medical field, including the Health Careers Academic Advancement Program (HCAAP) and Clinical Work-Study Summer Health Program. Both are known today as the North Carolina Health Careers Access Program (NC-HCAP). But the university was unquestionably most proud of the quality of instruction and personal attention given to its students. In a 1985 survey of graduates of all UNC system institutions, Pembroke State came out above the average for "Quality of Instruction in Major Field" and "Overall Quality of Instruction." Pembroke graduates were satisfied or moderately satisfied by 97.6 percent and 95 percent, respectively, for the two categories. Clearly, the university provided a high level of quality education, according to its current students and alumni. As a result of efforts to expand the curriculum and provide quality, personal instruction, the university began to attract an increasing number of high school seniors from the upper ranks of their graduating classes.

Another selling point was the affordability of attending the university. In 1989, annual tuition and fees for twelve or more undergraduate hours for in-state students was $716, and $3,782 for out-of-state students.

Tuition and fees for nine or more graduate hours was $716 for in-state students, and $4,088 for out-of-state students. Room and board for the year was $1,920.

During this period, Pembroke State students were successful not only in the classroom but also on the athletic field. Between 1980 and 1989 the university's athletic program continued to expand and excel in competition in the NAIA, NCAA Division II, and the Carolinas Conference. In 1982, women's teams left the AIAW to join the NAIA. With the addition of women's cross country in 1985 the university sponsored eight sports for men and five for women. The Braves continued their winning tradition of the 1960s and 1970s as teams won numerous conference and NAIA district championships. The men's basketball team won four conference and one district championship; the women's basketball team won four conference and two district championships; the men's cross country squad won one conference (began conference competition in 1989) and six district championships; the women's cross country team won one district championship; the softball team won two conference and three district championships; the men's outdoor track and field squad won eight conference and four district championships; the volleyball team won two conference championships; and the wrestling team won three conference and five district championships. Pembroke State came to be known as "The Campus of Champions."

There were other major team and individual athletic accomplishments. The 1980 men's cross country team finished second at the NCAA II nationals while the 1982 men's outdoor track and field team finished third at the NAIA nationals. The 1984 men's basketball team and the 1985 women's basketball team advanced to the final 16 of the NAIA national championship. The period also produced three individual national champions: Julius Meekins '82 won the long jump (NCAA II) in 1980, and Garry Henry '82 won both the 5,000- and 10,000-meter races in 1982. Henry also set the college world record for the marathon in December

FIGURE 5.2. *Pembroke State University Braves basketball team, which advanced to the final 16 of the NAIA National Basketball Championships in 1984.*

FIGURE 5.3. *Pembroke State University Lady Braves, who finished in the final 16 of the NAIA National Basketball Championships in 1985.*

1980 with a time of two hours, ten minutes, and nine seconds. The wrestling program produced four NCAA regional champions in 1985: Joe Stukes '89 (118 pounds), Roger Horton '89 (150), Thomas J. Cluchey '86 (158), and Jay Stainback '87 (190). Conference players of the year were Dee Major '86, volleyball, in 1983 and 1984, and Barbara Green '86, women's basketball, in 1984 and 1985. Pembroke State also produced eighty-three NAIA, NCAA, College Sports Information Directors of America (CoSIDA), and academic All-Americans, along with numerous all-conference players and conference and district coaches of the year. To honor its outstanding sports performers, the institution established an Athletic Hall of Fame. The inaugural class was inducted on February 16, 1980; it included Mike Carruthers '69, baseball; Joe Gallagher '68, basketball; Theodore Maynor '26, '28, '46, baseball, basketball, and football; Tom Oxendine '48, baseball, basketball, and football; and John W. "Ned" Sampson '53, baseball, basketball, and football. The Athletic Hall of Fame now includes seventy-four individuals representing twelve sports. On July 1, 1981, Larry Rodgers '73 became the first African American head coach at Pembroke State when he was hired to coach the cross country and track and field teams. Rodgers was a four-year track and field athlete and honorable mention All-American at Pembroke State. In recognition of the university's athletic success, Pembroke State was awarded the Joby Hawn Cup in 1984 and 1989 by the Carolinas Conference. The cup was presented to the conference member that showed the highest rating of excellence in all conference-sponsored sports.

Another goal of the Givens administration was improved community-campus relations. If the selection of Dr. Givens to head the institution strained relations between the Indian community and the university in 1979, the rededication of Old Main on February 16, 1980, did much to restore those ties. Old Main was gutted by a mysterious fire in 1973; the restoration was completed in 1979. At the rededication ceremony, six Lumbees—professor emeritus Clifton Oxendine '24; Jesse Oxendine, chair of the Board of Trustees; professor Adolph L. Dial '43; student LeJeana Hammond '80; Janie (Maynor) Maynor Locklear '66; and John Robert Jones, chair of the Old Main Commission—spoke on the meaning and importance of the historic structure. They were followed by remarks from former governor James E. Holshouser. On this occasion, Maynor Locklear, secretary of the Save Old Main movement and former member of the Board of Trustees, said the restoration of the building was "the fulfillment of a dream, the answer to a thousand prayers and a high moment in the history of a proud people." She went on to praise Old Main as "the intellectual mother of an entire people." Holshouser, who was governor at the time of the fire and an advocate of saving the facility, emphasized the importance of remembering the past, but he also stressed that "it would be tragic if, with this rededication of Old Main, we kept looking back in our thinking. We can't just look inside ourselves anymore," he said, "but must keep looking upward and outward. Be proud of your Indian heritage, but also be proud of the larger community we all live in. The best is yet to be. There is a better day, not just for Lumbees, but for all North Carolinians." A few days before the rededication, Stan Swofford of the *Greensboro Daily News* noted Old Main's place of prominence on the campus when he wrote, "[Old Main] still assumes, powerfully but unobtrusively, her customary position of quiet leadership at the center of the Lumbee Indian community. She remains as she always has been—at once a symbol of a proud but troubled past and a promise of brighter and more prosperous tomorrows."

Other efforts to improve the relationship between the campus and the community included the involvement of more local citizens in university projects, such as the Centennial Celebration. There was a conscious attempt to get people to the campus through cultural activities and special events, such as minority presence days. In 1980 Pembroke State first hosted a mathematics competition as part of a statewide competition that brought students from throughout the region to campus.

Winners in their categories advanced to the state regional finals. The following year, the university hosted the Region IV Science Fair, with winners advancing to the state competition. Another such event was the Robeson County Shootout basketball tournament, which featured high school teams from Robeson and surrounding counties. First held in December 1986 in the English E. Jones Health and Physical Education Center, the popular tournament brought many community members and prospective students onto the campus for the first time. Organized by Pembroke State's head men's basketball coach Dan Kenney, the tournament continued the campus tradition of hosting a community basketball tournament, beginning in 1940 when the Indian high school tournament was held in the old gymnasium. The Robeson County Shootout tournament continues today, now hosted on the campuses of Robeson County high schools and the university.

Under Dr. Givens, the university engaged in widespread landscaping activities. Dozens of trees and flowers were planted, a number of pleasant sitting areas were provided, and a carillon bell tower, made possible by a gift from professors Ira Pate Lowry '29 and his wife, Reba M. Lowry, was added to the Quad. At the May 10, 1981, dedication of the Lowry Bell Tower, Ira Pate Lowry remarked, "I hope that hearing [the chimes ring out] will bring you closer to God, to the university, and to others." Religion Professor I. Ruth Martin said, "As the tones roll across the area and

FIGURE 5.4. *Lowry Bell Tower. Named for professors Ira Pate Lowry '29 and his wife, Reba (Millsaps) Lowry. Erected April 28, 1981; renovated in 2003.*

rise into the skies, let them remind us of this educational institution and of fine people like Ira Pate and Reba Lowry, who contributed to the growth of Pembroke." The campus landmark chimes on the hour, and, each day at noon, plays various tunes, including the university's alma mater, which was written by the Lowrys. The Givens administration was seeking to create an ambience that was both intellectual and aesthetic. Today, the university has one of the most beautiful and well-maintained campuses in the UNC system.

In providing direction to the institution, Dr. Givens consistently drew ideas from the university community, including the previously mentioned Office of Economic Development and the Robeson County Shootout. Shortly after taking office he established twenty task forces to examine the university, discover its problems, and identify its strengths. Once that was accomplished, he set up a system of study commissions to offer specific recommendations for the future development of the institution. Working through the 1983–1984 academic year, the various commissions proposed hundreds of recommendations covering the spectrum of the university's operation. Many, such as the establishment of an Office of Advisement and Retention, were quickly adopted. The office developed the Early Alert Program, Freshman Seminar, and the Student Advocacy Program to promote the academic success of students. Through the Early Alert Program, a faculty or staff member could recommend that a student get assistance with a problem that threatened his or her academic success. Freshman Seminar was designed to introduce students to campus and college life. With the Student Advocacy Program, any student who became confused or frustrated by university practices could request that the office act as an intermediary or locate assistance or information. Today, the Center for Academic Excellence, the Hawk Alert Program, and Freshman Seminar continue to support the university's student retention and advising efforts. Other proposals set forth by the study commissions were included in the school's long-range plans, while some were dropped as undesirable or impracticable. In this way, Chancellor Givens's initiatives ensured that all segments of the university were given the opportunity to help shape the future of the institution.

The Givens administration witnessed many other significant developments. In 1981 the University of North Carolina system and the federal Justice Department settled an eleven-year desegregation suit with a consent decree. The Justice Department sued the UNC system in 1970 on the grounds that it had not worked hard enough to integrate its five predominantly black and eleven predominantly white colleges. Under the decree the UNC system agreed to establish twenty-nine new programs at the historically black institutions in an effort to attract more whites to them, while establishing racial goals at the white institutions to assure integration on those campuses. Critics argued that it was a self-defeating agreement that would continue segregated schools, while proponents hailed it as a victory for the state's right to control its own colleges. Ironically, Pembroke State was the odd school out. Although a historically minority institution, by 1981 its enrollment was 64 percent white, 24 percent Indian, and 12 percent black. Thus, it received none of the new programs because of the consent decree. Even so, it was, and remains today, the most racially diverse of the seventeen campuses in the UNC system.

In the 1980s Pembroke State acquired more of an international flavor when it recruited a number of foreign students to its campus. In 1982, for example, thirty-two international students from ten different countries were enrolled. These students introduced elements of new cultures to the campus. In this period, it also became possible for the university to offer its students greater access to outside resources when the Mary Livermore Library joined SOLINET (Southeastern United States Library Network). Additionally, the library received funds to establish a computer catalog system.

Another noteworthy event during the Givens administration reflected a change in attitudes toward women in leadership. In October

1983 Geneva (Everette) Parnell (1929–2006) of Parkton, North Carolina, became the first female elected chair of the Board of Trustees. Parnell was the third female trustee at a UNC system school to hold that distinction; the first two were elected just the year before, in 1982. The following year, on October 26, 1984, she became the first female trustee at a UNC system school to serve two terms as chair of the trustees. On September 15, 1989, Rosa (Revels) Winfree '60, a Lumbee, was the first Indian female elected chair of the trustees.

While the Givens administration promoted excellence in campus activities and witnessed much progress, not all of its efforts to implement change were successful. In 1983 Chancellor Givens proposed changing the name of the institution from Pembroke State University to the University of North Carolina at Pembroke. It was believed that the new name would more clearly identify the institution as a member of the UNC system, increase the prestige of its programs and degrees, and result in increased enrollment. Many Lumbees came out in opposition to the proposal, feeling that it was another example of de-Indianization, that it would further lessen the historical ties of the institution with the Indian community. The pros and cons of changing the school's name were vigorously debated by faculty, students, alumni, administrators, and citizens. A white columnist in the October 14, 1983 edition of *The Robesonian* expressed his deep discontent with the suggested change. He wrote:

> I find it appalling that Pembroke State University officials could even consider changing the name of their institution to the University of North Carolina at Pembroke. Only a naive or uninformed person could believe that such a name change could benefit the university or Pembroke or Robeson County. Pembroke State, my alma mater, has made tremendous strides in the past 20 years, increasing its enrollment, its campus facilities, and its overall standing

among the nation's academic centers. It is a special, friendly place, much better than what some ignorant people would believe. But apparently it has a stigma for some because it was formerly a "minority" school and remains located in a predominantly Indian community.

Although the columnist disagreed with the name change, his pride in the institution and the quality of its academic program was evident. A notable opponent of the change was Adolph L. Dial '43, chair of the Department of American Indian Studies.

A week later, on October 23, 1983, at a meeting of the Board of Trustees, Chancellor Givens recommended, and the trustees unanimously approved, that the name change be tabled indefinitely after the trustees requested more input in the matter. This action ran contrary to the results of a survey of alumni concerning the name change. Some 6,200 alumni were polled, with 1,147 responding. Of the respondents, 914 alumni or 79.6 percent favored changing the name of the school. Before making the recommendation to table the issue, Chancellor Givens expressed his own strong support for the idea. He reported, "You may not realize it, but people in our Admissions Office have to explain who we are. People ask them: 'Is this a private school?' They don't know we are a part of the University of North Carolina." Givens continued, "Some think a name change is a good idea; others think it would fail to recognize the Indian heritage of the school. I fail to see this logic. What sounds more Indian? Pembroke State University or the University of North Carolina at Pembroke?"

FIGURE 5.5. *Pembroke State University wordmark.*

After studying the issue and with the support of 80 percent of alumni, the Board of Trustees unanimously voted, one year later, on October 26, 1984, to endorse the name change. Sharing in the symbolism of Indians making the motion to change the name were trustees Dennis Lowery '64 and Burlin Lowry, both Lumbees. The motion was seconded by another Lumbee trustee, Ira Pate Lowry '29. As a result, Chancellor Givens added, "The excitement on this campus is the highest since I've been here. We are opening new doors, and may have opened a new door today."

President Friday took the trustees' endorsement of the name change to the Board of Governors, who in turn would decide whether to make a recommendation to the General Assembly. Authority for renaming the institution resided with the General Assembly. While awaiting a decision from the Board of Governors, Gene Warren, director of public information at the university, in a November 29, 1984, letter to the editor of *The Robesonian*, tied the name change to the progress made by the institution. He wrote, "The name change may be difficult for some people to understand. But, as has been pointed out, every name change of this institution has been to more clearly define what it was doing at that particular time. The institution has progressed through the years to its present level: of being really the University of North Carolina at Pembroke."

Following a February 7, 1985, meeting where supporters and opponents of the name-change issue spoke, the Board of Governors took no further action on the issue. Opposition to the change within the Lumbee community was a key reason. The idea, however, resurfaced with the Board of Trustees in September 1987 after chair Dennis Lowery '64 expressed concern about a recent effort by technical colleges to change their names to community colleges. He was worried about the "competitive aspect" of the move. At a January 6, 1988, meeting, the trustees voted, with one member abstaining, to "develop a systematic strategy for changing the name" of the university. However, no further action was taken by the trustees, as the institution's name remained Pembroke State University.

Despite the opposition to the name-change proposal at that time, it was generally recognized that Chancellor Givens provided capable leadership to the university, and that he worked diligently to establish high levels of excellence. Consequently, on May 11, 1985, the Board of Trustees voted to name the Performing Arts Center in his honor, making it the Paul R. Givens Performing Arts Center. Since the beginning of his tenure, Givens recognized the potential for the sixteen-hundred-seat Performing Arts Center to be a regional center for cultural and performing arts. Through his efforts, the 1980s saw the continued development of first-rate programming and growing audiences as the "GPAC" regularly brought outstanding musical, literary, and political personalities to its campus. Those included world-famous rhythm and blues musician Ray Charles, who performed two back-to-back shows on November 13, 1987, and the Reverend Jesse Jackson, a Democratic presidential candidate who spoke at GPAC in February 1988. In addition, the university reached out to the public with its drama group, The Pembroke Players; with its talented chorus and band, "The Singers" and "The Swingers;" through its faculty, who served as speakers and resource persons to community groups;

FIGURE 5.6. *Centennial Celebration logo (1987).*

and through its Native American Resource Center, with its displays and programs. As a result, Pembroke State became the focal point and facilitator of cultural events in the community and the region.

The high point of the decade came when Pembroke State marked its Centennial with a celebration from September 1986 through April 1987. Chaired by Dr. Gerald Maynor '59, professor of education, the theme was "Opening New Doors." The grand marshal was Rev. Charles W. Maynor '40, the first four-year graduate of the institution. The celebration was a period of great celebration and brought regional attention to the campus. It kicked off with the Centennial Convocation in GPAC on September 3, 1986. Dr. David Eliades and Linda Oxendine presented their research into the history of the university, and discussed the publication of *Pembroke State University: A Centennial History*, the first comprehensive history of the institution. Also during the convocation, Professor Emeritus Clifton Oxendine '24 and Joseph Sandlin, codirector of the university's Annual Giving campaign, were conferred honorary doctorates by the university.

The Centennial Celebration also included a three-day Festival of Native American Arts and Culture; concerts by the U.S. Marine Band, the Orlando String Quartet, and international opera star Costanzo Cuccaro; and performances of *Evita*, Les Ballets Trockadero de Monte Carlo, and *The Gilded Age*. On October 15, 1986, portraits of chief executives of the institution—W. L. Moore, Ralph D. Wellons, Walter J. Gale, English E. Jones, and Givens—were unveiled, and a thirty-minute video about the university, titled, *Pembroke State University: A Class by Itself*, premiered. Other events included a reunion of classes from 1905 through 1986, a symposium on Indian culture, Centennial Homecoming, and a reunion concert of the "The Singers" and "The Swingers." Former queens were invited to the Miss Pembroke State University pageant.

On March 5, 1987, the Centennial Founders' Day Convocation featured remarks by Gov. James Martin; the University Band's performance of "Centennial Ode," a musical composition written by Elliott Del Borgo; and Chancellor Givens reading a congratulatory letter from President Ronald Reagan. The highlight of the day was the unveiling of a statue of Hamilton McMillan, the state representative from Red Springs who introduced the legislation establishing the institution in 1887. The unveiling was the culmination of a four-year effort, began in January 1983, to raise twenty-five thousand dollars to procure the statue. The statue was created by art professor Paul Van Zandt. The campus landmark sits in front of historic Old Main, facing northwest while gazing across campus. The following day, on March 6, 1987, a Centennial Founders' Day Banquet was held. Eric Sevareid, a former CBS news commentator for four decades, was the keynote speaker. The Centennial Celebration concluded on April 8, 1986, with the dedication of the Special Collections Room of the Mary Livermore Library.

The celebratory mood on campus did not subside with the conclusion of the Centennial Celebration. The dedication of the James B. Chavis University Center on September 16, 1987, marked another milestone in the university's history. The University Center was considered the last link in meeting the essential needs of the university, especially since two-thirds of the institution's students were commuters. Today the heart of student activity on campus, the building features a large student lounge, dining hall, recreation center with bowling alley, chapel, faculty and chancellor's dining rooms, and offices for student government and other student services. Adjacent to the dining hall, the smaller snack bar was named "Bert's" in honor of Berteen (Oxendine) Prine (1923–2000), who served as the executive secretary for five administrations between 1943 and 1991. To mark the building's dedication, a time capsule was placed in the façade of the building to be opened in 2087. The spacious $5.5 million structure, then the most expensive campus building to construct, sits on the eight-acre site of the former Pembroke Graded School, which the university acquired in 1981. The Board of Trustees, earlier on May 9, 1987, named the building for Dr. James B. Chavis '63 (1936–2010), a Lumbee who served as vice chancellor for student affairs from 1979 to 1999. Chavis worked at the university for thirty-four years, including serving as director of the D.F. Lowry Student Center when it

FIGURE 5.7. *James B. Chavis '63. Vice chancellor for student affairs and namesake for James B. Chavis University Center.*

FIGURE 5.8. *Aerial view of the campus of Pembroke State University (circa 1988).*

opened in 1965. He guided the planning of the University Center, with its signature skylights, mezzanine, and vaulted ceilings.

Other innovations during the period enhanced student life. In 1981 the Baptist Student Union (BSU) was completed. A four-thousand-square-foot, one-story structure, it was built by the Baptists on land across North Odum Street / Prospect Road from the university, adjoining the Indian Burnt Swamp Baptist Association. The BSU was a $210,000 facility built by Baptist volunteers, and intended to be a home away from home for any student who wished to go there for fellowship, study, or relaxation. Known today as Baptist Campus Ministries, it has added another dimension to the university and to the quality of student life. In 1983 the Office of Student Activities was established. Now the Office of Student Involvement and Leadership, it coordinates and promotes activities for students. To encourage student involvement in extracurricular activities, a student activity period was initiated in 1986; one class period per week was designated solely for student activities, including organizational and academic major meetings.

With the opening of the Chavis University Center, the D. F. Lowry Building received a major renovation in 1988 that converted the former student center into space for the bookstore and offices. There was other campus construction during this period. In 1980 the Classroom North Building was completed. For the next two decades, it was the northernmost building on campus. In 1986 an area of the second floor of the Mary Livermore Library was renovated, as office and classroom space was eliminated to make additional room for book space. Renovations to the Admissions Building, today Hickory Hall, were completed in 1987. The following year, in 1988, the old gymnasium was razed, and work began on a $2.45 million addition to the Herbert G. Oxendine Science Building.

With the new construction and renovations to campus buildings during the 1980s, the campus, by 1989, had 33 buildings on 102 acres. At end of the decade, Pembroke State had an outstanding and modern physical plant; every campus structure had been built or remodeled since 1949. The total value of the university was calculated to be $50 million. The university also had more than 350 full-time or part-time employees, and the annual operating budget was $14 million.

On September 14, 1988, Chancellor Givens announced his retirement, effective July 1, 1989. As was customary at that time, chancellors at UNC system schools retired upon reaching age sixty-five; Givens turned sixty-five the following November. In making the announcement, Givens said the university had reason to be optimistic about the future. Enrollment that fall was at an all-time high of 2,835, "faculty and staff morale is excellent, and there are some new programs and new faces that add excitement to this grand institution." Acknowledging the supporting efforts of the campus and local community, Dr. Givens later remarked, "Anything Lee and I have accomplished has been done with a lot of help. We have not walked alone." To recognize Chancellor Givens's ten years of service to Pembroke State, the Alumni Association awarded him the Distinguished Service Award in February 1989. Upon retirement, Givens was awarded chancellor emeritus status. The Givenses retired to Temple Terrace, Florida, where he jokingly planned to "get up in the morning and make a list of the all the things I'm not going to do." Chancellor Emeritus Givens passed away October 24, 2004. The university held a memorial service in the Givens Performing Arts Center the following November 16 when Givens was eulogized by faculty, staff, and alumni.

At a May 12, 1989, appreciation dinner for Chancellor Givens and his wife, Lee, Dr. Ruth (Dial) Woods, a Pembroke native and member of the UNC system Board of Governors, captured the essence of his tenure at Pembroke State. She said he left behind "a legacy of educational excellence, progressive leadership, quality institutional programs, proud alumni, and faculty, and staff committed to continuing institutional growth and progress."

MAP 5.1. *Pembroke State University campus (1989).*

TIMELINE OF NOTABLE INSTITUTIONAL EVENTS (1979–1989)

1979   • Dr. Paul R. Givens named second chancellor.

1980   • Rededication of Old Main.
- Athletic Hall of Fame established.
- Classroom North Building completed; later renamed the Adolph L. Dial Humanities Building.

1981   • Campus size increased from 95 to 102 acres.
- Lowry Bell Tower erected.
- Chancellor's Scholars Program established.
- The Baptist Student Union, known today as Baptist Campus Ministries, opened.
- Awards Day implemented.
- Funding received to establish WPSU-TV; known today as WNCP-TV.
- First hosted the Region IV science fair.

1982   • Women's athletic teams leave AIAW and join NAIA.

1983   • Geneva (Everette) Parnell elected first female chair of the Board of Trustees
- Proposal to change the name of the institution to the University of North Carolina at Pembroke.
- Office of Student Activities established; known today as the Office of Student Involvement and Leadership.

1984   • The Board of Trustees unanimously voted to endorse the university's name change.
- Geneva (Everette) Parnell became the first female in the UNC system to serve two terms as the chair of the Board of Trustees.
- Centennial Giving Campaign begun.
- Francesca (Adler) Adler-Baeder '83, Miss Pembroke State University 1981, was crowned Miss North Carolina.
- Department of American Indian Studies authorized to offer a major.
- Pembroke State awarded the Joby Hawn Cup.

1985   • The UNC Board of Governors discussed the proposed name change but took no action.
- Women's cross country added.
- Givens Performing Arts Center named for Chancellor Paul R. Givens.

1986   · The Robeson County Shootout basketball tournament began on campus.
        · Student activity period established.
        · Renovations to second floor of Mary Livermore Library.
        · William H. Belk Endowed Chair of Business Management established.
1986–87 · Pembroke State University celebrated its Centennial.
1987   · James B. Chavis University Center opened.
        · The Admissions Building, today Hickory Hall, was renovated.
        · "Bert's" named for Berteen (Oxendine) Prine, who served as the executive secretary for five administrations between 1943 and 1991.
        · $1 million Centennial Giving Campaign goal reached.
        · Office of Economic Development established.
1988   · The Board of Trustees, with one abstention, voted to "develop a systematic strategy for changing the name" of the university; no further action was taken.
        · D. F. Lowry Building renovated.
        · Old gymnasium razed.
1989   · Pembroke State awarded the Joby Hawn Cup.
        · Dr. Paul R. Givens retired.

Chapter Six

1989–1999
NEW HORIZONS

*This validation by those who know us best convinces me that
UNC Pembroke is making the right moves, continues on the road
to progress, and stands ready to embrace the new millennium.*

Dr. Joseph B. Oxendine, chancellor,
University of North Carolina at Pembroke, response
to results of Student Satisfaction Survey (1999)

The last decade of the twentieth century at Pembroke State University was marked by a continued emphasis on excellence and the dawn of new horizons as the university, led by a chancellor with local roots, embarked on a path to engage the community, expand the university's visibility in the region and the state, and promote its status as a constituent institution of the University of North Carolina system.

Prompted by the retirement of Chancellor Paul R. Givens in the summer of 1989, the Board of Trustees established a fifteen-member search committee in October 1988 to screen applicants and nominees for the next university chancellor and to make recommendations to the Board of Trustees. Chair of the committee was Wayne Evans, who also chaired the Board of Trustees. Committee members included trustees, faculty, and presidents of the Alumni Association and the Student Government Association. After a six-month search, the board sent three names to C.D. Spangler Jr., president of the UNC system. On April 13, 1989, the Board of Governors, after accepting the nomination of President Spangler, unanimously voted to approve Dr. Joseph B. Oxendine, a professor and former dean of physical education at Temple University, as the third chancellor of Pembroke State University. Spangler noted that Dr. Oxendine "is precisely the right person for Pembroke State at this time." Board of Governors member Dr. Ruth (Dial) Woods, in her motion to appoint Oxendine, said, "In a county perceived as riddled by controversy, disruption, ambiguities, and contradictions, the appointment of Dr. Oxendine sends forth a message for reconciliation in Robeson County.... We welcome Dr. Oxendine home, and welcome his leadership and contributions in helping all of us achieve our vision of restoring Robeson County and the southeastern region of North Carolina to the

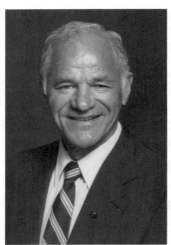

FIGURE 6.1. *Dr. Joseph B. Oxendine. Chancellor of Pembroke State University (1989–1996) and the University of North Carolina at Pembroke (1996–1999).*

greatness that it is and that it can become." Chancellor Oxendine led the university from 1989 to 1999.

Dr. Oxendine was a professor of physical education and former dean of the College of Health, Physical Education, Recreation, and Dance at Temple University in Philadelphia, Pennsylvania. Born March 31, 1930, he was a Pembroke native who, as a youth, had tended tobacco and cotton fields about one mile west of the campus. Oxendine's family had a long history of association with the institution. He was the great-grandson of J. (John) J. Oxendine, who was a member of the institution's first Board of Trustees. His father and many of his siblings attended and graduated from the institution. Oxendine's brother Tom Oxendine '48 was a distinguished graduate, and his sister Magnolia G. Lowry was a professor of business at the university.

Oxendine attended the county's segregated Indian schools, graduating from Pembroke High School in 1947. To earn money for college, Oxendine joined his brother Robert Oxendine and other Lumbees in Detroit, where he worked in an automobile factory for one year. While there, Oxendine decided to be an athlete at a small college. After some research, he discovered that Catawba College in Salisbury, North Carolina, had one of the best small college football programs in the nation. When Oxendine returned home from Detroit, he fondly recalled taking seventeen one-hundred-dollar bills—money for education—out of his shoe where he had stored them for safe keeping during the bus ride home. Oxendine enrolled at Catawba in the fall of 1948, where he excelled as an athlete. He was a three-sport athlete in varsity baseball, basketball, and football, earning all-state honors in football and baseball. He was later installed in the Catawba Athletic Hall of Fame in 1978. Oxendine earned a BA degree in health and physical education from Catawba in 1952. During the summers from 1952 to 1955, he was a professional baseball player in the Pittsburgh Pirates minor league system. Herbert G. Oxendine, namesake for the Oxendine Science Building, befriended Joe when they both played baseball on a Robeson County team. Herbert was a doctoral student at Boston University (BU) and encouraged Joe to get his master's degree there. Taking his friend's advice, Oxendine enrolled at BU and graduated in 1953 with an EdM degree in physical education. He was then drafted by the U.S. Army and served until 1955. Between 1955 and 1957, Oxendine was a public school teacher and coach of high school baseball, basketball, and football, and American Legion baseball in Lynchburg, Virginia. While teaching, Oxendine decided to become a college professor. Consequently, he enrolled in BU in 1957, completing a doctor of education degree in 1959.

Dr. Oxendine was a distinguished scholar and national authority on physical education teaching and research at Temple University between 1959 and 1989. From 1965 to 1974 he served as chair of the Department of Health, Physical Education, Recreation, and Dance. Between 1974 and 1981 Dr. Oxendine was the founding dean of the College of Health, Physical Education, Recreation, and Dance. He authored two books: *Psychology of Motor Learning* (1968; second edition, 1984) and *American Indian Sports Heritage* (1988; second edition, 1995). He also authored three dozen professional and research articles, five chapters in books on motor learning, and served as a consulting editor for *American Educator* encyclopedia. At Temple, Dr. Oxendine served as president of the Faculty Senate and president of the university's chapter of the American Association of University Professors.

Dr. Oxendine received numerous awards for his accomplishments. In 1978 he received the Alumni Award for Distinguished Public Service from Boston University. In 1979 he received an honorary doctor of science degree from Catawba College, and a doctor of laws degree from Sandhills Community College in 1996. Dr. Oxendine also received an Honor Award and Outstanding Teacher Award, both from the American Association of Health, Physical Education, Recreation, and Dance, in 1979 and 1966, respectively.

At the time of his selection, Chancellor Oxendine noted that Pembroke State had a "special meaning" to him. He added, "It is a great university, and I want it to be greater. I want to make sure it has an impact on the community—I want to do more." A finalist for the position ten years earlier, Dr. Oxendine said, "I feel I've worked the past few decades to prepare for this." At the time of his appointment, there was considerable racial unrest in Robeson County. Dr. Oxendine acknowledged the tensions, pledging to "make a difference on the total community," including all three races.

Dr. Oxendine, the second Lumbee to serve as chancellor of the university, began his duties on July 1, 1989. His first day coincided with the concluding Saturday of the weeklong Lumbee Homecoming, held annually in Pembroke. Embarking on a tour of "personal diplomacy," Dr. Oxendine won his age division in the four-mile road race and rode in the parade through the Town of Pembroke. Dr. Oxendine's tour continued that August as he addressed the teachers, supervisors, and administrators of the Public Schools of Robeson County, Pembroke State faculty and freshmen, civic clubs, and other organizations. He was also interviewed by former UNC system president William C. Friday for *North Carolina People*, a public television program that aired statewide.

Three days of inaugural festivities climaxed on October 27, 1989, with the formal installation of Chancellor Oxendine. Special guests included C.D. Spangler, who presided over the inauguration; Gov. James B. Martin; and Dr. Martin R. Levy, a professor of health education at Temple University and a longtime friend of Chancellor Oxendine. Dr. Levy, the keynote speaker, welcomed Dr. Oxendine home and praised his accomplishments when he said, "We're proud that you bring to this new position a hometown perspective on hard work, commitment, and a desire to succeed, and years of training, experience, and achievement to education."

During his installation remarks, Dr. Oxendine pledged to dedicate the university to the "pursuit of academic excellence, the promotion of racial harmony, and the fight against illiteracy in Robeson County." He said, "The pursuit of the mark of the high calling requires that at Pembroke State University we create a climate of academic excellence, with rigorous standards and a curriculum based on the liberal arts, not compromised by the rush towards vocationalism...." He also said the university would "reach out to our community—we are going to impact on our public schools and help to upgrade the quality of education for persons from preschool to the completion of high school." In addition, Dr. Oxendine pledged the support of the university in addressing economic and social issues affecting the area. "We're going to recognize the serious poverty in this area," he said. "We're going to reach out and address human relations in this community, a community often under strife and stress and threats." He continued, "We are going to use our resources to heal the wounds in this community. We will do that at Pembroke State University."

One of Chancellor Oxendine's primary goals was increased community outreach and regional engagement that would build better relations between the university and the community. To this end, the first effort began on campus on April 25, 1990, when the university, in conjunction with the Town of Pembroke and the Pembroke Chamber of Commerce, hosted the first Pembroke Day. Staged in the Quad, and open to the campus and local community, the purpose of the event was to improve relations between the university and the Town of Pembroke, particularly among the university's students and local businesses. Pembroke Day featured exhibitions by Indian dancers, booths staffed by local vendors and town businesses, entertainment for children, a health fair, free lunch, and singing. The event received regional radio and television coverage. It was carried live for four hours on WJSK-FM radio. *Carolina in the Morning*, a program of WECT-TV in Wilmington, broadcast that morning from campus. Staged on the last day of classes, Pembroke Day was similar to a "school breaking," held decades earlier to celebrate the end of the school year. It was a huge success. The second Pembroke Day was held October 2, 1991, at the beginning of the school year. Now an annual campus tradition, the twenty-third annual Pembroke Day was held in September 2012, attracting thousands of townspeople and students. In another expression of outreach to the community and the county's school system, the second annual Project Graduation, an all-night, drug-and-alcohol-free party for graduating seniors in Robeson County high schools, was held on campus in June 1990. Sponsored by the Public Schools of Robeson County, the event brought more than one thousand graduates to campus. The annual event has been held at the university since 1990. To reach out to alumni and friends of Pembroke State, the university began publication of *PSU Today* in the fall of 1990. Now known as *UNCP Today*, the magazine shares news and information about the university with over twenty-two thousand alumni and friends. That same year, Kristy (Woods) Maynor '92, who was crowned Miss Pembroke State University in 1989, became the first Miss PSU to compete in the Miss North Carolina Pageant. This brought additional visibility to the university. Although temporarily discontinued in 1993 and reinstituted in 2000, participation by Miss UNCP in the state pageant was again discontinued in 2012 because of concerns over the cost to the university and contestants. In 1995 the university launched the Regional Center for Economic, Community, and Pro-

FIGURE 6.2. *Chancellor Joseph B. Oxendine unveiling the new university logo in April 1992.*

fessional Development to function as the outreach arm of the university. Established to serve southeastern North Carolina, the Regional Center fosters collaboration, enhances business development through the Small Business and Technology Development Center, and empowers communities to improve the quality of life in the region.

The university's image was a priority for Chancellor Oxendine. He initiated efforts to rebrand the institution's image by updating the university and athletic logos, which modernized the university's graphic presence and brought consistency to images used to represent the school. Oxendine hoped the university's new image would enhance the school's visibility and attract students from outside the region. With the approval of the Board of Trustees on December 13, 1991, a new logo was adopted that featured a stylized Old Main, the oldest and most historic building on campus, with a black and gold starburst or sun over the left side of the building's roof. The words "Pembroke State University" appeared to the left of the building and "of the University of North Carolina" was

displayed across the bottom of the logo. Elements of the design represented the history of the school and emphasized its connection with
the UNC system. The logo replaced a wordmark from the mid-1980s
that featured the words "Pembroke State University" and a rendition
of Old Main. Chancellor Oxendine utilized the new logo in another
initiative to bring attention to the university. Taking advantage of a 1991
state law allowing collegiate license plates, Chancellor Oxendine, in May
1992, announced the issuance of a Pembroke State license plate by the
North Carolina Department of Motor Vehicles. The third UNC system
institution to take advantage of the law, the license plate featured the
new logo plus the letter "P" for Pembroke. A portion of the license plate
renewal fee was returned to the university to support scholarships. The
license plate provided the university with additional visibility and was
another way for alumni and friends to simultaneously show their pride
and financial support for the institution.

   An unexpected encounter between Chancellor Oxendine and the
university's mascot in 1992 brought Pembroke State unintended national
exposure, leading to a new mascot and its first official athletic logo. During a
January 23, 1992, home basketball game, Chancellor Oxendine was shocked
to see the university's "masklike" Indian mascot, with an "oversized head and

FIGURE 6.3. *Former
athletic logo repre-
senting the Braves.*

FIGURE 6.4. *Former
athletic logo representing
the Lady Braves.*

FIGURE 6.5. *First official
athletic logo, adopted in
1992, featured a Brave
and the red-tailed hawk.*

feathered headband." Concerned that the mascot was offensive to Indians and misrepresented the university's Indian heritage, Chancellor Oxendine immediately ordered that it not appear again until a study was completed. He appointed a committee of students, faculty, and alumni, representing all races, to recommend a resolution to the matter. Oxendine later said "inappropriate portrayals of American Indians in sports are disrespectful, insulting, and psychologically destructive to the Indian population." Many Indian students shared the chancellor's concerns. Soon, Chancellor Oxendine and the university were at the forefront of the national debate over Indian mascots. More importantly, it brought an awareness of the issue to campus, particularly how Indian mascots, athletic imagery, chants, and other behaviors promoted Indian stereotypes. Although Chancellor Oxendine intended to keep the "Braves" nickname, he seized the opportunity to select a new mascot and redesign the athletic logo.

Following a search for a new mascot, the university unveiled its first official athletic logo in July 1992. The design features an Indian brave, a red-tailed hawk, and the word "Braves." A prominent feature of the black and gold design is a circle, which ties all the elements together. The logo was drawn by local artist Gloria Tara Lowery '66 after Dr. Stanley Knick, professor of archaeology and American Indian studies at the university, suggested the design with the hawk as a companion to the brave. The new logo replaced earlier logos that depicted a "war whooping" Indian with a tomahawk and a female Indian used to represent the Lady Braves.

In September 1992 Chancellor Oxendine announced the selection of the red-tailed hawk as the university's mascot. The red-tailed hawk is indigenous to North America and can be seen soaring high above or perching in the pine trees surrounding campus. Its selection reflected the traditional relationship between Indians and animals. Indian traditions teach that some animals were sent by the Great Creator to serve as guardians and teachers for humans. Consequently, they are endowed with certain sacred qualities and powers that can be imparted to humans. The powers of specific animals are invoked by adding symbols and images on clothing and personal belongings. The Braves' athletic uniforms and other campus signage are now adorned with the mascot to invoke the qualities of the red-tailed hawk—speed, keen sight, focus, power, hunting prowess, and good luck. Regarding the selection, Chancellor Oxendine said, "We are excited about the Hawk as our mascot and the new logo portraying the partnership of the Brave and the Hawk. We feel good about projecting such an image of teamwork and the winning spirit of Pembroke State University, an image that does not denigrate but rather celebrates pride in our heritage as well as the joy of athletic competition." With the selection of a mascot, the university unveiled a costumed version of the red-tailed hawk during its first home basketball game in late November 1992. Donned in black and gold, the costumed hawk became a visible part of athletic and campus functions. The new athletic logo, red-tailed hawk mascot, and the costumed mascot, according to Oxendine, "received widespread popularity and acceptance."

The next step in the rebranding of the university came on February 26, 1993, when Pembroke State's official seal was modified to reflect the new

FIGURE 6.6. *Seal of Pembroke State University adopted in February 1993.*

university logo. Since 1940 the seal had featured the name of the school, its location, the year "1887" and an open book, with the words "knowledge," "wisdom," "devotion," and "service" added in the early 1970s. The book was replaced with the logo featuring Old Main and the phrase "of the University of North Carolina." It prominently denoted the university's relationship with the UNC system. The rebranding of the university through the adoption of new logos and a mascot, along with the redesign of the seal, were essential to bringing additional visibility to the university and its status as a constituent institution of the UNC system.

While rebranding the university's image was one way to attract a broader spectrum of students, particularly from outside the immediate region, another was to offer a wider variety of degree programs, particularly in the hot-button professions such as nursing. As a result, the curriculum was expanded to include new areas of study at the undergraduate and graduate levels. In 1992 Pembroke State began offering an RN-to-BSN program jointly with Fayetteville State University, designed to attract registered nurses with two-year degrees who wished to pursue a BS degree in nursing and unlock career opportunities. Other new undergraduate degree programs included community health education, mass communication, birth-to-kindergarten, American studies, athletic training, and criminal justice. At the graduate level, the university added a master of business administration (MBA) in 1995 and master of arts in school counseling and agency counseling. To support student academic success, the University Writing Center was opened in May 1994.

To augment the expanded curriculum and recruit highly qualified students, the university was awarded the prestigious North Carolina Teaching Fellows Program in November 1992. Established by the General Assembly in 1986, the program was the most ambitious teacher recruitment program in the nation, with a mission to recruit the "best and brightest" high school graduates into the teaching profession. The application process is highly competitive. Teaching Fellows are awarded a four-year scholarship valued at sixty-five hundred dollars per year for a total of twenty-six thousand dollars, and participate in year-round enrichment activities. They are obligated to teach four years in a North Carolina public school system. The first class began at Pembroke State in the fall of 1994. With the addition of the program, the university continues to support its historic mission as a teacher training institution, but more importantly, it enhances the quality of public school teaching in southeastern North Carolina. Today, the program is hosted by seventeen campuses across the state.

In conjunction with expanding and strengthening the curriculum, Chancellor Oxendine's administration emphasized faculty scholarship, and service to the university and the community. Prior to his arrival, Pembroke State was known as an institution that focused primarily on teaching. Consequently, the university dramatically increased its research, creative work, and grant activity. An Office of Grants, later renamed the Office of Sponsored Research and Programs, was established in 1992, and Gene Brayboy was hired as its director. That year, the university had twelve grant submissions and was awarded $425,000 for research or training programs. By 1998 the number of submissions had increased to seventy-three and awards had grown to more than $4.7 million. To promote faculty scholarship and attract nationally recognized scholars, two distinguished professorships, the Martha Humphrey Beach Chair in Art and the William C. Friday Chair in Molecular Biology and Biochemistry, were established in 1997. These $500,000 endowed professorships were made possible through the support of Martha (Humphrey) Beach '62, the General Assembly's Distinguished Professors Endowment Trust Fund, the C.D. Spangler Foundation Inc., and the university community. Beach (1917–2012) was a native of Fairmont, North Carolina, who nurtured a lifetime practice of helping people that led to a career in social work and counseling. The two new chairs joined the William H. Belk Endowed Chair of Business Management that was established in 1986. Although Chancellor Oxendine emphasized faculty research and scholarship, quality teaching remained a cornerstone of the Pembroke State experience. The university established the Teaching and Learning Center in 1996 to promote teaching excellence among the faculty by offering programs to foster continuous improvement in teaching and support for professional development opportunities. To recognize and reward teaching excellence at Pembroke State and other UNC system institutions, the Board of Governors established the UNC Board of Governors Award for Excellence in Teaching in 1994. The award, presented annually to a member of the faculty at each of the UNC system institutions, also includes a stipend. In 1995 Dr. Bonnie Kelley of the Department of Biology was the inaugural winner at Pembroke State. Throughout the period, faculty and staff greatly increased their community service to the public schools and health and social agencies, and in the areas of economic development and financial counseling. In 1998 the number of service hours to the public schools totaled eighteen hundred.

During the 1990s, under the auspices of University Computing and Information Services, the university saw a dramatic growth in the use of technology to provide for the academic and administrative needs of the campus. To support its technological infrastructure, a fiber optic loop was installed to connect every computer on campus and further enhance the integrity of the university's computer network. The 1990 *Indianhead* touched on other technological advances. It read, "Computerized registration has eliminated long lines and much frustration at the start of each semester.... The once laborious process of writing, typing, proofreading, and then re-typing a research paper has become less arduous with the aid of word processors." The most pronounced technological advancement was the integration of electronic mail or email and the World Wide Web into campus communication and work processes. During the late 1980s, the UNC system's General Administration ran Educational Computing Services (ECS), which provided system institutions with a number of services that included access to mainframe and minicomputer class machines and email service. ECS provided a small number of Pembroke State's staff with email accounts. The first campus-based email system was implemented in the late 1980s on the VAX/VMS system. This email system was a member of BITNET, a "store and forward" network largely made up of universities. By the 1990s, the university operated its own email servers, and began distributing email accounts to students, faculty, and staff. The email addresses included "farmer" and "papa," among others. This was a direct reference to the naming nomenclature used for the university's email servers, which were named after the Smurfs, popular cartoon characters from the 1980s. In 1995 the university joined the Internet, expanding its presence online, using Gopher, a text-based, nongraphic program designed for distributing, searching, and retrieving

documents over the Internet. The following year, Gopher was replaced
as the university connected to the World Wide Web, a system of hyperlinked documents that allowed users with web browsers to view and navigate hyperlinked webpages that contained text, images, videos, and other
media. Consequently, advances in technology and the Internet expanded
student opportunities for learning that were no longer limited to the
physical boundaries of the Pembroke State campus. With the installation
of the Interactive Video Facility (IVF) in the Business Administration
Building in 1995, the university offered distance learning opportunities
with a virtual interactive classroom and conference room via the North
Carolina Research and Education Network (NC-REN) and North
Carolina Information Highway. The IVF provides interconnectivity
to other universities, community colleges, K–12 institutions, and other
sites within the state. Technology changed how faculty taught and how
students learned. Recognizing the possibilities of the Internet and technology, Chancellor Oxendine remarked, "Together with more creative
use of the Internet, including video streaming, UNCP is preparing its
graduates for the rapidly changing technology in today's world." Today,
email and the university's website are the primary means for communication on campus. Technology contributed to greater productivity and
efficiency as the university moved toward a paperless campus.

Like technology, the campus physical plant evolved to meet the
present and future needs of the university and its students. In 1990,
renovations to Locklear Hall and a two-story addition to the Oxendine Science Building, which included computer labs, classrooms, and
office space, were completed. Funding for the construction of a new
administration building and an addition to the Business Administration
Building were part of a $510 million bond referendum approved by state
voters in November 1993, to make improvements at UNC system institutions. A two-story addition to the Business Administration Building,
which included a new classroom, offices, and an elevator, was completed

in 1997. In 1995 construction of a new administration building, located north of the English E. Jones Health and Physical Education Center, was completed. The $7 million, four-story building consolidated numerous administrative offices that were spread across campus, thereby improving student service and administrative efficiencies. It included offices for the chancellor and vice chancellors, undergraduate and graduate admissions, financial aid, registrar, student accounts, human resources, and the offices for academic affairs, business affairs, student affairs, and development and university relations. During Lumbee Homecoming in 1996, Chancellor Oxendine announced that the building would be named Lumbee Hall in honor of the tribe for whom the institution was established. Lumbee Hall replaced Sampson Hall, which had served as the administration building since 1949. Sampson Hall was razed in 1995 to make room for an expansion of the Mary Livermore Library. The seventeen-thousand-square-foot expansion was completed in 1997 and included a new entrance facing the Quad, a two-story reading room with a massive glass ceiling, additional space for books and offices, a computer lab, a computer classroom, and a Special Collections room to house the university's historical collections and the Charlie Rose Collection. In 1996 the university was selected to house the papers of retired congressman Charles G. "Charlie" Rose III, who represented North Carolina's Seventh Congressional District from 1973 to 1997. Although Sampson Hall was razed, Rev. O. R. Sampson's name was not forgotten. The library was renamed the Sampson-Livermore Library in 1995 by the Board of Trustees, despite some opposition from trustees, the campus, and the community over combining the names. At the dedication of the "state-of-the-art information center" on April 22, 1998, Dr. Clarence Toomer, director of library services, remarked, "Libraries, like this one, continue to stand at the forefront of information literacy. This library empowers our university community and improves the quality of intellectual life of the university and the region that surrounds it."

Other construction projects during the 1990s included the addition of the first electronic sign at the corner of North Odum and Third Street, renovations to the Moore Hall auditorium in 1998, and a new main entrance in front of Lumbee Hall that coincided with the widening of North Odum Street/Prospect Road to a five-lane road in 1999. Pine Residence Hall was completed in 2000 shortly after Chancellor Oxendine's retirement. The three-hundred-bed facility was the university's first coed residence hall and first new residence hall since 1972. To accommodate future growth, the university, in 1996, purchased 18 acres of land along University Road, directly west of the Jones Center. The purchase increased the size of campus from 102 to 120 acres.

The construction of Lumbee Hall in 1995 facilitated the addition of another landmark to campus. Named *Font (Lumbee River)* and located in the lobby of Lumbee Hall, the black terrazzo sculpture was commissioned by the North Carolina Artworks for State Buildings Program. The sculpture, a six-and-a-half-foot vessel-shaped piece symbolizes the Lumbee River—the Indian name for the Lumber River—and its indigenous plant life. Created by artist Kenneth Matsumoto of San Jose, California, the bronze leaves embedded in the sculpture represent the lush vegetation seen throughout the Intercoastal Plains of North Carolina. Inside the opening at the top of the sculpture is water from the Lumber River. Another campus landmark, the Tommy Statue, was placed between the Jones Center and the James B. Chavis University Center in February 1999. The life-size bronze statue of the university's mascot was a gift from the class of 1999. The statue, created by art professor Paul Van Zandt, is twenty-two inches tall with a fifty-seven-inch wingspan and weighs 150 pounds. Dubbed the largest gift in the history of the university, the statue sits on a pedestal of raw granite, weighing close to sixteen tons, and stands over nine feet tall. During the statue's dedication, Chancellor Oxendine remarked, "The red-tailed hawk symbolizes the courage, speed, power, and vision for athletes and all students to aspire to." A 1999 alumni magazine explained how rubbing the rock for good luck became a campus tradition. It read, "The Tommy Statue was in place for just four days when its legend took hold. Senior Braves basketball player Chavis Rachel ['99] was photographed by a passing *Fayetteville Observer* photographer climbing the rock to touch the hawk for good luck before the Homecoming game on February 13, 1999. With the Braves down by two points, Rachel launched a desperation three-point attempt that—perhaps guided by an unseen hand—found nothing but net to win the game. Rachel's visit with the hawk was not revealed until the following Thursday when the photograph was published by the newspaper."

While the Braves continued their winning ways in the early part of the decade, the 1990s brought significant change to the university's athletic program. Team sports were added while others were discontinued. Softball moved to fast pitch in 1990, and women's outdoor track and field was added in 1995. Men's and women's tennis was discontinued after the 1992 season. Women's tennis was reinstated for the 1996–1997 season. By the end of the decade, the university offered seven sports for men and six for women. Between 1990 and 1992 the Braves excelled in the NAIA, NCAA Division II, and the Carolinas Conference. Teams won numerous conference and NAIA district championships. Winning one conference championship were the men's and women's basketball, women's cross country, and volleyball teams. The men's cross country team won two conference and two district titles; the softball team won three conference championships; and the men's outdoor track and field squad won one district championship. In addition to winning the 1992 conference championship, the women's basketball team advanced to the Sweet 16 of the NAIA national championships for the second time in the previous seven years. Pembroke State was awarded the Joby Hawn Cup for the third time in 1992. The cup was presented to the conference member that showed the highest rating of excellence in all conference-sponsored sports.

A new era in athletics began on July 1, 1992, when Pembroke State began full-time competition in NCAA Division II as a member of the Peach Belt Athletic Conference, one of the premiere Division II conferences in the nation. The move provided the university with more visibility in the region and the nation. The Peach Belt's fourteen-member schools—twelve state-supported and two private—are located in North Carolina, South Carolina, Georgia, Alabama, and Florida. The remainder of the decade was a period of transition for the university's athletic program as the 1993 volleyball team won the university's first and only Peach Belt Conference championship during the decade. That year, Debbie McNamara '95 was named the conference volleyball player of the year. In 1995 the wrestling program produced two NCAA regional champs: Brent Campbell at 126 pounds and Buddy Watson (HWT). In 1997 Christene White '97, in women's cross country and track and field, was named the female Peach Belt Scholar-Athletes of the Year. During the decade, the university produced fifteen NAIA and NCAA All-Americans. Another highlight was the June 1994 election of Chancellor Oxendine as the fifth president of the Peach Belt Conference. He served as vice president the previous year.

As the campus continued to change, the university received external and internal validation of the progress made in its quest for academic excellence. The Carnegie Foundation for the Advancement of Teaching reclassified the university from a Comprehensive II to a Comprehensive I institution in 1994. The Carnegie Foundation is the national classifier of institutions of higher education according to mission. Earlier, in 1972, it classified Pembroke State as a General Baccalaureate University. To qualify for the new classification, the university had to graduate at least forty master's-degree students in three different fields. The new classification resulted in additional per-pupil state funding and higher faculty salaries. According to Chancellor Oxendine, the Comprehensive I classification "generated immense pride within and outside of the university."

The university's graduating seniors and sophomore students affirmed excellence in teaching and learning at the university. The 1996 Graduating Senior Survey, administered by UNC General Administration at all UNC system institutions, measured the level of satisfaction of recent graduates in forty categories. The university rated higher than any other UNC system institution in eighteen of the categories, with no other institution receiving more than five of the highest ratings. The university received the highest ratings in the quality of instruction. A 1998 survey of sophomores and grad-

FIGURE 6.7. *Chancellor Joseph B. Oxendine holding an issue of the September 1998* US News & World Report *that ranked UNC Pembroke as the second-most-diverse university in the South.*

uating seniors administered to all campuses in the UNC system again showed that Pembroke's students were more satisfied than students at any other institution in an overwhelming number of categories. Chancellor Oxendine felt that "this validation by those who know us best convinces me that ... [the university] is making the right moves, continues on the road to progress and stands ready to embrace the new millennium."

The university's affordability attracted a more diverse student body to the campus. In 1999, annual tuition and fees for twelve or more undergraduate hours was $1,796 for in-state students, and $9,066 for out-of-state students. Tuition and fees for nine or more graduate hours was $1,670 for in-state students and $8,940 for out-of-state students. Room and board was $3,358. Enrollment became more diverse during the period. In the fall of 1989, enrollment broke the 3,000 mark for the first time in school history, peaking at 3,133 the following year. However, for the remainder of Chancellor Oxendine's tenure, it hovered around 3,000 students. The African American student population grew from 10 percent to 15.6 percent. The Indian population saw a slight increase to 25 percent, while the Hispanic population increased from 0.5 to 2 percent. The university's diversity was cited by *US News & World Report* in 1998, rating the university as the second-most-diverse campus in the South and the most diverse in North Carolina. The study also showed that the university had the largest percentage of Indians among all colleges and universities in the study. The campus grew in other areas as well. The number of full-time faculty and staff increased as faculty grew from 160 to 192 while staff increased from 224 to 339.

Another notable but less visible event spoke to Chancellor Oxendine's desire to improve the quality of the student experience in Pembroke. The CSX east-west train, long vital to the development of the town of Pembroke and the impetus for the campus's move to Pembroke in 1909, had for decades been an annoyance to students and employees trying to get to campus on time for class or work. The train would stop in front of campus, blocking the two railroad crossings, so the engineer could grab a bite to eat from a local restaurant. Many students and even an employee had crawled beneath the stopped train cars to get to campus. During the fall of 1989 Chancellor Oxendine contacted CSX about this matter. Although CSX issued directives to stop the practice, the train continued to stop in front of the campus. In response, the chancellor mandated that he be notified when the train stopped. At such times, he rushed out to the stopped train, confronted the engineer, and threatened to report him to national headquarters. After repeating this several times, the practice ceased.

Perhaps the most noteworthy accomplishment of Chancellor Oxendine's tenure was the university's name change in 1996 from Pembroke State University to the University of North Carolina at Pembroke. Although an attempt to change the university's name in the 1980s failed because of opposition from the Lumbee community, there was a renewal of interest in the name change in 1995, which reflected how far the university had come over the previous decade. Dr. Adolph L. Dial '43, a professor of American Indian studies and history at the university and one of the strongest opponents of the earlier name-change effort, proved to be its biggest proponent in 1995. In a surprise address to the Board of Trustees on September 1, he called for the name of the university to be changed, and to do it "with all deliberate speed." Dr. Dial said he made a mistake in 1984. "I was wrong and I apologize," he said. "I wouldn't be here if more than 90 percent of the people I talked with over the past few months didn't agree with the change." Dr. Dial noted, "It would help enrollment and that will help build the university. When it is better to change—you change. It's time for a change."

The Board of Trustees then held a special hearing on October 17, 1995, in the auditorium of Moore Hall to get public response to the name change. Unlike the 1980s, the vast majority of those in attendance supported the name change. Rev. Welton Lowry '33, '48 said, "The University of North Carolina—that carries something with it." He also said, "I've seen the name change…[numerous] times and if it changes again it will rest." Dial also attended that meeting and said, "We should change the name. It will benefit all of us. That's where I stand, and that's where many people stand." According to Chancellor Oxendine, "No one, past or present, did more to make it [the name change] possible than did Professor Dial." Dial died two months later on December 24, 1995, before he could enjoy the fruits of his labor, but not before the Board of Trustees voted unanimously in favor of the name change on December 2, 1995. The issue was then forwarded to the Board of Governors.

On February 16, 1996, the Governance Committee of the Board of Governors, tasked with studying the issue, also held a hearing on the name change in the auditorium of Moore Hall. They wanted to make sure there was no opposition to the name change before any decision was made. As with the previous forum, there was resounding support for the name change from the standing-room-only crowd of students, faculty, staff, alumni and community. The results of a university survey, conducted in November, were distributed at the hearing. According to the survey, the great majority of all constituents overwhelmingly supported the change: faculty (89 percent), administration and staff (76 percent), students (76 percent), and alumni (71 percent). On April 12, 1996, the Board of Governors approved the name change, and the issue was then taken up by the General Assembly, which had final decision on the matter.

While awaiting a decision by the General Assembly, *The Robesonian* ran an editorial on April 15, 1996, which highlighted the importance of traditions over names. It said, "What the university's supports have seemingly realized is that the name of Pembroke State University is not as important as the tradition of Pembroke State University. Pembroke State University is far more than just a name. The spirit, the tradition, the pride that is Pembroke State University will live on no matter what the university is called."

The General Assembly took action on the name change in May 1996. The Democratic-controlled senate, on May 16, approved a bill changing the name, and the Republican-controlled House took similar action the following day. The name change received insignificant opposition as bills sped through both chambers. The issue, oddly, deadlocked after chamber leaders disagreed over whether the senate Democratic bill or the House Republican bill would be signed into law. On June 20, 1996, the senate agreed to accept the Republican bill. After a month of wrangling, the House bill was ratified the following day. The name change, from Pembroke State University to the University of North Carolina at Pembroke, became effective on July 1, 1996.

The unveiling of the university's new name was held July 6, 1996, in conjunction with Lumbee Homecoming. The ceremony was held on the steps of historic Old Main, which had

FIGURE 6.8. *Seal of the University of North Carolina at Pembroke.*

prominently carried the name of the institution on its façade since the late 1920s. A crowd eagerly awaited as a banner, which hung above the columns, was unfurled to display the new name "University of North Carolina at Pembroke." David Weinstein, chair of the Board of Trustees, credited Dr. Adolph L. Dial '43 with the vision for the name change. According to Weinstein, Dr. Dial "loved this university, and through his leadership, this name change was presented to the Board of Trustees." Weinstein also thanked the community for its support of the change. Chancellor Oxendine then said, "The idea, long in germinating, blossomed with momentum, energy, and excitement. The new name has given us increased recognition and a clearer perception in the minds of our public that we are indeed an integral part of the University of North Carolina." The following year, the Classroom North Building was renamed the Adolph L. Dial Humanities Building on February 14, 1997, in honor of Dr. Dial and his service to the university.

The university's name change affected the campus in other ways. The university's logo was tweaked. The sun was moved to the right side to reflect a rising sun, and the letters U-N-C-P were added to the base of Old Main with "The University of North Carolina at Pembroke" appearing below it. WPSU-TV changed its call letters to WNCP-TV. By 1997, WNCP-TV, aided by the addition of a major in mass communication with concentrations in broadcasting, journalism, and public relations, produced about two hundred programs annually, including news, entertainment, and public affairs, and was reaching more than 2.5 million North Carolinians.

The year 1998 proved to be a memorable one for the university. Comedian Bill Cosby, known for his character, Dr. Cliff Huxtable, in the television sitcom *The Cosby Show*, was the featured speaker at the May 16, 1998, Commencement. Located on the baseball field, the ceremony was the largest Commencement ever held by the university, with approximately seven thousand in attendance. When asked by reporters why he agreed to come to UNC Pembroke, Cosby said, "The chancellor [Oxendine] has my college transcript and has threatened to expose my grades." Chancellor Oxendine was a new professor in Temple University's physical education program and Cosby was in his class. "Bill is the type of student who stood out at Temple," said Chancellor Oxendine. "He was an outstanding athlete and a little older than the average student because of his tour of duty in the navy. He was also something of a character in class, although not a disruptive student." UNC Pembroke conferred an honorary doctorate—a doctor of humane letters—on Cosby. The visit by Cosby generated much excitement and brought the university much publicity throughout the region.

A few months later, on September 3, 1998, Chancellor Oxendine announced his retirement, effective July 1, 1999. During the announcement, he remarked, "It has been a great honor for me to serve as chancellor of this outstanding university. The support of faculty, administrators, staff, Board of Trustees, General Administration, and the many friends outside the university has been strong and unwavering. I will forever be grateful for having had this rare opportunity." On June 30, 1999, at a farewell party held on his last day on the job, Dr. Charles Jenkins, provost and vice chancellor for academic affairs, offered a toast in honor of Chancellor Oxendine. He said that Dr. Oxendine "has done a lot for UNCP and for the region. He has represented the university and the region well. He has made his mark on this institution and certainly has made a tremendous contribution to this university. He is leaving things in good order. This is a good time for a smooth transition for a new chancellor." When Chancellor Oxendine walked out of his office for the last time that Wednesday afternoon, he left three things on his desk: a letter, a note, and a bottle of Bufferin, all for his successor. The note explained the Bufferin. It said: "When I arrived here 10 years ago, my predecessor, Paul Givens, left me a bottle of aspirin. I only used half of them, all in the first month. Feel free to use them as needed, Joe." With that note, Chancellor Oxendine, who was later awarded chancellor emeritus status, retired to Pinehurst, North Carolina.

Between 2000 and 2010 Chancellor Emeritus Oxendine taught part-time in UNC Pembroke's departments of American Indian Studies and Health, Physical Education, and Recreation. In January 2011 he was named the interim president of Catawba College, his alma mater. Dr. Oxendine served in that capacity from March 2011 through May 2012.

As the twentieth century came to a close, the University of North Carolina at Pembroke was positioned for unprecedented growth and expansion.

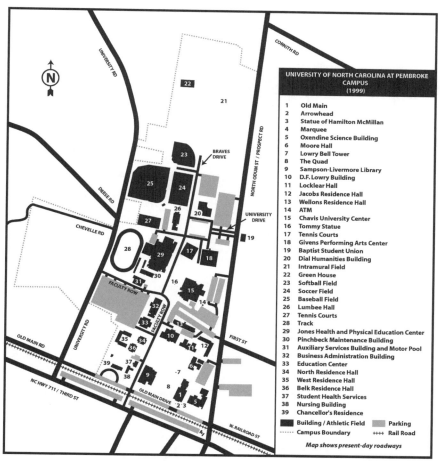

MAP 6.1. *University of North Carolina at Pembroke campus (1999).*

TIMELINE OF NOTABLE INSTITUTIONAL EVENTS (1989-1999)

1989
- Dr. Joseph B. Oxendine named third chancellor.
- Enrollment broke three thousand for the first time.

1990
- Miss Pembroke State University first competed in the Miss North Carolina pageant.
- Softball moved to fast pitch.
- First Pembroke Day held.
- Pembroke State first hosted Project Graduation.
- *PSU Today*, the alumni magazine, first published. Later renamed *UNCP Today*.
- Locklear Hall renovation and addition to Oxendine Science Building completed.

1991
- New university logo adopted.

1992
- Indian mascot discontinued.
- Pembroke State University license plate issued.
- First official athletic logo adopted.
- Red-tailed hawk chosen as new mascot.
- Costumed red-tailed hawk mascot appeared for first time at a basketball game.
- Awarded the North Carolina Teaching Fellows Program; first class began in 1994.
- Office of Grants, known today as the Office of Sponsored Research and Programs, established.
- Men's and women's tennis discontinued.
- Pembroke State awarded the Joby Hawn Cup.
- The university began full-time competition in NCAA Division II and joined the Peach Belt Conference.

1993
- The university's seal was changed to feature the new university logo.

1994
- Reclassified as a Comprehensive II university by the Carnegie Foundation, resulting in increased financial support for students and faculty salaries.
- University Writing Center opened.

1995
- The Regional Center for Economic, Community, and Professional Development was established.

- Dr. Bonnie Kelley of the Department of Biology was named the inaugural recipient of the UNC Board of Governors Award for Excellence in Teaching.
- Interactive Video Facility opened in the Business Administration Building.
- Pembroke State joined the Internet via Gopher.
- A new administration building, later renamed Lumbee Hall, was completed. It included the sculpture *Font (Lumbee River)*, a campus landmark.
- Sampson Hall razed.
- Mary Livermore Library renamed Sampson-Livermore Library.
- Women's outdoor track and field added.

1996
- Selected to house the papers of Charles G. "Charlie" Rose III, who represented North Carolina's Seventh Congressional District from 1973 to 1997.
- Launched a website to connect to the World Wide Web.
- Teaching and Learning Center established.
- Women's tennis reinstated.
- Name changed to the University of North Carolina at Pembroke.
- Campus size increased from 102 to 120 acres.

1997
- The Martha Humphrey Beach Chair in Art and the William C. Friday Chair. in Molecular Biology and Biochemistry were established.
- Additions to the Business Administration Building and the Sampson-Livermore Library completed.
- Classroom North Building renamed the Adolph L. Dial Humanities Building in honor of Dr. Adolph L. Dial '43.

1998
- Moore Hall auditorium renovated.
- Recognized by *US News & World Report* as the second-most-diverse campus in the South.
- Comedian Bill Cosby was the Commencement speaker.
- UNC system adopted Focused-Growth Initiative; UNC Pembroke designated "focused-growth institution."

1999
- North Odum Street/Prospect Road widened.
- Fiber optic loop completed.
- Tommy Statue donated by the class of 1999.
- Chancellor Joseph B. Oxendine retired.

Chapter Seven

1999-2010
BUILDING ON THE DREAM

The University of North Carolina at Pembroke has a long and distinguished history of providing a high quality education with the personal touch.

Dr. Allen C. Meadors, chancellor,
University of North Carolina at Pembroke,
Academic Catalog (2007)

The University of North Carolina at Pembroke began the 21st century with a mission of growth that transformed the campus. In April 1998 the Board of Governors of the University of North Carolina system adopted a ten-year enrollment plan to ensure that the system would be prepared to accommodate projected enrollment growth for the first decade of the twenty-first century. As part of the Focused-Growth Initiative, seven system institutions—including UNC Pembroke—were designated "focused-growth institutions." When Molly C. Broad was named system president in 1997 she found these seven institutions "had serious problems with outmoded buildings and deteriorating capital facilities. With flat or declining enrollment and inadequate resources to launch new academic degree programs, they faced a challenging future in an increasingly competitive higher education environment." The seven campuses agreed to aggressive enrollment growth of 20 percent or more by 2003.

In April 1999 the Board of Governors approved *Building for the New Millennium*, a report that "documented woefully outmoded buildings, mounting deferred maintenance, and a looming shortage of critical science, technology, and study facilities." The report identified $6.9 billion needed to meet the current needs of the system and accommodate the projected enrollment growth. In response, the General Assembly in May 2000 authorized a statewide referendum on a $3.1 billion construction bond for the UNC system and the state's community colleges. The bond included $2.5 billion for UNC system campuses and its affiliates. That November, North Carolinians overwhelmingly supported the measure. Passage of the 2000 Higher Education Bond Program "ushered in a new era of rebuilding and expansion across the University [UNC system]." UNC Pembroke's share of the bond was $56.9 million.

Coupled with the passage of the bond referendum and the infusion of enrollment growth and other special funding from the General Assembly, the UNC General Administration worked closely with the seven institutions to implement the Focused-Growth Initiative. The principles of the plan included the addition of degree programs that helped to meet the state's emerging workforce needs and attract a broader range of students, the upgrade and expansion of technology infrastructure, the enhancement of capacities and fund-raising efforts of the Office of Advancement, the development of research opportunities and increase in the participation of underrepresented populations in science and engineering, and an increase in faculty research and sponsored program activity.

With Chancellor Oxendine's retirement announcement in September 1998, the search for the next chancellor of UNC Pembroke commenced in October 1998 when a fifteen-member search committee was organized. Led by Roger Oxendine, who also chaired the Board of Trustees, the search committee comprised representatives from the trustees, faculty, staff, and community, and included the chair of the Faculty Senate and presidents of the Student Government Association and the Alumni Association. The search committee held two forums on October 27 and 29, 1998, to gather input from students, faculty, staff, alumni, and the community on characteristics desirable in the next chancellor. Opinions were varied. Some suggested the next chancellor should be an Indian, a businessperson, a scholar, or a people person, while others sought a "change maker" who would raise the university's profile in the region and in the state. Faced with the challenge of finding a chancellor who had the dynamic leadership skills to grow the university according to the focused-growth plan, the search committee hired a firm to assist with the search and the development of the job description. After six months, the search committee submitted recommendations to the Board of Trustees who then submitted

FIGURE 7.1. *Dr. Allen C. Meadors. Chancellor of the University of North Carolina at Pembroke from 1999 to 2009.*

three finalists to President Broad. Upon recommendation by President Broad and with the approval of the Board of Governors, Dr. Allen C. Meadors, the chief executive officer and dean of Penn State Altoona, was named UNC Pembroke's fourth chancellor on April 9, 1999. Dr. Meadors began his duties on July 1, 1999, and led the institution until 2009.

A native of Van Buren, Arkansas, who was born on May 17, 1947, Dr. Meadors had a broad educational and professional background that included careers in the air force, the health-care industry, and higher education. From 1969 to 1973 he served in the Medical Service Corps of the U.S. Air Force. A hospital and clinic administrator, he achieved the rank of captain. After an honorable discharge, Chancellor Meadors received a bachelor's degree in business administration from the University of Central Arkansas in 1969; a master of business administration from the University of Northern Colorado in 1974; a master of public administration from the University of Kansas in 1975; master's degrees in psychology/human relations and health services management, both from Webster University, in 1979 and 1980, respectively; and a PhD in administration and education from Southern Illinois University in 1981. Dr. Meadors also received an associate's degree in computer sciences from Saddleback College in 1981, and certificates in the Health Services Administration Program at Trinity University Graduate School, and health systems management from the Sloan School of Management of the Massachusetts Institute of Technology, in 1974 and 1977, respectively. He was also a Fellow of the American College of Healthcare Executives (FACHE).

Prior to Dr. Meadors's tenure as CEO and dean of Penn State Altoona from 1994 to 1999, he served as professor and dean of the College of Health, Social, and Public Services at Eastern Washington University from 1990 to 1994; professor and dean of the College of Public Health at the University of Oklahoma (1989–1990); professor and chair of the Department of Health Administration in the College of Public Health at the University of Oklahoma (1987–1990); executive director of the Northwest Arkansas Radiation Therapy Institute (1984–1987); associate professor and director of the Division of Health Administration in the School of Allied Health Sciences at the University of Texas, Galveston (1982–1984); western regional coordinator for Southern Illinois University (1980–1982); adjunct professor and program coordinator with Webster University (1978–1982); assistant professor and program director at Southern Illinois University (1977–1982); health consultant (1977–1982); assistant director of Health for Kansas City, Missouri (1976–1977); assistant director of Health Services Development for Blue Cross and Blue Shield of Kansas (1975–1976); and manager of Institutional and Drug Review with Blue Cross and Blue Shield of Kansas (1973–1975).

Dr. Meadors had written and spoken widely on health-care issues and was a member of an array of professional and civic organizations. He won a number of honors, including two outstanding faculty awards and an outstanding professional service award, all from the University of Texas, and Penn State's Ben Lane Award for outstanding contributions to student affairs.

During the announcement of Dr. Meadors's election, President Broad said, "Allen Meadors has compiled an enviable track record of stimulating and managing growth in a variety of academic settings." She continued, "He brings to UNC Pembroke great energy, enthusiasm, and strong commitment to reinforcing and strengthening UNCP's historic ties to the local community and the region's public schools." President Broad also outlined four goals for UNC Pembroke that Dr. Meadors was "well-qualified to meet." They included enrollment growth, connections with the public schools, ties to the community, and the development of the regional economy.

Dr. Meadors quickly won broad approval in the community, especially among Pembroke's Indian community after his two sons enrolled at Purnell Swett High School in Pembroke. Both sons played on the school's football team, and Dr. Meadors, a fan of athletics, regularly attended their games.

On December 15, 1999, Dr. Meadors was installed as UNC Pembroke's fourth chancellor. The installation coincided with the introduction of two new traditions—the school's first winter Commencement was held in response to a request by the Student Government Association, and the UNC Board of Governors Excellence in Teaching Award recipient first served as the winter Commencement keynote speaker. During his remarks, Chancellor Meadors promised to lead the school with "passion" and "optimism" and "not to forget the university's past."

To accommodate General Administration's vision for the future growth in enrollment at UNC Pembroke, changes began in 1998 with Chancellor Joseph B. Oxendine, who planned a structural reorganization of the university's academic departments into three new schools and a college: School of Business, School of Education, School of Graduate Studies, and College of Arts and Sciences. Deans would lead each entity. The plan became effective October 1, 1999, during Meadors's tenure. According to Chancellor Meadors, the restructuring promoted "greater operating efficiencies, effectiveness, and communication within the university and to external constituencies." Prior to the restructuring, the numerous department heads reported directly to the provost and vice chancellor for Academic Affairs.

Chancellor Meadors embraced UNC Pembroke's designation as a "focused-growth institution." His first goal was to grow enrollment, particularly the Indian enrollment, and improve the Scholastic Aptitude Test (SAT) average for entering freshmen. To this end, his administration developed and implemented an aggressive recruiting and marketing plan, and, in 2001, established the Office of Enrollment Management with a vice chancellor at the helm. Buttressed by focused-growth funding, UNC Pembroke's unprecedented marketing efforts expanded the university's visibility online and throughout North Carolina and the eastern United States. UNC Pembroke branded itself as a university "where learning gets personal"—a direct reference to its small class sizes and low student-faculty ratio. During the fall of 1999, the university's enrollment was 3,062. General Administration's focused-growth plan called for that number to increase to 4,200 by 2007. The university's aggressive marketing and recruiting efforts paid off, and quickly. The university eclipsed the 4,200 mark in the fall of 2002 with 4,432 students. In 2005 enrollment broke 5,000, and three years later, in 2008 enrollment passed 6,000. By the fall of 2009, enrollment was 6,661—more than double its enrollment in 1999. Enrollment increased every year between 1999 and 2009 as UNC Pembroke, for the second time in its history, was recognized as the fastest-growing university in North Carolina.

UNC Pembroke unexpectedly gained additional visibility throughout the state with the assistance of the Miss North Carolina pageant. Lorna

(McNeill) Ricotta '01, '08 was crowned Miss North Carolina in 2000, and two years later, Rebekah (Revels) Lowry '01, '11, Miss UNCP 1998, was crowned Miss North Carolina 2002. They were the second and third UNC Pembroke students to win the crown. In 2008 UNC Pembroke students again fared well in the pageant. Jamee (Hunt) Freeman '08, Miss UNCP 2008, was named first runner-up, and Erica Dellinger '07, competing as Miss Forsyth County, was a top-ten finalist.

The rapid increase in enrollment brought other enrollment-related changes to the student body. The average freshmen class size increased from 460 to more than 1,100, while entering freshmen SAT scores increased nearly 40 points. Graduate enrollment increased from 256 in the fall of 1999 to 751 in the fall of 2009. Out-of-state enrollment grew from 92 to 218. Transfer students rose from 291 to 578. Consequently, the student body became more racially diverse. Although Indian enrollment increased from 685 to 1,100, their percentage of the student body declined from 22 percent to 17 percent. African American student enrollment grew from 497 to 1,918, expanding from 16 percent to 29 percent of the student enrollment. Hispanic student numbers increased from 58 to 252—an increase from 2 percent to 4 percent of the student body. As a result, UNC Pembroke was recognized by *US News & World Report* throughout most of the decade as one of the most diverse among southern universities. In its 2009 and 2010 reports, UNC Pembroke was the most ethnically diverse campus in North Carolina and the South.

The increased enrollment also resulted in larger graduating classes, accommodated by the addition of a winter Commencement ceremony. During the 1999–2000 academic year, 559 degrees—477 undergraduate and 82 graduate—were conferred. During the 2008–2009 academic year, 933 degrees—739 undergraduate and 194 graduate—were awarded, an 83 percent increase. According to *Diverse* magazine, UNC Pembroke ranked nationally—eighth in 2007 and sixth in 2008—for all undergraduate degrees earned by Indians. Commencement ceremonies featured prominent and well-known speakers. They included U.S. senators Elizabeth Dole and John Edwards, Congressman Mike McIntyre, all representing North Carolina; authors Pat Conroy and Scott Turow; television personality Charlie Rose; and UNC system presidents Molly Broad and Erskine Bowles.

The curriculum was expanded to attract a wider range of students and to help meet the needs of the state's emerging workforce—another goal of the Focused-Growth Initiative. At the undergraduate level, new degree programs were added in applied physics in 1999, Spanish (2003), environmental science (2004), musical theatre (2005), interdisciplinary studies (2007), information technology (2007), and athletic training (2008). In 2005 UNC Pembroke became the first university in North Carolina to offer an undergraduate degree in biotechnology. After offering an RN-to-BSN program jointly with Fayetteville State since 1992, UNC Pembroke began offering a four-year, prelicensure bachelor of science in nursing (BSN) degree in 2005. Southeastern Regional Medical Center in Lumberton gave the program a home in a ninety-eight-hundred-square-foot Instructional Technology Center located at the hospital. The undergraduate curriculum was also expanded with additional minors, including gender studies in 2004, and an entrepreneurship minor and certificate in 2008. By 2009 UNC Pembroke offered forty-one undergraduate degree programs, fifty-seven minors, and eighteen concentrations.

The number of graduate degree programs almost doubled to seventeen by 2009. Graduate programs expanded to include art education in 1999, physical education (2000), social studies education (2000), science education (2000), elementary education (2002), and music education (2003). A master of arts in teaching (MAT) and the master of social work (MSW) were added in 2004 and 2007, respectively. The master of business administration (MBA) launched a day program in 2004. During the period, the master of public administration (MPA) was the fastest-growing graduate program.

Chancellor Meadors also set a goal to provide increased support to academics. As the number of degree programs increased, so did the requisite number of faculty and support staff positions. Full-time faculty and staff positions increased 96 percent from 437 in 1999 to 841 in 2009. The number of nonteaching staff increased from 291 to 519, while the full-time faculty more than doubled from 146 to 322. In recognition of the growth and expansion of the Sampson-Livermore Library, the position of university librarian was elevated to dean of library sciences in 2006. In 1999 the Staff Council was organized to advocate for nonteaching staff, and facilitate communication between staff and the university's administration. The first edition of the *Brave Bulletin* was published in February 2000 to keep faculty and staff informed of university news.

Faculty research and scholarship also increased and expanded. Over thirty books were published, and grant awards increased from $1.6 million

FIGURE 7.2. *Biotechnology Research and Training Center. Located in the Regional Center, the facility provides faculty and students with research opportunities and innovative training.*

in 2000 to $4.3 million in 2009. During the period, a total of $36.6 million in grants were awarded to UNC Pembroke. To develop innovative training and research opportunities, the Biotechnology Research and Training Center (BRTC) was dedicated in 2009. The forty-six-hundred-square-foot laboratory was located at the Regional Center for Economic, Community, and Professional Development at the Carolina Commerce and Technology Center (COMtech) in Pembroke. A three-year, $600,000 grant from the National Science Foundation helped pave the way for the center. Also that year, faculty from UNC Pembroke and North Carolina A&T State University received a $750,000 appropriation to develop affordable alternative energy for farmers. The overarching goal of the UNCP Biofuels Project was to make it possible for farmers in southeastern North Carolina to grow crops from which they could produce biodiesel for their farm equipment, saving them money and increasing their energy independence. Robeson Community College's BioAg Center partnered in the project. In 2009 Dr. Ben A. Bahr, a scientist with an international reputation in Alzheimer's disease research, accepted the William C. Friday Distinguished Professorship in Molecular Biology and Biochemistry. A tenured member of the Biology and Chemistry Departments, Dr. Bahr also had laboratories and offices in the BRTC.

To attract additional distinguished scholars and promote faculty scholarship, five distinguished professorships were established during the period, bringing the total at UNC Pembroke to eight. They were the Brenda B. Brooks Distinguished Endowed Professorship in Nursing, the BB&T Distinguished Endowed Professorship in the Philosophical Foundations of Free Enterprise, the Joseph B. Oxendine Distinguished Professor of Education, the Anne Reynolds Belk Endowed Professorship in Nursing, and the Thomas Family Endowed Professorship in Entrepreneurship. The Brooks Professorship was established in 2006 after Healthkeeperz, a Pembroke comprehensive home health-care company, pledged $250,000 to the Nursing Department. The endowment honored Brenda B. Brooks

'65, the late wife of company founder and Chairman Howard Brooks '63. The BB&T Professorship was established in 2007 after a $500,000 gift from the BB&T Corporation of Winston-Salem, North Carolina. That same year, the Oxendine Professorship was established with a $250,000 donation by the C.D. Spangler Foundation Inc. to honor Chancellor Emeritus Joseph B. Oxendine. In 2008 the Belk Professorship was made possible through a $250,000 gift from Irwin Belk, a former president and CEO of Belk Stores Inc. and one of North Carolina's foremost philanthropists. The late Anne (Reynolds) Belk was married to Carl Grotnes Belk, Irwin Belk's son. Also in 2008 the Thomas Family Professorship was established after a $500,000 gift from the Thomas Family Foundation, founded by Los Angeles real estate developer and Pembroke native James A. Thomas and his wife, Sally. Matching funds for the five distinguished professorships were provided by the General Assembly's Distinguished Professors Endowment Trust Fund and the C.D. Spangler Foundation Inc. The distinguished professorships endowed two faculty positions in nursing, two in business, and one in education.

The expansion in enrollment, degree programs, and faculty and staff positions necessitated additional classroom and office space. Approximately $200 million in new construction and renovations transformed the campus. The transformation touched all corners of the campus, which grew from 120 acres and twenty-six buildings in 1999 to 169 acres and forty-six buildings just ten years later. Most existing campus buildings were also renovated. Additional land was purchased alongside University Road and north of campus as the university's footprint grew north along Prospect Road. The construction boom improved the campus's physical plant and infrastructure, but more importantly, it accommodated the growth and expansion of the university and the increased needs of the student body. Funding for the projects included UNC Pembroke's $56.9 million share of the bond referendum, focused-growth funding from the General Assembly, and federal and private monies.

Efforts to enhance the physical appearance of the campus began with beautification projects. New sidewalks and signage were installed throughout campus. The tennis courts adjacent to the Quad and west of the Givens Performing Arts Center were removed to make way for sidewalks and other enhancements. In 2001 an information kiosk was constructed at the southern entrance to campus to provide visitors with a map of campus and a phone directory. The following year, on February 16, 2002, the water feature and amphitheatre, with its trademark fountain and bridge, were dedicated. Located on the site of the old gymnasium, it quickly became a focal point of campus interest and activity. In 2007 the bridge was named the Alicia and Whitney Jones ['10] Bridge after a gift from their parents, Jeff, a Pembroke businessman, and Robin Jones. That same year, the walkway in front of Old Main was reconfigured and the Heritage Walk was constructed. Dedicated July 7, 2007, during Lumbee Homecoming, the monument featured the names of more than five hundred graduates of the institution between 1905 and 1954. Additional marquees or electronic signs were constructed in front of the James B. Chavis University Center in 2005 and the Givens Performing Arts Center in 2009. The electronic sign at the intersection of North Odum and Third Streets was replaced in 2009 with a modern marquee encased in stone that resembled that in the Arrowhead in front of Old Main. On April 15, 2009, a new campus landmark was installed in front of the Chavis University Center, nestled between the crape myrtle trees. The rock sculpture by California artist Katsuhisa Sakai rested on a concrete base. The artwork was titled *Tanza*, which, according to Sakai, meant "to sit straight and follow your thoughts." He said, "It's about focus and problem solving, so I thought it a good concept for students."

Earlier, in 2003, another campus landmark received a facelift. The Lowry Bell Tower, situated in the Quad, had sat quiet since the mid-1990s. The tower's black and gold panels were replaced with new panels that featured black and gold geometric designs that, according to facilities designer Frank Britt, were inspired by architect Frank Lloyd Wright's stained-glass windows. According to Britt, Wright drew heavily upon Indian designs. A second inspiration, according to Britt, was the glass and metal work found in the dome of the U.S. House of Representatives wing of the Capitol. The top of the bell tower contained the UNC Pembroke and UNC system seals and a stylized rendition of a hawk's head looking skyward. Chancellor Meadors remarked, "The Lowry Bell Tower is a landmark on our campus and should be maintained in a manner that represents the spirit and love in which it was given to the university." The bell tower soon had a new "old" tune to play.

In 2004 the university's alma mater, which had not been heard on campus in many years, was dusted off and renamed "Hail to UNCP" to reflect the new name of the institution. Among those who labored over the song's revival were Lawrence T. Locklear '05, '12, the university's web publisher, and Dr. Larry Arnold and the late Dr. Gary Wright, both faculty in the Music Department. Dr. Arnold characterized the song as embodying a "spirit of reverence" and "an attitude of aspiration." Dr. Wright, the choral director, tweaked the tune to make it more "comfortable" for the chorus by removing some "odd" notes. With its revival, "Hail to UNCP" returned to its intended place as an integral part of campus ceremonies.

The first campus building to be renovated was the chancellor's residence. The 1999 remodeling and expansion was directed by Barbara Meadors, wife of Chancellor Meadors. The remodeling included the addition of a small library designated for alumni and faculty who have authored or coauthored books. Enhancements to the residence facilitated expanded community engagement through functions hosted at the home. In 2003 the dining hall and Chancellor's Dining Room in the Chavis University Center were renovated and expanded. That same year, an elevator and additional rooms were added to Student Health Services. On August 25, 2004, the Herbert G. Oxendine Science Building was dedicated after the completion of a $17 million renovation. The building's interior was gutted, and a three-story wing was added to the north side of the structure. A green house and observatory with a telescope were constructed north of the new wing. That same year, the Adolph L. Dial Humanities Building reopened after mold remediation was completed and windows were replaced.

Three renovation projects were completed in 2005. The $8.8 million renovation of the English E. Jones Health and Physical Education Center was dedicated on February 2. The two-story Dobbs Enterprises Lobby was constructed as a new main entrance on the west side of the building after the track was relocated across University Road to make room for a new parking lot. Also, new classrooms, offices, the Mac and Sylvia Campbell Wellness Center, an athletic training facility, and racquetball courts were added to the facility. A $1.1 million two-story addition was added to Locklear Hall, which included a new art gallery, painting studio, elevators, and offices. A $1.1 million renovation of Moore Hall added choir and band practice rooms.

The following year, in 2006, the former Auxiliary Services Building was razed and the former Pinchbeck Maintenance Building was renovated, expanded, and renamed to make room for the UNCP Bookstore, which relocated from the D.F. Lowry Building. The new $4.1 million Auxiliary Services Building included the 18,000-square-foot bookstore and a convenience store, along with the Mail Center, Printing, and Business Services offices. In 2007 the D.F. Lowry Building was renovated to add classroom, office, and dining space. Jacobs Residence Hall was converted to office space in 2001. Wellons Residence Hall was also converted to office space. They were renamed Jacobs and West Halls.

While two residence halls closed, three new modern residential facilities were constructed. Pine and Oak residence halls were completed in 2000 at a cost of nearly $9 million and in 2007 at $15 million, respectively. Both were located west of the Business Administration Building. Pine, a 300-bed facility, was the campus's first coed residence hall. Oak has a capacity of 360 beds. An apartment complex was also constructed on campus. University Village Apartments, located north of the Dial Humanities Building, was completed in 2003, and consists of six buildings with 354 beds. The construction of additional residential facilities increased the number of on-campus beds from 779 in 1999 to 1,721 in 2009. As a result, UNC Pembroke became more of a residential campus. Four private off-campus apartment complexes, located within a short walk of the campus, were also built during the period. In 2001 University Courtyard Apartments was constructed on the west side of University Road. It offered ninety-six apartments with 336 beds, a clubhouse, and a pool. On July 1, 2012, the university assumed management of the facility.

In 2007 the first classroom building constructed on campus since 1980 was completed. On July 16, it was dedicated as the O.R. Sampson Academic Building. The $4.8 million, two-story structure, built north of the Dial Humanities Building, was named for the Reverend O.R. Sampson who served as chair of the Board of Trustees for thirty years. As a result, the name of the Sampson-Livermore Library reverted to its original name—Mary H. Livermore Library. This marked the third campus building to bear Sampson's name. The first was Sampson Hall, which served as the university's administration building from 1949 to 1995. Other academic space was added to campus during the period. In 2002 the Outdoor Education Center was constructed on the north end of campus. The facility consisted of a fifty-foot ropes tower, a climbing wall, and six shorter stations. It was later razed to make room for campus expansion. In 2003 a temporary complex of mobile units was erected northeast of the Dial Building to serve as classrooms, laboratories, and office space while the Oxendine Science Building was renovated. Of those temporary units, Mimosa and Sirius served the campus through the remainder of the decade.

Other construction included a new Walter J. Pinchbeck Facilities Planning and Maintenance Complex, located on the north end of the campus. Dedicated May 26, 2004, the $5 million complex, with four buildings and sixty thousand square feet, replaced the Pinchbeck

Maintenance Building constructed in 1977. The University Center Annex, a $5 million, nineteen-thousand-square-foot structure, was completed in 2007. It includes office and meeting space, and features a large multipurpose room with high ceilings, a wood dance floor, a stage, and audio and video and food preparation areas. The sixty-two-hundred-square-foot room accommodates banquet seating for three hundred and conference seating for nearly five hundred. A water tower was completed on the north side of campus in 2009. It was painted white and prominently features the university's seal and athletic logo.

The university acquired additional properties that served as office space. Located along the southern edge of University Road were West Office Building, acquired in 2001; Dogwood Building (2004); International Programs and International Guest House (2006); and Magnolia House (2008). The home of the late Rev. Welton Lowry '33, '48, known as the Lowry House, was leased and served as a guest house from 2005 to 2011. In 2008 Carter Hall, the former main building for the Odum Baptist Home for Children, located across North Odum Street/Prospect Road from campus, was leased to house the Division of Information Technology.

The expansion of the campus's footprint saw changes and new names for many campus streets. The segment of Braves Drive between the Jones Center and the Chavis University Center was closed to accommodate the expansion of the Jones Center and to make campus more pedestrian friendly. The southern entrance to campus along Faculty Row was closed and a roundabout later installed north of the railroad tracks. University Drive and Old Main Drive continued their same course. New street names included Alumni Lane, Hawk Drive, Dogwood Lane, Facilities Drive, PSU Court, and UNCP Place. The entrance to the new athletic complex along University Road was named Curt Locklear Drive in 2007 in honor of Curt Locklear Sr. '49 (1924–2011), the founder of Pembroke Hardware in 1955, and a member of the 1947 football team, after a gift from Locklear and his wife, Catherine '48.

The expanded campus included other naming opportunities for prospective donors. A primary goal of the Focused-Growth Initiative was to enhance advancement and fund-raising efforts at each of the focused-growth institutions. As a result, the campuses were provided with resources essential to increasing their fund-raising capacities. At UNC Pembroke, such efforts produced dramatic results: five distinguished professorships and numerous academic and athletic scholarships were endowed, while donor gifts supported the construction of campus buildings and facilitated the renaming of numerous structures. The university's endowment tripled, and the Office of Advancement raised $14.6 million, including fifteen of the largest gifts in the history of the university. A cornerstone of those fund-raising efforts was the five-year "First and Ten: Campaign for Football and Athletic Excellence." Kicked off in 2005 the campaign raised $4 million to support the return of football and the enhancement of the university's athletic facilities. In 2004 the university held the first Scholarship Awards Dinner to recognize scholarship donors and student academic achievement. More importantly, the awards dinner provided donors and scholarship recipients with an opportunity to meet. At the 2007 dinner, Chancellor Meadors thanked the donors for their gifts. "This event brings together our most precious resources—our students—with our most precious friends—our donors," he said. "The opportunity to get a college education is priceless, and to make it possible for another person is to change history." Chancellor Meadors exhorted the students to "remember this day and the help you received, and give back when it is your time."

The philanthropy of another donor supported the development and growth of UNC Pembroke's Honors College. The Chancellor's Scholars Program was expanded and renamed the Honors College in 2000, and a dean was added later. It opened in the fall of 2001 with a mission to attract top scholars to the campus and provide them with academic and cultural enrichment. In 2006 Esther (Graham) Maynor '38 (1921–2005), a native

of Pembroke and resident of Mount Airy, North Carolina, who finished
high school at Cherokee Normal in 1938, bequeathed the university $1.2
million, the largest gift in university history. On September 13, 2006, the
Esther G. Maynor Honors College was dedicated in her honor. At the
ceremony, Mary Alice (Pinchbeck) Teets '58, Maynor's cousin, said it was
Maynor's "wish and prayer that our students will grow strong, blossom,
and bear good fruit." Maynor's gift endowed the Esther G. Maynor
Scholarship, established to benefit a student in the Honors College who
demonstrated financial need. In 2007 Sara Pack '11 was named the first
recipient. The Maynor Honors College is a vital part of the campus's
intellectual backdrop.

The Focused-Growth Initiative also sought to ensure that UNC
Pembroke achieved its full potential through the use of targeted funding
to upgrade and expand the university's technology infrastructure.
Consequently, there were numerous technological advancements on the
campus. Improvements in high-speed connectivity brought Internet 2
to UNC Pembroke, enabling it to participate in a UNC system inter-
campus grid computing initiative. UNC Pembroke joined the University
of North Carolina at Wilmington and Fayetteville State University
in a regional collaboration called Southeast Education and Research
Networking (SERNet). The collaboration provided network upgrades
to each campus that offered enhanced research, education, and high-
performance computing resources that were at least four times faster
than the previous infrastructure. The foundation for the initiative was
an upgrade of the southeastern portion of the statewide North Carolina
Research and Education Network (NCREN), developed and operated
by the Microelectronics Center of North Carolina (MCNC) in partnership with the UNC system. Other technological advances included the
installation of wireless Internet or Wi-Fi on campus and the addition of
an Internet portal called Braveweb, which enables students to register
for classes, pay tuition and fees, and check grades and staff to complete

timesheets. Another portal called Blackboard provides faculty with the ability to supplement classes with online materials, and facilitate the offering of online courses. An online master University Calendar provided the rapidly growing university community with a centralized tool for staying abreast of campus events. To assist with the rapid growth and development of campus technology, the Help Desk was established by University Computing and Information Services (UCIS) to provide the campus with telephone-based technical support. In 2003 UCIS implemented the BraveTech program. Staffed with student workers who made on-site technical support available to the campus, the program provided the students with experiential learning opportunities. In 2007 UCIS was renamed the Division of Information Technology or DoIT.

With advances in technology and the expansion of the university's curriculum, distance education, through off-campus sites and online courses, played a pivotal role in the university's ability to attract students. In 1999 the Office of Distance Education was instituted to provide statewide access to UNC Pembroke through alternatives to place-bound, nontraditional students. Consequently, programs designed for distance education delivery were offered through face-to-face, interactive video, online, and hybrid formats.

By the late 1990s UNC Pembroke was one of the first UNC system institutions to offer classes at community colleges in the region. In the summer of 1996 UNC Pembroke began offering off-campus baccalaureate programs in areas underserved by the state through a pilot program funded by the General Assembly. The university offered undergraduate degree coursework at Sandhills Community College in Pinehurst and Richmond Community College in Hamlet. Consequently, UNC Pembroke developed close relations with the region's community colleges, resulting in the establishment of additional off-campus sites at Bladen Community College in Dublin, Brunswick Community College in Bolivia, Cape Fear Community College in Wilmington, Fayetteville Technical Community

College in Fayetteville, Fort Bragg in Fayetteville, and Robeson Community College in Lumberton. UNC Pembroke also established off-campus sites at Southeastern Regional Medical Center in Lumberton and Cape Fear Valley Medical Center in Fayetteville. At off-campus sites, students took courses and completed their degree programs without having to come to the Pembroke campus.

With the addition of off-campus sites, UNC Pembroke also expanded its online/Internet-based degree programs. The first interactive class was offered over the information superhighway in 1996, while the first online class was offered in 1999. By 2002, seventy classes were available online. Technology precipitated the establishment of interactive classroom facilities at the various off-campus sites. More than ten classrooms at UNC Pembroke had the same functionality as the Interactive Video Facility in the Business Administration Building. The master of public administration (MPA) was the fastest-growing graduate program, in part because of its online availability. GetEducated.com named the MPA program the most affordable online graduate program in the nation in 2007 and a "Best Buy" in 2008. By 2009, students could complete the MPA entirely online.

In 2013, online courses account for about 22 percent of the courses taken at UNC Pembroke, the largest percentage in the UNC system. Online undergraduate degree programs include business administration, with a concentration in management; criminal justice; and the bachelor of interdisciplinary studies in applied information technology, applied professional studies, economic development, and financial administration. At the graduate level, the MPA and the MAEd in elementary education are available online. Several stand-alone courses are also delivered fully or partially online to fulfill varying student needs. The Office of Distance Education collaborates with the Southern Regional Education Board (SREB) Electronic Campus by posting the university's online courses and programs on the Electronic Campus dashboard each semester for participation by e-learners from SREB states. As technology continues to advance and evolve, so does UNC Pembroke's opportunities to expand to students in the region, state, and around the globe.

The Meadors administration also worked to improve students' academic, extracurricular, and residential living experience. As enrollment grew and the number of on-campus residential facilities increased, UNC Pembroke was transformed from a primarily commuter campus to more of a residential campus. Living and learning communities, which facilitated the academic, social, and extracurricular development of students, were instituted to attract students to on-campus living. Communities were established for first-year freshmen, nursing, and the Honors College, along with an international community comprising a mix of U.S. and international students.

Student activities were broadened with the addition of a Nostalgia Concert Series in the Givens Performing Arts Center (GPAC), and the establishment of a Distinguished Speaker Series. The Nostalgia Concert Series, launched in 2000, featured performers such as the Commodores, Tony Orlando, 1964–The Tribute, Larry Gatlin and the Gatlin Brothers, the Fifth Dimension, Crystal Gayle, and Glen Campbell. The Broadway and More Series and the On Stage for Youth Series continued to entertain audiences. The Broadway series featured shows such as *A Christmas Carol, Footloose, Rent, Hairspray, Death of a Salesman, Sweeney Todd, To Kill a Mockingbird*, and numerous others. The youth series included entertainment tailored for youth and school-age children. Shows included *Seussical, the Musical*, the Chinese Golden Dragon Acrobats, *The Lion, the Witch, and the Wardrobe*, and *Cinderella*. These performing artist series thrilled sell-out crowds that drew students and members of the community from throughout the region and the state.

In 2000 the Office of Student Activities (today Student Involvement and Leadership) launched the Distinguished Speaker Series to bring nationally recognized speakers to campus. The first season featured television journalist Deborah Norville, political consultant James Carville, political activist Julian Bond, and retired Lt. Col. Oliver North. Other speakers included environmental activist Erin Brockovich, consumer advocate Ralph Nader, poet Dr. Maya Angelou, authors Sherman Alexie and Nicholas Sparks, actors Henry Winkler and James Earl Jones, actress Rita Moreno, sports commentator Dick Vitale, and former National Football League quarterback Doug Flutie.

The student academic experience was strengthened through opportunities for research and experiential and service learning. During this period, undergraduate and graduate student research, like faculty, increased exponentially. As an example, a UNC Pembroke and University of North Carolina at Charlotte team of Lumbees, dubbed the "Weightless Lumbees," were selected in 2002 to participate in NASA's KC-135A Reduced Gravity Undergraduate Research Program. They conducted scientific experiments aboard a reduced-gravity aircraft. Advisor and physics professor Dr. Tim Ritter said the project provided students with "a very full research experience, including proposal writing, experiment design, equipment construction, testing, data acquisition, analysis, and report writing." The team expanded to include non-Lumbees and continued to conduct research throughout the decade. In 2006 the Undergraduate Research Center was established to promote the expansion of undergraduate research. Later renamed the Pembroke Undergraduate Research and Creativity (PURC) Center, it encouraged student involvement in mentored research experiences with faculty and other regional, national, and international scholars, and cultivated the development of research skills necessary for professional fields and graduate study. In 2007 the first PURC Forum, later the PURC Symposium, was held to celebrate student creativity and research. Undergraduate students showcased their research through poster, art, music, and oral presentations. UNC Pembroke's Research Initiative for Scientific Enhancement (RISE) also stimulated student research by training students for careers in scientific research. The UNCP-RISE program was funded through a grant from the National Institutes of Health and targeted students who were considering a career in biomedical research. In 2007 the first Graduate Research Poster Session gave graduate students the opportunity to showcase their scholarship. Students also presented research at various campus, state, and national conferences, including UNC Pembroke's Southeast Indian Studies Conference, which was initiated by the Department of American Indian Studies in 2005. The conference provides scholars, students, and all persons interested in American Indian studies with a forum for the discussion of a variety of issues pertinent to Indians in the Southeast.

UNC Pembroke's student publications, WNCP-TV, and WNCP Radio served as learning laboratories to supplement student's academic studies. In 2001 *The Aurochs*, a student literary magazine, began publication. *The Pine Needle* went online in 2003. The print edition expanded to include additional pages, color photography, and a sports section. Student publications received numerous awards for their quality many times during the decade. The 2000 edition of the *Indianhead* was awarded the All-Columbia Scholastic Press Association's silver medal for overall excellence and top awards in the areas of concept and design. In 2009 *The Pine Needle* won top honors from the American Scholastic Press Association. It was rated one of the top newspapers in the nation among two thousand entries nationwide.

WNCP-TV returned to cable in 2000. After a generous gift from Time Warner, WNCP-TV began operation of the community access channel—cable channel 6—in Robeson County. That May, WNCP-TV produced its first-ever live Commencement when broadcast journalist Charlie Rose spoke. The channel allowed WNCP-TV and the university to access more viewers on cable television than ever before. Consequently, in 2004, because of the installation of a fiber optic link to the Jones Center, WNCP-TV began to broadcast Braves home basketball games and wrestling matches live on cable channel 6. In 2006 WNCP-TV and *The Pine*

Needle launched online video podcasts. WNCP-TV broadcast student-produced talk shows, newscasts, sports, and special event coverage in 2013, including live broadcasts and webcasts of Commencement. In 2006 WNCP-Radio, the university's student-produced Internet radio station, began broadcasting. Dubbed "The Hawk," the station included music, talk, sports, and other student programming.

Student service and volunteerism increased during the period. In 2000 the Leadership Service Opportunity Program was established to facilitate service on campus and in the community. It was later renamed the Center for Leadership and Service and then the Office for Community and Civic Engagement (CCE). Nine hundred students contributed more than twelve thousand volunteer service hours in 2006, while 560 students performed more than fourteen thousand hours of service in 2008. Through CCE's efforts, UNC Pembroke was named to the President's Higher Education Community Service Honor Roll for 2006, 2007, and 2008. This was the highest honor a university could receive for its commitment to volunteering, service learning, and civic engagement.

Community service also found its way into the classroom with service-learning programs offered by faculty. Service learning is a teaching and learning strategy that provides students with opportunities to apply the concepts, skills, and information learned in the classroom to real-world problems through meaningful community service. In 2007 the position of director of service learning was established to facilitate such opportunities on campus.

Chancellor Meadors also sought to enhance the student experience through the globalization of the student body and the campus. He hoped to expose students to the global society by increasing the number of international students on the campus and opportunities for students, faculty, and staff to study abroad. An Office of International Programs was established in 2001. Consequently, there was a significant increase in international student enrollment, study abroad, and faculty exchanges. International student enrollment dramatically increased from 19 in 1999 to 114 in 2009. While 64 of the students in 2009 came from China, nineteen nations were represented on campus. UNC Pembroke hosted students, administrators, and faculty from universities in China, France, Germany, Russia, South Africa, South Korea, and Taiwan, among others. UNC Pembroke signed agreements with institutions in these countries, establishing formal relationships that resulted in student, faculty, and administrative exchanges as well as other programs. As a result, UNC Pembroke offered its MPA program to students at the China University of Mining and Technology. At the December 11, 2004, Commencement, three Chinese students—Cui Lan, Wu Gang, and Wang Yan Qui—received their master of public administration degrees after successfully completing UNC Pembroke's first international degree program. UNC Pembroke also joined the China Center for International Education Exchange, a consortium of Chinese and U.S. universities, who were represented by the American Association of State Colleges and Universities. In conjunction with the increased number of international students, particularly from China, the university first hosted Asia Day in 2005 to celebrate the diversity of Asian culture. The presence of international students was no more evident than in 2003 when a half-dozen exchange students from Germany helped the men's soccer team achieve its first-ever NCAA tournament invitation and a top-ten national ranking. Many of the team's American players studied abroad in Germany the following spring semester.

The university also made efforts to attract and improve the college experience for other groups. In 2005 Congress established the Defense Base Closure and Realignment Commission (BRAC) to consolidate military bases in the United States, resulting in the expansion of troops stationed at Fort Bragg in Fayetteville. As a result, UNC Pembroke made a concerted effort to attract these veterans with the establishment of an off-campus site at Fort Bragg. In 2008 the university held its first Veterans Appreciation Banquet to celebrate its student veterans.

The Office of Military and Veteran Services was established in 2009 to assist veterans with their higher education needs. As a result, *Military Advanced Education* magazine rated UNC Pembroke as one of the top military-friendly universities in the United States in 2007 and 2008. The university also reached out to other student groups. In 2000 the Office of Disability Support Services was established to create a more inclusive, accessible community for students with disabilities. To support its more diverse student body, the Office of Multicultural and Minority Affairs was established in 2003 to support cultural diversity, encourage increased cultural competency, and prepare students to interact in a diverse global community. To better coordinate fraternity and sorority activities on campus, the Office of Greek Life was established in 2006. Today, there are nineteen social fraternities and sororities on campus.

Affordable tuition rates continued to attract students from throughout the region and the state. Although tuition, fees, and room and board rose during the period, UNC Pembroke remained one of the most affordable universities in North Carolina and the nation. In 1999, annual tuition and fees for twelve or more undergraduate hours was $1,796 for in-state students and $9,066 for out-of-state students. Tuition and fees for nine or more graduate hours was $1,670 for in-state students and $8,940 for out-of-state students. Room and board was $3,358. By 2009, undergraduate in-state tuition and fees was $4,222 and out-of-state was $13,428. Graduate tuition and fees for in-state students was $3,902 and out-of-state was $13,229. Room and board varied from $5,740 to $7,090 based on the selected residence hall and room (double, single-private, double-private). Apartments cost $4,000 annually. *US News & World Report*, in its annual publication "America's Best Colleges," ranked UNC Pembroke as one of the most affordable southern regional universities for graduates with lowest debt in 2000, 2005 (second among North Carolina public universities and twelfth for all universities in the South), 2006, 2007, and 2008.

As UNC Pembroke's athletic program expanded, the new century brought challenges to the university's use of the "Braves" nickname and athletic logo. In 2001 a national Indian organization was critical of UNC Pembroke's use of the nickname. In May of that year, the Board of Trustees, and its six Indian members, voted unanimously to support the university's nickname. Chancellor Meadors summed up the board's feelings when he asked, "Does this community want the Brave to remain part of the university?" "It is my feeling," Meadors said, "that the community feels very strongly about keeping the Brave—alumni, too." The following year, the board again voted unanimously to support the nickname after UNC Pembroke was one of thirty-one schools identified by an NCAA committee as having a mascot or logo that could be considered controversial. In 2005 the NCAA went a step further and asked the university to study of the use of its athletic logo and nickname and submit a report to the NCAA governing body by May 1. A six-member campus steering committee was formed to respond to the NCAA's request. Chancellor Meadors remarked, "We are following the community's lead on this." He said, "If the community says we should change our nickname and logo, we will do it." The Board of Trustees again voted unanimously to support the nickname. The university had widespread support for its use of the nickname and athletic logo. On February 15, 2005, the Lumbee Tribal Council voted unanimously to support the logo and nickname. A student-led petition garnered over two thousand signatures supporting the campus tradition. On August 5 the NCAA ruled that UNC Pembroke was the only school that would be allowed to use an Indian mascot, nickname, or imagery at NCAA-sanctioned postseason events. Seventeen universities were banned from using their Indian athletic symbols in postseason tournaments because they were judged "hostile or abusive." According to the NCAA, UNC Pembroke "made a very compelling case to retain its nickname and imagery."

The number of athletic teams increased as three sports were added during the decade. Women's soccer and women's golf began competition

FIGURE 7.3. *Football was reintroduced in 2007.*

in 2001 and 2007, respectively. The reintroduction of football in 2007 was perhaps the athletic highlight of the decade. The institution fielded a football team between 1946 and 1950. In October 1962 President English Jones mentioned the possibility of football returning to campus; the student body was "anxious" to get football started. He appointed a committee to study the issue, but no further action was taken. On December 1, 2004, the Board of Trustees approved the return of football, generating a buzz of excitement that rippled across campus and throughout southeastern North Carolina. The "First and Ten: Campaign for Football and Athletic Excellence" kicked off on September 22, 2005, with a pep rally and boisterous crowd of sixteen hundred Braves fans. The goal was to raise $4 million to support the university's athletic program and the return of football. Honorary campaign cochairs were Kelvin Sampson '78, a Pembroke native and head coach of the University of Oklahoma's men's basketball team, and National Football League great Dwight Clark. As a testament to the region's excitement, the campaign exceeded its $4 million goal. In 2007, competing as an independent NCAA Division II team, football won its first home game, defeating Greensboro College 26-20, and also won its first fall Homecoming game, a 31-21 victory over Webber International. In just its third season, Braves football became the fastest program in NCAA history to receive a playoff bid. The Braves finished the 2009 regular season with nine wins and one loss for the second year in a row; they were also undefeated at home in 2008 and 2009. Also in 2009, the Braves began a home-and-away series with Fayetteville State University dubbed the Two Rivers Classic. The Braves went undefeated in the budding rivalry's first four games. At the end of Chancellor Meadors's tenure, the university supported sixteen athletic teams: eight for men and eight for women.

Football was a huge success for the school and the region. The coaching staff recruited local talent, and football became a rallying point for bringing alumni and the community back to campus. Fund-raising, a primary goal of the UNC system's Focused-Growth Initiative, also benefitted greatly. Numerous campus facilities were constructed and named for donors as a result of gifts made during the First and Ten Campaign. The track and soccer complex, built in 2002 as the home for men's soccer and the track and field teams, became the home of Braves football and track and field. A new soccer complex was constructed on the north end of campus in 2006. Thanks to donations from alumni and friends, most athletic facilities were named during this period. The track and soccer complex was renamed the Irwin Belk Athletic Complex in 2002. It comprised Grace P. Johnson Stadium (2007), the Dick and Lenore Taylor Track (2002), the Lumbee Guaranty Bank Field (2002), the Bob Caton Fieldhouse (2007), and the First Bank Chancellor's Box (2008). The complex was named for Irwin Belk, former president and CEO of Belk Stores. The stadium was dedicated in honor of Grace P. Johnson on September 6, 2008, after a $1 million gift from her husband, Marvin, and family, who own House of Raeford, a national turkey processor headquartered in nearby Duplin

County. The stadium's playing field was named for Lumbee Guaranty Bank, headquartered in Pembroke, on April 20, 2007, while the press box was dedicated to First Bank, headquartered in Troy, North Carolina, when it was constructed in 2008. Taylor Track was named after Lenore and Dick Taylor, a Lumberton businessman, while Caton Fieldhouse, dedicated on February 19, 2007, was named for Bob Caton, a Lumberton businessman. The ultramodern stadium has seating for more than forty-eight hundred fans. The home of Braves baseball was renamed Cox Field in 2006 after a gift from local businessman Sammy Cox '76 and his wife, Onita. That year, the softball stadium was renamed LRA Field for donor Lumberton Radiological Associates.

UNC Pembroke's other athletic teams began to flourish in the NCAA Division II and the Peach Belt Conference (PBC). The men's soccer team advanced to the NCAA Final Four for the first time in 2004 after winning the regular season and conference tournament championships. They also earned invitations to the NCAA tournament in 2003 and 2005. The women's basketball program won a conference division championship in 2005, while the softball team won a conference championship and also made the NCAA tournament in 2008. Other teams that made NCAA tournament appearances during the period included men's golf (2001—first time ever, 2005, and 2006), women's soccer (2008), and women's track and field (2008). Along with team championships, there were numerous individual accomplishments. Wrestling produced ten NCAA regional champions: 2003—Dwayne Coward (165 pounds) and Derek Brunson '07 (184); 2004—Curry Pickard (125), Roylando Lucas (133), and Dwayne Coward (165); 2005—Curry Pickard (133), Dwayne Coward (165), and Derek Brunson '07 (184); 2007—Derek Brunson '07 (197); and 2008—Joe Mavins '10 (125). Members of the men's golf team also qualified for the NCAA regionals: 2002—Matt Drye; 2004—Gregg Dobbins '05 and Mark Long; and 2007—Matthew Morrison. Dobbins qualified for the national tournament in 2005. Pardon Ndhlovu '13 qualified for the men's cross country NCAA championships in 2009. Danielle Richardson was named the women's basketball conference Player of the Year in 2005. Four UNC Pembroke students were also named the conference Scholar-Athlete of the Year: 2003—men's soccer player Brian Young '03; 2006—men's golfer Lee Nejberger '06 and women's soccer player Katie Stokes '06; and 2007—tennis player Natalies Dies '07. Dan Kenney was named the 2007 Athletic Director of the Year by his peers at a meeting of the National Association of Collegiate Directors of Athletics. The period also produced eleven conference and regional coaches of the year, and ninety-three academic and athletic All-Americans.

Chants of "Go-Braves-Go!" greeted the football team in 2007 after the marching band was reinstated in 2004. Absent since the early 1980s, the band was a nonmarching band for its first three years. In 2007 it transitioned to a marching band with the reintroduction of football, and was renamed the Spirit of the Carolinas Marching Band. Chancellor Meadors believed that some of the strongest alumni at most universities

FIGURE 7.4. *The Spirit of the Carolinas Marching Band.*

were former members of the marching band, and that marching band and football were part of the total package of a destination school. With the return of the marching band, Michael Raiber, a professor of music education at the University of Oklahoma, was commissioned to write a fight song in 2004. Fans now rally the Braves with chants of "Go Braves! Go-Braves-Go!" The university also fielded one of the premier pep bands in the Peach Belt Conference, winning the Band Division Championship in 2010, 2011, and 2012. They were first runner-up in 2009 and 2013.

Another goal of Chancellor Meadors was to improve town-and-gown relations between the university and the town of Pembroke. To this end, he established a Town and Gown Committee and hosted numerous gatherings and receptions at the chancellor's residence. In 1999 he initiated the Alumni Holiday Drop-In, inviting alumni to the residence for a Christmas reception. As another form of outreach, Relay for Life was launched on campus in 2008. The university's economic impact on the town of Pembroke and the region expanded with the university. This spurred a business boom in Pembroke with the addition of a Walmart, several chain restaurants, and other local businesses. The town's growth reflected Chancellor Meadors's goal to bring new jobs and businesses to the community. To stimulate additional job growth, the university partnered in 2000 with the Carolina Commerce and Technology Center (COMtech), a business park located east of Pembroke. In 2004 a new facility for the university's Regional Center for Economic, Community, and Professional Development opened at COMtech. Later renamed the Regional Center, it housed the Small Business and Technology Development Center, which provided individualized consulting to new and expanding businesses. In 2006 the Thomas Family Center for Entrepreneurship (TFCE) was established after a gift from the foundation established by Pembroke native James Thomas and his wife, Sally. TFCE serves the community through its commitment to entrepreneurship education and development. To that end, the university created an entrepreneurship minor for undergraduate business majors, an entrepreneurship track in the MBA program, and a certificate program available to students with any major. In recognition of its commitment to collaboration with the local community, UNC Pembroke was selected for the 2008 Community Engagement Classification by the Carnegie Foundation for the Advancement of Teaching. The national recognition confirmed the university's support for education, social and economic growth, and its civic and cultural engagement in the region.

There were other notable events during Chancellor Meadors's tenure. On July 5, 2005, UNC Pembroke was designated "North Carolina's Historically American Indian University" when the General Assembly approved a bill introduced by local representative Ronnie Sutton. Also, during the 2008 presidential campaign, former president Bill Clinton spoke to a standing-room-only crowd in the main gym of the Jones Center on April 4 during a rally for candidate Hillary Clinton. Clinton, however, was not the only U.S. president to visit Pembroke. On May 1, 1912, Howard Taft became the first president to visit the town of Pembroke when he stopped during a train trip through town while en route from Florence, South Carolina. According to *The Robesonian*, President Taft "walked out on the rear of his car and exchanged words with a few of the boys that were at the [Pembroke train] station."

FIGURE 7.5. *President Bill Clinton speaking at the English E. Jones Health and Physical Education Center in 2008.*

On June 16, 2009, Chancellor Meadors announced his retirement, effective June 30, 2009, to take the helm of his alma mater, the University of Central Arkansas. Under his leadership, UNC Pembroke experienced ten years of growth as enrollment more than doubled, the physical face of the campus was transformed, football returned, records for giving were shattered, and the town of Pembroke blossomed.

As a testament to Chancellor Meadors's leadership, UNC Pembroke was awarded several top state and national honors. Between 2000 and 2002, UNC Pembroke was one of two schools of education in North Carolina—out of forty-eight—to be ranked "exemplary" for three years by the State Board of Education. *US News & World Report* recognized UNC Pembroke throughout the decade for its high proportion of classes with under twenty students, the number of international students, and the economic diversity of its students. The *Princeton Review* designated UNC Pembroke a "Best Southeastern College" four times from 2006 to 2009. The National Survey of Student Engagement in 2008 noted that more than eight of ten students surveyed said UNC Pembroke placed "substantial emphasis on academics." The transformation of UNC Pembroke during Chancellor Meadors's tenure raised the university's status and visibility in the region and throughout North Carolina. As a tribute, Chancellor Meadors was granted emeritus status upon his retirement.

Dr. Meadors served as president of the University of Central Arkansas from 2009 through 2011. He was a senior fellow with the American Association of State Colleges and Universities from 2011 through 2012. Since 2011 Dr. Meadors has served as a senior consultant with Global Leadership Group, and in 2013 he was named the executive director of the Higher Education Coordination Council in the United Arab Emirates.

To continue the university's progress, Dr. Charles R. Jenkins, a former provost and vice chancellor for Academic Affairs at UNC Pembroke, was named chancellor on an interim basis on June 22, 2009, by UNC system president Erskine Bowles. According to Bowles, Dr. Jenkins "has unmatched knowledge of UNCP and the surrounding region, and he has earned the trust and respect of his faculty colleagues, the students, the local community, and other key campus constituencies." Bowles continued, "UNCP will be in very capable hands during the search for a permanent chancellor." Dr. Jenkins had served the university in many capacities, including twenty-six years in senior administration, since joining the faculty in 1971. He was as a faculty member in the Department of Education

(1971–1974 and 1976–1977), director of admissions (1975–1976), director of student teaching (fall 1974 and 1976–1977), assistant to the vice chancellor for academic affairs (1977–1978), dean of academic affairs for programs and faculty development (1978–1980), academic dean (1980-1985), provost and vice chancellor for academic affairs (1986–2000), and professor of educational leadership (since 2000). In August 2007 he was named professor emeritus, and continued to teach in the School of Education as a clinical professor of educational leadership. Before coming to the university, he taught at Scotland High School in Laurinburg, North Carolina, from 1967 to 1970. Dr. Jenkins served as interim chancellor from July 1, 2009, to June 30, 2010.

FIGURE 7.6 *Dr. Charles R. Jenkins. Interim chancellor of the University of North Carolina at Pembroke from 2009 to 2010.*

Born on September 27, 1944, Dr. Jenkins was a native of Rockingham, North Carolina, and a resident of Laurinburg. He earned BA and MAEd degrees in education from East Carolina University in 1966 and 1967, respectively, and an EdD in educational administration and supervision from Duke University in 1975. Concerning his tenure as interim chancellor, Dr. Jenkins said, "We will not be in a holding pattern." He continued, "There are real challenges this year, especially with the budget." But, he also noted, "There are many opportunities as well, and we will move forward this year."

UNC Pembroke continued its forward progress under Chancellor Jenkins's leadership as evidenced by many notable challenges and accomplishments during his tenure. The university had to deal with cuts in the state budget appropriation resulting from the Great Recession, and a change in the General Administration's funding formula. The new formula reflected a new emphasis on retention and graduation rates over increases in enrollment. As a result, Dr. Jenkins appointed a

university-wide task force to address the university's retention and graduation rates. Consequently, admission standards were raised, including
increased grade point averages for entering students.

UNC Pembroke, however, continued to grow, expand, and earn
honors. Enrollment reached an all-time high of 6,944 in 2010. In
February, UNC Pembroke announced a collaborative effort with East
Carolina University (ECU) to host two doctor of education (EdD)
programs in higher education and in K–12 educational leadership, offered
by ECU, beginning in fall 2010. UNC Pembroke continued to receive
accolades for its achievements. The university was rated by the *Princeton
Review* as one of the best colleges and universities in the Southeast for
2010. *US News & World Report* ranked UNC Pembroke first in the South
for the diversity of its student body, and *G.I. Jobs* magazine named the
university a "Military Friendly School for 2010." *The Pine Needle* won a
national award presented by the American Scholastic Press as one of
the best college and university newspapers in the United States. Also in
March 2010 the Science Education Program was recognized as one of
the top performers in the state according to a report published by the
Carolina Institute for Public Policy. The Nursing Department received
notice for the 95 percent passing rate of its graduates on the National
Council Licensure Examination (NCLEX-RN). Again, in March 2010,
the Commission on Colleges of the Southern Association of Colleges
and Schools (SACS) Visiting Reaccreditation Team came to campus to
evaluate UNC Pembroke, including the evaluation of the university's
Quality Enhancement Plan (QEP), which focused on the improvement of student writing skills across the curriculum. UNC Pembroke
received a very favorable evaluation and was reaffirmed for accreditation.
This endeavor was led for the second time by Dr. Elizabeth Normandy,
director of the Teaching and Learning Center.

UNC Pembroke athletes continued to excel during the 2009–2010
season. In 2010 the university was named a corecipient of the Peach Belt

Conference's Wachovia Foundation Creative Connection Education Award for service to the community and the Public Schools of Robeson County. UNC Pembroke was also awarded the conference's Presidents' Academic Award in recognition of its student-athletes who led the league in classroom performance with the highest grade point average. The baseball team won a share of the Peach Belt East Division championship, while Jordan Walor '12 won the conference individual championship in men's golf. The women's soccer team and numerous individuals qualified for the NCAA championships. They included Maurice Eubanks (100 meters, men's track and field); men's track and field 4x100 relay team (Brandon Eaddy '12, Karlos Jordan '11, Tyrie Webb, and Maurice Eubanks—Devan Cureton was the alternate); and Pardon Ndhlovu '13 (men's cross country). Kyera Tennyson (high jump) was the first in the history of the women's track and field program to qualify for the NCAA championships. Qualifiers in wrestling included Russell Weakley '11 (125 pounds), J.J. Davis (174), Mike Williams (157), and Shane Nolan '12 (197). Williams won the NCAA regional championship. The season also produced one conference coach of the year and twenty-six academic and athletic All-Americans.

The ninth and tenth distinguished professorships were also established during Chancellor Jenkins's tenure. In 2009 the Allen C. Meadors Distinguished Professorship in Mathematics Education was made possible by a $250,000 gift from the C. D. Spangler Foundation Inc. The BB&T Distinguished Endowed Professorship in the Morality of Capitalism was established after the Winston-Salem, North Carolina, bank made a $500,000 gift to the university. This was the second distinguished professorship endowed by BB&T at UNC Pembroke, bringing their total gift for both endowments to $1 million. The Meadors and BB&T distinguished professorships were matched by the General Assembly's Distinguished Professors Endowment Trust Fund.

Two events, to benefit and enhance the student experience, began in 2009. The S.O.S. Beach Party was first held August 7 to raise funds for student scholarships. The fund-raiser was a call to friends of the university to "Support Our Students." It was a creative response by the Office of Advancement to the Great Recession that temporarily left UNC Pembroke's Endowment unable to provide scholarships. The Honoring Native Foodways gathering was also first held that fall on November 12. The event celebrated and showcased traditional and contemporary Indian foods. The campus and local community were encouraged to bring healthy food for attendees to sample. Now annual events, they were both huge successes. In 2010 the Office for Advancement won a major national award from the Council for the Advancement and Support of Education (CASE). The office, which supports fund-raising and alumni efforts, received the 2010 CASE Educational Fundraising "Overall Improvement Award" for its performance over the previous three years.

Chancellor Jenkins left a lasting mark on the campus with the establishment of Founders' Day in 2010. Now an annual tradition, the March 17, 2010, ceremony honored the history and the heritage of the institution, the first Board of Trustees, and graduates through 1950. Dr. Jenkins described the gathering as a "seminal event." He proclaimed, "We all have a great deal to celebrate, and this event will lead up to a larger celebration of the 125th year."

With his successor named in April 2010, Dr. Jenkins returned to the faculty in the School of Education on July 1, 2010.

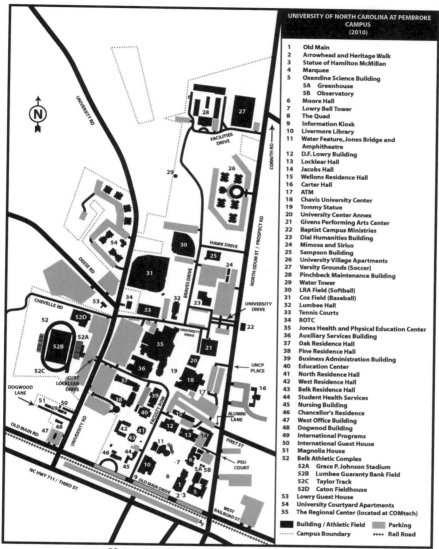

UNIVERSITY OF NORTH CAROLINA AT PEMBROKE CAMPUS (2010)

1	Old Main
2	Arrowhead and Heritage Walk
3	Statue of Hamilton McMillan
4	Marquee
5	Oxendine Science Building
5A	Greenhouse
5B	Observatory
6	Moore Hall
7	Lowry Bell Tower
8	The Quad
9	Information Kiosk
10	Livermore Library
11	Water Feature, Jones Bridge and Amphitheatre
12	D.F. Lowry Building
13	Locklear Hall
14	Jacobs Hall
15	Wellons Residence Hall
16	Carter Hall
17	ATM
18	Chavis University Center
19	Tommy Statue
20	University Center Annex
21	Givens Performing Arts Center
22	Baptist Campus Ministries
23	Dial Humanities Building
24	Mimosa and Sirius
25	Sampson Building
26	University Village Apartments
27	Varsity Grounds (Soccer)
28	Pinchbeck Maintenance Building
29	Water Tower
30	LRA Field (Softball)
31	Cox Field (Baseball)
32	Lumbee Hall
33	Tennis Courts
34	ROTC
35	Jones Health and Physical Education Center
36	Auxiliary Services Building
37	Oak Residence Hall
38	Pine Residence Hall
39	Business Administration Building
40	Education Center
41	North Residence Hall
42	West Residence Hall
43	Belk Residence Hall
44	Student Health Services
45	Nursing Building
46	Chancellor's Residence
47	West Office Building
48	Dogwood Building
49	International Programs
50	International Guest House
51	Magnolia House
52	Belk Athletic Complex
52A	Grace P. Johnson Stadium
52B	Lumbee Guaranty Bank Field
52C	Taylor Track
52D	Caton Fieldhouse
53	Lowry Guest House
54	University Courtyard Apartments
55	The Regional Center (located at COMtech)

■ Building / Athletic Field ▨ Parking
······ Campus Boundary +++ Rail Road

MAP 7.1. *University of North Carolina at Pembroke campus (2010).*

TIMELINE OF NOTABLE INSTITUTIONAL EVENTS (1999–2010)

1999
- Dr. Allen C. Meadors named fourth chancellor.
- Distance Education established; first online class offered.
- Administrative reorganization of academic departments into College of Arts and Sciences, School of Business, School of Education, and School of Graduate Studies.
- Staff Council organized.
- Graduate degree program in art education added.
- Applied physics undergraduate degree program added.
- Chancellor's residence renovated and expanded.
- Alumni Holiday Drop-In first held.
- First winter Commencement held following the installation of Chancellor Allen C. Meadors. The UNC Board of Governors Excellence in Teaching Award recipient has since served as the winter Commencement keynote speaker.

2000
- Chancellor's Scholars Program was expanded and renamed the Honors College; named the Esther G. Maynor Honors College in 2006.
- *Brave Bulletin*, the faculty and staff newsletter, was first published.
- Lorna (McNeill) Ricotta '01, '08 crowned Miss North Carolina.
- Graduate degree programs in physical education, social studies education, and science education added.
- WNCP-TV returned to Time Warner Cable.
- UNC Pembroke partnered with the Carolina Commerce and Technology Center (COMtech).
- Disability Support Services established.
- Distinguished Speaker Series launched.
- Leadership Service Opportunity Program established; renamed Community and Civic Engagement.
- Pine Residence Hall completed.
- North Carolinians overwhelmingly supported Higher Education Bond referendum.

2001
- *The Aurochs* first published.
- Women's soccer added.
- University Courtyard Apartments and information kiosk constructed.
- West Office Building acquired.

2002
- Water feature and amphitheatre along with Heritage Walk constructed.
- Enrollment passed four thousand.
- Rebekah (Revels) Lowry '01, '11, Miss UNC Pembroke 1998, was crowned Miss North Carolina.
- "Weightless Lumbees" organized.
- Graduate degree program in elementary education added.
- Outdoor Education Center constructed; later razed.
- Irwin Belk Athletic Complex completed, comprising the Grace P. Johnson Stadium (2007), the Dick and Lenore Taylor Track (2002), the Lumbee Guaranty Bank Field (2002), the Bob Caton Fieldhouse (2007), and the First Bank Chancellor's Box (2008).

2003
- Spanish undergraduate degree program added.
- Graduate degree program in music education added.
- *The Pine Needle* goes digital with launch of website.
- Lowry Bell Tower renovated.
- Student Health Services and the Chavis University Center dining hall expanded.
- University Village Apartments constructed.

2004
- Alma mater revived and renamed "Hail to UNCP."
- Men's soccer reached NCAA Division II Final Four.
- Marching band reinstated; renamed the Spirit of the Carolinas Marching Band in 2007.
- Fight song written by Michael Raiber.
- Master of arts in teaching added.
- Environmental science undergraduate degree program added.
- Scholarship Awards Dinner first held.
- The Regional Center for Economic, Community, and Professional Development constructed at COMtech. Later renamed the Regional Center.
- Herbert G. Oxendine Science Building renovated and expanded.
- Walter J. Pinchbeck Facilities Planning and Maintenance Complex completed.
- Dogwood Building acquired.
- Three Chinese students received MPA degrees after completing UNC Pembroke's first international degree program.

2005   · Enrollment broke five thousand
        · Chavis University Center marquee constructed.
        · Designated "North Carolina's Historic American Indian University"
          by the General Assembly.
        · NCAA allowed UNC Pembroke to use "Braves" nickname and ath-
          letic logo during NCAA-sanctioned postseason events.
        · Southeast Indian Studies Conference first held.
        · Bachelor of science in nursing program added along with undergrad-
          uate degree programs in musical theatre and biotechnology.
        · First and Ten: Campaign for Football and Athletic Excellence kicked off.
        · English E. Jones Health and Physical Education Center, Locklear
          Hall, and Moore Hall expanded.
2006   · Brenda B. Brooks Distinguished Endowed Professorship in Nursing
          endowed.
        · WNCP-Radio "The Hawk" began broadcasting.
        · Pembroke Undergraduate Research and Creativity (PURC) Center
          established.
        · Greek Life established.
        · Cox Field and LRA Field dedicated.
        · Thomas Family Center for Entrepreneurship established.
        · Former Walter J. Pinchbeck Maintenance Building renovated, expanded,
          and renamed the Auxiliary Services Building to include new bookstore.
        · International Programs and International Guest House acquired.
2007   · BB&T Distinguished Endowed Professorship in the Philosophi-
          cal Foundations of Free Enterprise and Joseph B. Oxendine Distin-
          guished Professor of Education endowed.
        · Football reintroduced. First fall Homecoming held.
        · Women's golf added.
        · First Pembroke Undergraduate Research and Creativity (PURC)
          Center Symposium and Graduate Research Poster Session held.
        · Sara Pack'11 named first recipient of the Esther G. Maynor Scholarship.
        · Master of social work added.
        · Interdisciplinary studies and information technology undergraduate
          degree programs added.

- D. F. Lowry Building renovated.
- Oak Residence Hall and O.R. Sampson Academic Building constructed; library renamed Mary H. Livermore Library.
- University Center Annex, Grace P. Johnson Stadium, and Bob Caton Fieldhouse completed.

2008
- Anne Reynolds Belk Endowed Professorship in Nursing and Thomas Family Endowed Professorship in Entrepreneurship established.
- President Bill Clinton spoke at the Jones Center.
- Enrollment passed six thousand.
- Athletic training undergraduate degree program added.
- Magnolia House acquired.
- Carter Hall leased.

2009
- Marquees constructed in front of the Givens Performing Arts Center and at the intersection of Third and North Odum Streets.
- *Tanza* statue erected.
- Biotechnology Research and Training Center opened.
- Water tower constructed.
- Dr. Charles R. Jenkins named interim chancellor.
- Allen C. Meadors Distinguished Professorship in Mathematics Education endowed.

2010
- Enrollment reached all-time high of 6,944.
- UNC Pembroke announced a collaborative effort with East Carolina University to host two doctor of education (EdD) programs offered by ECU.
- Southern Association of Colleges and Schools (SACS) accreditation reaffirmed.
- BB&T Distinguished Endowed Professorship in the Morality of Capitalism established.
- Founders' Day celebration established.

Chapter Eight

2010–2013
SOARING TOWARD THE FUTURE

As we expand and define our role in southeast North Carolina, we must reaffirm our commitment to improving lives through education, and we must weave our American Indian heritage into the fabric of this regional comprehensive university. We acknowledge and embrace this fact: A small school, created for a singular purpose, has become a university for all.

Dr. Kyle R. Carter, chancellor,
University of North Carolina at Pembroke,
Installation Program (2011)

As UNC Pembroke raced toward its 125th year of service to the region, it faced a series of internal and external challenges in 2010. The Great Recession, a global financial crisis that lasted longer and was more severe than previous recessions, led to double-digit cuts in the university's state appropriation. Also, the University of North Carolina system's General Administration changed its funding formula to reflect an emphasis on retention and graduation rates over enrollment growth. As a result, the university began to address retention and graduation rates, admission requirements, and the academic standing policy.

To find the next chancellor who would navigate these challenges while continuing the university's forward momentum, the Board of Trustees on September 17, 2009, appointed a fifteen-member Chancellor Search Committee. Chaired by Dr. Freda Porter '78, who also chaired the Board of Trustees, the committee included five trustees, three faculty, a staff member, an alumnus, the president of the Student Government Association, one member of the UNCP Foundation Inc., and three members of the community. Less than one week later, during the committee's first meeting on September 22, 2009, Erskine Bowles, president of the University of North Carolina system, charged the committee to find a new chancellor who would "build on the incredible work" of Chancellor Emeritus Meadors. President Bowles also tasked the committee to find a leader with people skills who would have the "respect of the entire community," see the university's rural setting as an asset, and respect the institution's proud heritage. More importantly, Bowles exhorted the committee to find a chancellor to address UNC Pembroke's "disappointing" retention and graduation rates. Speaking to retention, he said, "It's about more than getting them in the door." At the meeting, the committee hired a firm with national experience in higher education to assist with the search for UNC Pembroke's next chancellor.

Between October 13 and 20, 2009, the Chancellor Search Committee hosted a series of forums on campus to gather input from students, faculty, staff, alumni, and the community on qualities desirable in the next chancellor. After a seven-month search, the Board of Trustees submitted the names of three finalists to President Bowles. On April 9, 2010, Dr. Kyle R. Carter, provost and senior vice chancellor for Western Carolina University, was elected the fifth chancellor of UNC Pembroke by the UNC system Board of Governors after President Bowles placed Dr. Carter's name into nomination. In recommending him to the Board of Governors, President Bowles said, "Kyle Carter brings to the task more than three decades of academic and leadership experience at respected public universities, including one of our own UNC institutions. At each step along the way, he has proven himself to be an engaged and effective leader who promotes collaboration and strategic thinking, academic excellence, and student success. He has also earned a reputation for great integrity, sound judgment, and an unwavering commitment to community engagement and outreach." Bowles concluded, "I am convinced that Kyle Carter brings the right mix of experience, skills, and passion needed to be a truly great chancellor for UNC Pembroke, and I am thrilled that he has agreed to join our leadership team." Immediately after the announcement, Chancellor Carter made the two-hour drive to Pembroke to greet the campus community. At the reception, he said he was drawn to Pembroke because of its "compelling" story, its rich history, and 123 years of service to a "very diverse citizenry." As a testament to developing a shared vision for the university, Carter remarked, "I will invite the entire Pembroke community to help chart the future course of the university." He also pledged "to honor and preserve the core values of the past."

Dr. Carter had served as provost and vice chancellor of Western Carolina since 2004. A native of Atlanta, he was born on January 29, 1948. Carter earned a BA degree in psychology with a minor in biology from Mercer University in 1970, and MA and PhD degrees in educational psychology from the University of Georgia in 1971 and 1974, respectively. He had more than thirty-five years of experience in higher education, particularly with regional universities set in rural communities. Dr. Carter began his career on the faculty of Valdosta State College, today Valdosta State University, as an assistant professor of psychology from 1974 to 1976. At the University of Northern Colorado, he taught educational psychology from 1976 to 1998, achieving tenure and the rank of full professor in 1985. Dr. Carter served as a full-time faculty member for more than thirteen years before moving into administration, including director of the Division of Research, Evaluation, and Development from 1985 to 1987; associate dean of the College of Education (1987–1989);

interim dean of the Graduate School (1990); president of the Research Corporation (1990–1996); dean of the Graduate School and University Research (1990–1996); and associate vice president for Research and Graduate Studies and dean of the Graduate School (1996–1998). While at the University of Central Missouri, Dr. Carter served as the provost and vice president for Academic Affairs from 1998 to 2004, and two months as acting president in 2002. His scholarship interests are the cognitive development of gifted and talented children, program evaluation, and transitioning the comprehensive university. Throughout his career Dr. Carter served on a number of boards and statewide committees and was actively engaged in community outreach and service.

FIGURE 8.1. *Dr. Kyle R. Carter. Chancellor of the University of North Carolina at Pembroke since 2010.*

Soon after beginning his duties as chancellor at UNC Pembroke on July 1, 2010, Chancellor Carter and his wife, Sarah, became prominent fixtures on campus and in the region. Along with their dog, Dooley, the Carters could be seen walking the campus each morning. Chancellor Carter's visibility and outreach began with the campus and the town of Pembroke and then extended to the region. Just two days after arriving to campus, the Carters participated in Lumbee Homecoming in Pembroke by walking the entire length of the parade route. This became an annual tradition; Dooley even joined them one year. Chancellor Carter also held open forums on campus to discuss issues affecting the campus. He visited and addressed numerous

FIGURE 8.2. *First Lady Sarah Carter. Wife of Chancellor Kyle R. Carter.*

civic and community organizations, including the Pembroke Chamber; Rotary Clubs in Lumberton, Red Springs, and Southern Pines; Lumberton Kiwanis; St. Paul's High School; the Robeson County Municipal Association; the North Carolina Indian Unity Conference; and the Cape Fear Council of Boy Scouts. He also continued to be active on boards and in the community, serving on the Board of Directors for the Southeastern Regional Medical Center in Lumberton, the International Student Exchange Program, and the North Carolina Campus Compact. On March 24, 2012, Chancellor Carter put on his dancing shoes and partnered with Shanita Wooten '11 to support Robeson County United Way's "Dancing with the Stars" fund-raiser.

First Lady Sarah Carter became very engaged in the campus and the community, serving as an integral part of the administration's outreach and engagement efforts. Aside from her customary duties as hostess for functions at the chancellor's residence, Carter expanded the role of the First Lady by serving on several on- and off-campus committees, including the 125th Anniversary Committee, the HEALTH (Helping Employees Achieve Lifetime Total Health) Committee, the Board of Governors Planning Committee, the Hospice of Scotland County Board, and the Southeastern Health Foundation's Planning Committee, among others. She also found time to promote her passions for education, health and wellness, and sustainability. Consequently, she worked with campus food service provider Sodexo to create healthier menus; helped to establish the Hawk Walk, a one-and-a-half-mile trail around campus; and increased awareness of recycling by encouraging the placement of bins outside buildings. As another initiative, on November 30, 2012, Chancellor and Sarah Carter, along with Lumbee tribal chair Paul Brooks lit the university's holiday tree, located in front of the University Center Annex. In 2013 she helped form the Chancellor's Ambassadors, a group of outstanding students who act as hosts for events held by the Office of the Chancellor and the university. Working with the ambassadors provided Carter with an opportunity to get to know students on a more personal level. A former elementary school teacher, Carter also supported children's literacy programs on and off campus.

Chancellor Carter's first official address to the campus community was his inaugural University Address on August 18, 2010, in the Givens Performing Arts Center. Speaking to the purpose of the address, Chancellor Carter said, "I intend to make this fall gathering a tradition for our university. It will be a time when we can take stock of our past accomplishments, discuss current challenges, and chart our future." During the address, attended by more than eight hundred students, faculty, staff, alumni, and members of the community, Chancellor Carter began to formulate a vision for the university. He charged those in attendance to help build "a shared vision of the future." He said, "Today's address starts our relationship, and it lays a foundation upon which we can build that relationship." Carter described how he would use the next three hundred days to "discuss the future of the university" by holding conversations with the local and regional community that would establish a "baseline of information as we go forward to build our vision." He continued, "The result that emerges will be a shared vision and strategic plan that fits our university and this region." To that end, the university conducted an online stakeholders' survey and Chancellor Carter led a Listening Tour of the region that fall.

In October and November 2010 Chancellor Carter conducted a nine-stop Listening Tour throughout UNC Pembroke's service region to gather information to guide the development of the university's vision and strategic plan for the future. The tour made stops at community college campuses in Bladen, Columbus, Hoke, Moore, Richmond, Robeson, and Scotland Counties as well as UNC Pembroke and Fayetteville State University in Fayetteville. Results from the survey and the Listening Tour demonstrated that UNC Pembroke was "well regarded" throughout the region. Chancellor Carter said that at all nine stops, "We heard over and over again about how the UNCP faculty and staff provided great service and helped change lives. We also learned about a few challenges and opportunities along the way." Speakers suggested the university add new programs in health care, including physical therapy, pharmacy, occupational therapy, public health, gerontology, and health information management. Others speakers suggested programs and outreach in public affairs with government and nonprofit organizations, and more online programs and training in engineering and technology for industry. The university was also asked to reach out to develop small business and support economic and community development. Other priorities mentioned included building partnerships with the region's thirteen hospitals, other health-care agencies, and youth development programs, and forging stronger ties with community colleges to facilitate student transitions to UNC Pembroke.

The shared vision and strategic plan for the university had taken shape by the time of Chancellor Carter's installation, held the week of April 11–15, 2011. Dubbed Installation Week, the theme for the festivities was "Honoring Traditions. Securing Our Future." Consequently, the week's activities celebrated the institution's history; the successes of students, faculty, and staff; and the installation of the chancellor. A memorable event was the first "Last Lecture" delivered on April 13, 2011, by Dr. Joseph Lakatos, a member of the faculty in the School of Business. Based on a last lecture made popular by the late Randy Pausch in his well-known lecture and book, Chancellor Carter shared the idea for the lecture: "What would you say in your last lecture to a group of people that you hold in very high esteem?" Dr. Lakatos was diagnosed with follicular lymphoma in 2004 and bravely continued to teach. Although he acknowledged the disease and the challenges it brought him—describing in detail the horrendous regime of radiation and chemotherapy that saved his life, but left him shaken to the core—he explained the true purpose of his talk when he said, "This is not about cancer. This is about inspiring you." Dr. Lakatos continued, "In your lifetime, you will have challenges; things will come at

FIGURE 8.3. *Chancellor Kyle R. Carter with flute player Jonathan Ward and the 2010 Lumbee Ambassadors—Teen Miss Lumbee Taylor Smith, Junior Miss Lumbee Erika Locklear, Little Miss Lumbee Nevaeh Locklear, and Miss Lumbee Brandi Scott—after April 15, 2011, installation.*

you. One day you will stand up and say, 'This is what I'm passionate about.' At the end of the day," he said, "C equals P. Your core has to equal your passion." The Last Lecture became an annual campus event.

Chancellor Carter's installation on April 15, 2011, was the high point of the week's activities. The ceremony in the Givens Performing Arts Center opened with reverence for the university's heritage and the traditions of the Lumbee people as a Lumbee flute player and the Lumbee Ambassadors, dressed in regalia, led the processional party onto the stage. Other special dignitaries included Hannah Gage, chair of the Board of Governors, and Dr. Robert C. Dickeson, the keynote speaker, who was president of the University of Northern Colorado when Dr. Carter joined the faculty. UNC system president Thomas Ross presided over the installation.

Joined by his wife and family on stage, Chancellor Carter took the oath of office. During his remarks, Dr. Carter "affirmed that he would carry the torch of the institution's remarkable history into a bold new future that will be loaded with challenges and possibilities." He said, "UNCP's heritage marks its character and shapes its future. UNCP is unique in this regard. Many institutions leave their past behind as they mature and change. Understanding UNCP's past matters as we move into the future." Chancellor Carter noted that although the rapid growth of the university during the past decade "positioned us well for the future," it presented the university with challenges that stressed the institution's systems. He emphasized that the university's "systems, practices, and culture . . . [must be] aligned to support our evolving responsibilities and expectations." He also outlined the shared vision and strategic plan for the university that would be fulfilled during his tenure.

Since the first University Address in August 2010, Chancellor Carter has emphasized four goals essential to the future of the university: (1) the "new normal"—efficient and effective use of resources, (2) student success, (3) becoming an "institution of choice," and (4) enhanced regional engagement. The Great Recession presented the university and the new Carter administration with a number of challenges: five straight years of budget cuts, salary freezes, increased tuition and fees, and the loss of veteran employees through retirement and seeking new opportunities. The new normal that Chancellor Carter invoked meant the university had to do more with less. He initiated measures to enhance the efficient and effective use of the university's human and nonhuman resources. To that end, the student activity period, a campus practice since 1986, was eliminated to maximize class offerings and classroom space utilization. Effective fall 2011, the move positioned the university to utilize all times throughout the week for course scheduling. Other efficiencies and effectiveness initiatives included the renegotiation of leases and a scaled-back use of off-campus facilities for university events. Numerous campus committees were consolidated, eliminated, or reduced in size to clarify the university's committee structure and promote more efficient use of human resources.

Chancellor Carter challenged the campus to maximize student success and improve student retention and graduation rates. To that end, as he noted, the university "advanced higher expectations in the classroom, tightened academic policies, increased admissions standards, and made organizational shifts to enhance academic support." Effective for the fall semester 2011, a new academic standing policy for undergraduate students was adopted. It required them to maintain a cumulative 2.0 grade point average to remain in good standing. The university enhanced student support services, which had not kept pace with the rapid growth of the university. Improvements were made to financial aid, advising, tutoring, and other services critical to retention and timely graduation. Many student support services were relocated and centralized in the D.F. Lowry Building. The College Opportunity Program (COP) was doubled in size, and the Advising Center and the number of professional advisers were expanded. The College of Arts and Sciences launched three initiatives designed to promote student success. The "2+2" program encouraged faculty to pair up and join pairs of students at campus events. The "Reach 3 Challenge" called on faculty to reach out to students who may be struggling. Finally, the "Go-to Faculty" was a group of more than twenty faculty members who served as informal resources to students, helping them work through academic, social, or other problems that threatened their success at the university. A CARE (Campus Assessment, Response, and Evaluation) Team comprising administrators and staff was organized in 2011 to work closely with students who were struggling with academic or social issues. The university also took steps to safeguard the quality of graduate student life, including academic progress, when the Graduate Student Organization was established in the spring of 2012. When Starbucks opened in the D.F. Lowry Building in 2011, it became a popular place.

The global financial crisis also proved to be a barrier to student success as many students were forced to "stop out"—taking a temporary leave of absence for financial reasons. The financial crisis combined with a reduction in state and federal financial assistance, and higher tuition and fees, made it more difficult for students to continue in school. These conditions along with a large number of students failing to show satisfactory academic progress resulted in an enrollment drop from the all-time high of 6,944 in the fall of 2010 to 6,251 two years later. However, the university took steps to abate the effects of the financial crisis as well as academic progress. In the fall of 2011, the textbook rental program was

FIGURE 8.4. *The class of 2015, along with Chancellor Kyle and Sarah Carter and the Lumbee Ambassadors, posing for a class photo on the Quad in the fall of 2011.*

implemented as an alternative to purchasing expensive textbooks. The Hawk Assistantship Program, begun in the fall of 2012, provided students with employment and financial assistance, and the campus profited by student workers applying classroom skills to meaningful work experiences, often related to their major at a time when fewer resources was the norm. To encourage higher student performance, Carter encouraged faculty to raise expectations, increased admissions standards incrementally over the next three years, and modified the institution's gradated good-standing policy to a 2.0 for all undergraduate students.

Chancellor Carter also believed that student engagement is a great factor in students' overall success at the university. He said, "Experiences in residence life, in student life activities, in our campus environment itself, and in the relationship students have with one another and with faculty and staff" serve to promote student success. Consequently, in 2011, the "#BraveNationCelebration" was initiated to encourage residential students to remain on campus and stay engaged for the weekend. Chancellor

Carter also reminded the university that "our institutional trademark must continue to be 'Where Learning Gets Personal.' …We must retain the personal interaction with our students in as many ways as possible." Emphasis was placed on undergraduate and graduate students engaged in mentored research with faculty to enhance the student academic experience. Students continued to develop research skills in the UNCP Biofuels Project, RISE (Research Initiative for Scientific Enhancement) Program, and Biotechnology Research and Training Center. Programs like living and learning communities in the residence halls and service learning were expanded. As an example of engaged learning, a team of four master of business administration (MBA) students in 2012 developed a plan to revitalize the Laurinburg-Maxton Airport. Chancellor Carter heralded the new "teacher-scholar" model of faculty instruction when he said that UNC Pembroke was "a university where research informs our teaching and enhances student learning." Endowed professorships, by bringing world-class scholars to campus, are another way to increase faculty scholarship. To that end, the Marion Bass Distinguished Professorship in Science, Technology, Engineering, and Mathematics was endowed after a $250,000 gift from the C.D. Spangler Foundation Inc. The gift was matched by the North Carolina General Assembly's Distinguished Professors Endowment Trust Fund. This was UNC Pembroke's eleventh endowed distinguished professorship, and the fourth funded by the Spangler Foundation.

Chancellor Carter also initiated several traditions to enhance the student experience and their affinity for the campus. In the fall of 2010, prior to the start of classes, first-year students had a class photograph taken on the Quad and then embarked on the "Brave Walk" northward over the Jones Bridge to First Year Student Convocation in the Givens Performing Arts Center. The northward crossing of the bridge symbolizes the students' entrance into the university community. At graduation, the students walk south across the bridge, a symbolic passage into a future rich with possibilities. In the spring of 2011, separate undergraduate and

FIGURE 8.5. *Brave Walk. As freshmen, students' northward crossing of the Jones Bridge symbolizes the students' entrance into the university community. At graduation, students walk south across the bridge, a symbolic passage into a future rich with possibilities.*

graduate Commencement ceremonies were first held. The spring undergraduate ceremony was held outdoors in the Quad. As with Chancellor Carter's installation ceremony, a Lumbee flute player and the Lumbee Ambassadors led the processional and recessional. Another tradition introduced a new name to campus. The need to replace the damaged costume for the university's red-tailed hawk mascot prompted a discussion of the mascot's unofficial name of "Tommy Hawk." On February 23, 2013, the costumed mascot was officially named "BraveHawk." As a play on the word "tomahawk," many believed the term "Tommy Hawk" promoted stereotypes of Indians as savages. BraveHawk, which combined the athletic nickname and mascot, was selected by an overwhelming majority of students, faculty, staff, and alumni who responded to a survey.

Efforts to promote student success began to show signs of progress. Increased admission standards, along with the new academic standing policy and higher expectations, resulted in improved retention rates and increased student performance, improvements that laid the foundation for improved graduation rates.

The Carter administration also recognized student successes in other ways. On May 5, 2012, the chancellor presented twenty-three graduating veterans with honor cords and university challenge coins. He said, "We are proud of you and proud that we have been of service to the men and women of the U.S. military. We take great pride in being a military-friendly school, and we hope to provide even better service to veterans and active-duty soldiers in the future." The ceremony became an annual tradition. Also that fall, former Student Government Association presidents gathered to dedicate the SGA Presidents' Wall of Honor, which featured bronze etchings of every SGA president dating back to 1947. The wall is located on the second floor of the James B. Chavis University Center near the student government offices. In March 2013 SGA president Robert Nunnery was elected president of the Association of Student Governments. The ASG represents the students of all UNC system universities. Nunnery is UNC Pembroke's first ASG president. In December 2012 UNC Pembroke named the first class of Chancellor's Ambassadors. The ambassadors are a select group of outstanding scholars and student leaders who serve as student representatives at events sponsored by Chancellor and Sarah Carter.

As a tribute to its emphasis on student success, UNC Pembroke continued to receive and to celebrate the national recognition it was receiving for student achievements. *The Aurochs* was named one of the best student literary magazines in North Carolina in 2010 by the North Carolina College Media Association. UNC Pembroke was named a "2012 Military Friendly School"—for the fifth consecutive year—by *G.I. Jobs* magazine. In 2013 Military Advanced Education named the school to its "2013 Guide to Military-Friendly Colleges & Universities." The university's 2011 and 2012 nursing graduates recorded a 100 percent passing rate on the National Council Licensure Examination (NCLEX-RN).

In 2013, for the fifth time since 2007, UNC Pembroke was placed on the President's Higher Education Community Service Honor Roll. Also that year, *The Pine Needle* won first place in the American Scholastic Press Association national contest and was recognized for the fifth consecutive year as one of the best college and university newspapers in the nation.

The Braves continued to excel in athletic competition in the NCAA Division II and the Peach Belt Conference (PBC) between 2010 and 2013—a period that was filled with innumerable team and individual accomplishments. The 2010–2011 season proved to be the best overall since UNC Pembroke joined the PBC in 1992. The athletic program achieved its highest-ever finish in the Learfield Sports Directors' Cup Standings. The Braves finished at number 61—out of 235 teams, and third best in the conference. The individual athletic highlight of the period occurred when wrestler Mike Williams won the 2012 national championship at the 165-pound weight class. He was UNC Pembroke's first national champion in wrestling and the university's first national champion in any sport since 1982. The following year, Williams finished in third place and Daniel Ownbey (141) in eighth place at the 2012–2013 NCAA championship. Women's golfer Meghan Moore finished in second place in the 2012 NCAA national tournament. The Braves also won numerous team conference championships. They included baseball (2011), men's golf (2012), and women's golf (2011). Katja Dammann '11 won the individual conference championship in women's golf in 2011. Golfers Jordan Walor '12 and Moore were named the PBC men's and women's Golfer of the Year in 2012. Cross country runners Pardon Ndhlovu '13 and Livia Mahaffie '13 were named the men's and women's PBC Runner of the Year in 2011.

FIGURE 8.6. *BraveHawk.*

The following season, Ndhlovu was again named the men's Runner of the Year while Mahaffie won individual PBC titles. Ndhlovu was also recognized as the USTFCCCA (US Track & Field and Cross Country Coaches Association) Male Athlete of the Year for the Southeast Region for the 2011-2012 season. He set the school record for the 8K cross-country race in 2012. By the time of his graduation in 2013 Ndhlovu recorded the eight best times in school history.

Numerous teams and individuals also earned invitations to the NCAA tournament. The men's basketball team, after making a run to the 2011 PBC tournament championship game, received the program's first invitation ever from the NCAA. Two years later, in 2013, they made a second appearance in the NCAA tournament. Other teams invited to participate in the NCAA tournament included baseball (2011), men's cross country (2010, 2011, 2012), women's cross country (2010, 2011, 2012), men's golf (2011, 2012), women's golf (2011, 2012), men's soccer (2012), men's track and field (2011, 2012, 2013), women's track and field (2011), and wrestling (2011). Individuals receiving bids to the NCAA tournament during the 2010–2011 season were Ndhlovu (men's cross country), women's golfer Dammann, Jonathan McCurry '12 (men's golf), Maurice Eubanks (men's track and field—100m, 200m), and wrestlers Mike Williams at the 165-pound weight class, Russell Weakley '11 (125), Brendon Parker-Risk (157), and Timdarius Thurston (133). Williams won the regional wrestling championship. Participating in their respective national tournaments in 2011–2012 were Walor (men's golf), Moore (women's golf), men's cross country runners Ndhlovu and Chris Schroll, and wrestlers Ownbey (141) and Shane Nolan '12 (197). During the 2012–2013 season, Braves invited to the NCAA tournament were women's golfer Moore, and wrestlers Ownbey (141), Justin Pencook (157), Blaze Shade (165), and Williams (174). Ownbey and Pencook won regional championships.

There were other athletic achievements during the period. Five UNC Pembroke coaches were named PBC Coach of the Year. Fifty Braves were named All-Americans for their athletic and academic achievements. Dammann (women's golf) was named the 2010–2011 PBC Scholar-Athlete of the Year, and UNC Pembroke received the 2011 Presidents' Academic Award—its second consecutive season—for the highest overall grade point average among student-athletes. UNC Pembroke also set a school record and led the league with 159 student-athletes named to the PBC Presidential Honor Roll during the 2012–2013 season. It marked the fourth straight season that UNC Pembroke had been represented by 100 or more student-athletes on the honor roll.

Another goal essential to the future success of UNC Pembroke was the establishment of a culture and climate that would make it the first choice or "institution of choice" for students in the region and state. Chancellor Carter recognized that students chose a university for a number of reasons—academic programs, on-campus amenities, student life, facilities, affordability, proximity, and welcoming environment. To boost UNC Pembroke's distinctiveness and appeal, new academic and administrative programs were launched to expand the curriculum, enhance student services and the campus's educational environment, and, more importantly, create a robust campus experience. In the spring of 2013 the university also undertook a project to rebrand its image through the development of a new logo, "wordmark," and tagline. Efforts were also initiated to revamp the university's online presence with a redesign of the university's website that will focus on engaging prospective students, alumni, and donors.

UNC Pembroke's curriculum broadened on February 8, 2013, when the UNC Board of Governors approved the university's proposal to offer a master of science in nursing (MSN). The Department of Nursing enrolled twenty students in the first cohort in the fall of 2013. The program offers three concentrations: nurse educator, clinical nurse leader, and rural case manager. Other academic minors and concentrations were added during the period. With the addition of the MSN, UNC Pembroke offers a total of forty-one undergraduate and eighteen graduate degree programs. Several academic programs earned key accreditations, making the university more appealing to undergraduate and graduate students. Most notably, the School of Business was accredited by the AACSB International (Association to Advance Collegiate Schools of Business). The Art Department earned accreditation from the National Association of Schools of Art and Design (NASAD). The department became one of only five NASAD-accredited institutions in North Carolina. The master of social work (MSW) program won full accreditation from the National Council on Social Work Education. The Clinical Mental Health Program and Professional School Counseling Program earned accreditation from the Council for Accreditation of Counseling and Related Education Programs (CACREP). As Chancellor Carter noted, the accreditations symbolized the "quality and excellence" of UNC Pembroke's academic programs.

The construction of state-of-the-art facilities and the presence of cutting-edge technology in the classrooms also distinguish UNC Pembroke from other universities in the region. On August 14, 2012, the $29 million Health Sciences Building opened on the north end of campus. The eighty-seven-thousand-square-foot structure is home to the Nursing and Social Work Departments. The bachelor of science in nursing (BSN) program, housed since 2005 in Lumberton on the campus of Southeastern Regional Medical Center, relocated to the new facility. In addition to being the greenest building on campus and LEED (Leadership in Energy and Environment Design)–certified silver, the Health Sciences Building features an atrium and $3 million in technology with smart classrooms and seven clinical learning centers with simulated nursing environments, including an operating room, obstetrics, intensive care, pediatrics, psychiatry, and home health. Remote-controlled mannequins or patient simulators, which talk, have heart attacks, and give birth, serve as patients, while nursing faculty control them from observation rooms. The building also houses a food court with Papa John's Pizza and Einstein Brothers Bagels—complements to the Starbucks Coffee brought to campus by Carter in 2011. State Sen. David Weinstein of Lumberton played a key role in making the building a reality. Chancellor Carter described Weinstein as a "great friend of higher education and of this university." Senator Weinstein called the building his greatest accomplishment as a legislator. The construction of the Health Sciences Building, coupled with an outstanding passing rate on the NCLEX-RN, led Chancellor Carter to proudly proclaim UNC Pembroke nursing as "one of the top programs in the state." The Health Sciences Building also features a new campus landmark funded through the generous gifts of donors. Embedded in a terrazzo floor at the entrance to the building is a medicine wheel carried on the back of a turtle. The medicine wheel represents the university's connection to its founding by Lumbee Indians. It is also an ancient symbol of health, balance, and well-being, which is fitting in a building devoted to health. The turtle is the symbol of the creation story of Eastern Woodland Indians.

FIGURE 8.7. *Medicine Wheel. Located in the floor of the lobby in the Health Sciences Building.*

In the fall of 2011 Cypress Residence Hall, an ultramodern, five-story, 476-bed residential facility, opened on the north end of campus. It features 119 four-person suites. Of those, 94 have two double-occupancy bedrooms, and 25 suites feature four single-occupancy rooms. In each suite, there is a shared common area and a shared bathroom. The construction of Cypress Hall coupled with the university's assumption of management of the University Courtyard Apartments on University Road on July 1, 2012, brought the number of bed spaces on campus to more than 2,000.

To accommodate the need for more administrative office space, Lindsay Hall, the former administration building for the Odum Baptist Home for Children, located across North Odum Street/Prospect Road from campus, was leased to house the offices of Advancement, Alumni Relations, University Communications and Marketing, the School of Graduate Studies, and Sponsored Research and Programs. The university also purchased 64 acres along Prospect Road on the north side of campus. The purchase increased the size of campus from 169 acres and forty-six buildings in 2010 to 230 acres and forty-nine buildings in 2013. Consequently, on February 20, 2012, a new master plan was displayed, detailing a greener and more pedestrian-friendly future that will be more welcoming to students and visitors. Over the next fifteen years, the plan called for the construction of a new library or "information commons," a new School of Business building, and a new athletic complex on the north end of campus.

Another quality of UNC Pembroke that continues to make it an institution of choice is its cost. Historically, UNC Pembroke has been one of the most affordable universities in North Carolina, which boasts the least expensive state-funded universities in the nation. Although costs associated with attending college in the United States continued to rise during the period, UNC Pembroke remained one of the most affordable in the state and nation. In 2012, annual tuition and fees for twelve or more undergraduate hours was $6,275 for in-state students and $15,482 for out-of-state students. Tuition and fees for nine or more graduate hours was $6,374 for in-state students and $15,701 for out-of-state students. Annual room and board ranged from $7,010 to $8,610 based on the residence hall and room (double, single-private, double-private). Apartment costs ranged from $4,450 to $5,650 annually.

From the beginning of his tenure, Chancellor Carter embraced UNC Pembroke's Indian heritage, a quality that made the school distinct among institutions of higher education in the United States. During his installation, Chancellor Carter remarked, "UNCP's heritage marks its character and shapes its future." In 2012 an innovative and bold move, rooted in the institution's past, served to shape the future of the institution and the region. While standing between the columns of historic Old Main on March 15, Chancellor Carter announced the establishment of the Southeast American Indian Studies (SAIS) Program with a goal to serve as the premier center for the study of Indians in the southeastern United States. The university, with its unique status as "North Carolina's Historically Indian University" and existing Indian programs, made an ideal setting for SAIS. Chancellor Carter said the program's "academic, research, and outreach missions will benefit all tribes in the Southeast and serve as a resource to all who are interested in American Indian life." He also remarked, "Within the UNC Pembroke campus, the program will act as the intersection between disciplines outside of American Indian studies to promote interdisciplinary curricula, research, and outreach about and for the American Indian." Chancellor Carter announced his intent for SAIS to become a stand-alone school alongside the schools of Business, Education, and Graduate Studies when it had fully established itself.

The Southeast American Indian Studies Program is a high-profile example of the Carter administration's efforts to engage the region—the final goal of the shared vision and strategic plan for UNC Pembroke. Chancellor Carter believes the university should be committed to using its programs and resources to improve the quality of life throughout southeastern North Carolina. He learned from the Listening Tour that citizens of the region want the university to become even more engaged in addressing regional issues related to education, health care, welfare, and economic development. To that end, members of the university community, as noted by Chancellor Carter, engaged with the local community to "bring their expertise and creative solutions to local problems." Chancellor Carter cultivated a close relationship between the university and the Lumbee Tribe. On October 20, 2011, he addressed the Lumbee Tribal Council and invited them to work with the university to increase the number of Indian high school graduates who attend college. Chancellor Carter also established the UNC Pembroke–Lumbee Tribe Advisory Committee. In an earlier effort to strengthen the connection between the university and the Lumbee community, Special Collections in the Mary Livermore Library announced the establishment of the Elmer W. Hunt Photograph Collection in 2010. The collection contained more than fifty-three thousand negatives of longtime community photographer Elmer Hunt '53, who also served as the university photographer from 1969 to 1973. In 2012, over fifteen thousand of the photos were made available to the public online. The collection generated quite a buzz in the Lumbee community, especially when the Library staged several special events for the community to identify individuals in the thousands of photos.

UNC Pembroke initiated other outreach and engagement efforts in the region. The Regional Center continued to expand the university's reach into the region through programs and courses, particularly its Continuing Education Program. Service-learning courses and opportunities expanded for students. UNC Pembroke, in partnership with the Public Schools of Robeson County and Communities in Schools, established a Literacy Commons to facilitate stronger community literacy in Robeson County through reading and writing. The service-learning opportunity allowed UNC Pembroke students to mentor Robeson County schoolchildren while simultaneously putting into practice theories learned in their coursework. UNC Pembroke also signed a number of articulation agreements with its community college partners—Bladen, Fayetteville Technical, Richmond, Robeson, and Sandhills—to foster a seamless transfer of students and their coursework to the university. As a result, Special Forces soldiers at Fort Bragg were provided with a pathway to complete degree programs online.

Faculty and student research also served to improve the quality of life and health of the region. In late 2011 UNC Pembroke joined a consortium of universities and other organizations to fight diabetes in North Carolina. That same year, graduate students in the elementary education program won a grant to purchase iPad tablets for classrooms in neighboring Bladen and Sampson Counties. Also that year, the university offered "locational advantage" grants that supported projects and efforts that took advantage of the university's location. As an example, in 2013 the Local Foods Connections Conference was held to support local foods in Robeson County, tout sustainable economic opportunities for farmers and rural communities, and promote healthy foods for consumers.

Another outreach effort sought to revitalize downtown Pembroke and give the university a presence there. Announced in February 2012, UNC Pembroke's Entrepreneurship Incubator would establish a business incubator in a renovated space that would house the university's Small Business and Technology Development Center and the Thomas Family Center for Entrepreneurship. Chancellor Carter described the effort as "a transformative project" that would "be a showcase for the town and the university." He saw the project as "the start of something really positive." The project was made possible through private funding and grants from the Golden Leaf Foundation and the U.S. Department of Commerce. Final funding was received in the summer of 2013.

The most exciting outreach and engagement program of the period was also the longest and largest celebration in the university's history. UNC Pembroke marked its 125th anniversary with a fourteen-month-long celebration from March 2012 to May 2013. The celebration was chaired by Patricia Fields '97, '10, executive director of

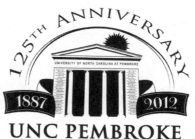

FIGURE 8.8. *125th Anniversary Celebration logo (2012).*

the Givens Performing Arts Center, and Lawrence T. Locklear '05, '12, web publisher with University Communications and Marketing. Honorary cochairs were Mickey Gregory '88, executive director of the Lumberton Visitors Bureau; Alphonzo McRae '74, vice president for Institutional Services at Robeson Community College; and Dr. Linda E. Oxendine, professor emeritus of American Indian studies at UNC Pembroke. The planning committee comprised students, faculty, staff, alumni, and members of the community. The theme of the celebration was, "Honoring Our Heritage, Soaring Toward Our Future!" To that end, the events celebrated the rich history and heritage of the institution while simultaneously showcasing the accomplishments of students, faculty, staff, and alumni. Contributing to the festive atmosphere and proclaiming the university's anniversary were black, gold, and white banners that lined the streets of campus and the town, and three banners, with a large 1-2-5, that were hung between the columns of historic Old Main. Heritage T-shirts,

FIGURE 8.9. *Unveiling of the 125th Anniversary celebration banners between the columns of historic Old Main on March 12, 2012.*

featuring each of the seven names the institution has had during its history, were sold throughout the celebration.

In recognition of UNC Pembroke's anniversary, the Lumbee Tribe in 2012 declared March 7 as a tribal holiday to be known as "UNC Pembroke Day." That same day, North Carolina congressman Mike McIntyre paid special tribute to UNC Pembroke during remarks from the floor of the U.S. House of Representatives. North Carolina governor Beverly Perdue also sent a letter of congratulations. There were also resolutions and proclamations honoring the university from the North Carolina Senate and House of Representatives, the Pembroke Town Council, and the Robeson County Board of Commissioners.

With motorcycles rumbling and the largest cake in the history of the university—perhaps even Robeson County—the celebration kicked off on March 14, 2012, with fanfare as the university community gathered in the Main Gym of the English E. Jones Health and Physical Education Center. A five-motorcycle procession, led by Chancellor Carter, roared into the gym to launch the celebration. Chancellor Carter was followed by his wife, Sarah, and the honorary chairs. Also in attendance were three of the institution's oldest living alumni: Beulah Mae (Ransom) Cormier '39, '52; Cattie Mae Hunt '41; and Tessie Hunt '42. They had front-row seats as cheerleaders rolled in a massive birthday cake. The kickoff featured performances by the Pep Band, cheerleaders, and Dark Water Rising, a local band led by Charly Lowry. The following day, Chancellor Carter announced the establishment of the Southeast American Indian Studies Program.

The celebration featured more than fifty events. To celebrate the university's heritage, the 125th Anniversary Celebration Powwow was held April 19, 2012. Kevin Gover, a member of the Pawnee Indian Nation and director of the Smithsonian's National Museum of the American Indian, was the featured speaker at the Spring 2012 undergraduate Commencement held in May in the Quad. In conjunction with the 125th celebration, the color of the tassel was permanently changed to gold, beginning with the May 2012 ceremony. Also, graduates wore special zipper pulls during the three Commencement ceremonies held during the 125th anniversary. That same month, Magdaline (Chavis) Canady '35, the university's oldest living graduate, celebrated her one hundredth birthday on May 30 with a party at her home attended by family, friends, and members of the UNC Pembroke staff. On October 22, 2012, "Reflections: A Review of UNCP's First 125 Years" featured a panel of alumni and faculty from the 1950s through the 1970s, including Larry Barnes '71, the first African American student to enroll at the university; longtime faculty member Dr. James Ebert; and alumni Emma Locklear '62, Pandora Strickland '61, Mary Alice (Pinchbeck) Teets '58, and Nat Tolar '70, who reflected on their experiences at the university. Also during Homecoming that fall, a "125th Choir," comprising 125 students, alumni, faculty, and staff, conducted by Chancellor Carter, sang the national anthem and the alma mater before the Braves October 27, 2012, football game against Newberry College.

There were other notable 125th Anniversary events. 2012 Olympic gold medalist Gabby Douglas spoke to a sold-out audience in the Givens Performing Arts Center as part of the Distinguished Speaker Series on February 25, 2013. Old Main's ninetieth anniversary was celebrated on March 5, 2013. Immediately following the Founders' Day Ceremony in the Givens Performing Arts Center on March 7, 2013, the Heritage Oak was dedicated in the Quad. Afterward, the Hawk Walk, a one-and-a-half-mile trail that snakes its way through campus, was officially opened. An attempt to break the Guinness World Record for the Longest Handshake Relay was held March 20, 2013. Although the world record was not broken, a UNC Pembroke record for the longest handshake relay was set with 387 participants. BraveHawk began the handshake relay and Chancellor Kyle and Sarah Carter completed the relay. The 125th Fun Run was held March 23, 2013. It featured a three-mile run/walk from the center of the current campus to the site of the original campus at Pates and back.

A one-mile run/walk was held on a portion of Hawk Walk trail. On March 27, 2013, "UNCP's African American Firsts: Celebrating Their Legacy!" recognized African American student firsts at UNC Pembroke, which included the first to enroll (Larry Barnes '71) and graduate (Sylvia [Baugham] Banks '69), and the first Student Government Association president (Delthine Watson '84) and Miss Pembroke State University (Renee Steele '93). On April 28, 2013, composer James Hosay's *Sing, Pray, Shout: A Lumbee River Revival* was premiered by the UNCP Concert Band. Commissioned for the 125th celebration, the work highlighted the influences of gospel music in the area and the importance of the Lumbee River—the Indian name for the Lumber River.

The Board of Governors honored the university's 125th anniversary by holding its April 10–12, 2013, meeting on campus. UNC Pembroke show-cased its academic programs, state-of-the-art campus, and engaged student body to the UNC system's leadership—many of whom had never visited the Pembroke campus. Gov. Pat McCrory took advantage of the moment to address the board on April 11 and make his first official visit to campus. Before his speech, Governor McCrory wished UNC Pembroke a happy birthday. He proclaimed, "You should be proud of the heritage and your history, and what you're doing for this region."

FIGURE 8.10. *Chancellor Kyle R. Carter (left) with Gov. Pat McCrory during an April 2013 visit to campus.*

The 125th Anniversary Celebration came to a close during Commencement weekend, held May 3–4, 2013. Baccalaureate degrees were conferred on 605 graduates on Saturday morning, and master's degrees were conferred on 184 graduate students on Friday evening; both were university records. The undergraduate ceremony was held Saturday, May 4, in the Quad and marked the final 125th Anniversary event. Father John Gillespie set the tone for the ceremony during the invocation when he noted the vision of the founders of the institution. He said, "We...give thanks...for the founders of this institution. One hundred and twenty-five years ago, it was their vision...that freed others to have different dreams for the future." Also recognized and in attendance were family members of the class of 1940, the first graduates to receive four-year degrees; the family of Christian White, the first white graduate in 1954; and Sylvia (Baugham) Banks, the first African American graduate in 1969. The inaugural Chancellor's Award of Excellence was presented to Patricia Fields and Lawrence T. Locklear, cochairs of the 125th Anniversary Committee, for service rendered to the university during the fourteen-month celebration.

The keynote speaker was Arlinda Locklear, a Pembroke native and Lumbee Indian, and the first Indian woman to argue a case before the U.S. Supreme Court. She is a nationally recognized advocate for Indian rights, and for many years, the Washington, DC-based attorney represented the Lumbee Tribe's efforts to win federal recognition. Prior to her remarks, she was conferred an honorary doctor of laws degree.

FIGURE 8.11. *Dr. Arlinda Locklear. Keynote speaker and recipient of an honorary doctor of laws degree at the Spring 2013 undergraduate Commencement ceremony.*

Locklear drew on the lessons of the university's founders to challenge the next generation of graduates "to live lives of purpose." She said the founders were simple men who did extraordinary things. "They were able to do these things because they led lives of purpose, and by their purpose, blessed you all with the university from which you graduate today." She noted, "A life of purpose begins with a vision, a goal, a notion of what is not

FIGURE 8.12. *Graduates celebrating at the conclusion of the Spring 2013 undergraduate Commencement ceremony.*

now but what could be." Locklear continued, "The founding trustees of this university knew that a vision requires hard work. It requires dedication. It requires commitment. It requires persistence. When you apply these qualities to a vision, anything is possible." She exhorted the graduates, "Apply the same purposefulness going forward, and you will reflect well on the legacy of the founding fathers." Locklear then said, "What I ask now is that you make a leap of imagination for the future. Imagine what you would like to see in the world and set about to make it so. This is precisely what the founding trustees of this campus did with their lives. Now, 125 years later, we celebrate them and their accomplishment. Dare to be as bold as they were, and perhaps 125 years hence, this campus will celebrate your accomplishments and lives."

At the end of its first 125 years of service, the University of North Carolina at Pembroke looked to its past to measure how far it had come and to guide it for the future. The school had faced many problems and obstacles, but it endured; it became a source of hope and opportunity, first for Indians, later for all people. Since 1887 the university had produced twenty-two thousand alumni, all justifiably proud of UNC Pembroke's past and confident in its future. While adversity and controversy had visited its history, progress has been the shining star, guiding its path. From its inception as the Croatan Normal School in 1887 to become a constituent institution of the University of North Carolina system, UNC Pembroke has had a proud history, indeed a remarkable history. As the 2013 *Indianhead* proclaimed, "What once was a dream is now a living legacy."

Hail to UNCP!

TIMELINE OF NOTABLE INSTITUTIONAL EVENTS (2010–2013)

2010
- Dr. Kyle R. Carter named fifth chancellor.
- Awarded the CASE (Council for the Advancement and Support of Education) Educational Fundraising "Overall Improvement Award."
- Elmer W. Hunt Photograph Collection established.
- First-Year Student Convocation initiated.
- Brave Walk begun.
- University Address first held.

2011
- First "Last Lecture" held.
- Spring undergraduate Commencement held in the Quad.
- Cypress Residence Hall opened.
- UNC Pembroke–Lumbee Tribe Advisory Committee established.

2012
- Mike Williams won the NCAA Division II national championship in wrestling in the 165-pound weight class.
- Entrepreneurship Incubator in downtown Pembroke announced.
- 125th Anniversary Celebration kicked off.
- Southeast American Indian Studies Program established.
- Marion Bass Distinguished Professorship in Science, Technology, Engineering, and Mathematics endowed.
- Health Sciences Building opened.
- SGA Presidents' Wall of Honor dedicated.
- First Class of Chancellor's Ambassadors named.

2013
- Costumed mascot named "BraveHawk."
- Master of science in nursing added.
- UNC system Board of Governors held meeting on campus; Gov. Pat McCrory addressed the board and made first official visit to campus.
- 125th Anniversary Celebration concluded.

Appendix A

AN ACT TO ESTABLISH A NORMAL SCHOOL
IN THE COUNTY OF ROBESON

The General Assembly of North Carolina do enact:

SECTION 1. That W. L. Moore, James Oxendine, James Dial, Preston Lock-lear, and others who may be associated with them, and their successors, are hereby constituted a body politic and corporate, for educational purposes, in the county of Robeson, under the name and style of the trustees of the Croatan Normal School, and by that name may have perpetual succession, may sue and be sued, plead and be impleaded, contract and be contracted with, to have and to hold school property, including buildings, lands, and all appurtenances thereto, situated in the county of Robeson, at any place in said county to be selected by the trustees herein named, provided such place shall be located between Bear Swamp and Lumber River in said county; to acquire by purchase, donation, or otherwise, real and personal property for the purpose of establishing and maintaining a school of high grade for teachers of the Croatan race in North Carolina.

SEC. 2. That the trustees at their organization shall elect one of their own number president of the board of trustees, whose duties shall be such as develops upon such officers in similar cases, or such hereafter be defined by said trustees.

SEC. 3. That said trustees shall have full power to rent, lease, mortgage or sell any real or personal property for the purpose of maintaining said school, discharging indebtedness, or reinvesting the proceeds for a like purpose: *Provided*, that the liabilities of said trustees shall affect only the property owned by said trustees for educational purposes and shall not affect the private credit of said trustees.

SEC. 4. That the trustees whose names are mentioned in the first section of this act shall have the power to select three additional trustees from the Croatan race in such manner as they may determine.

SEC. 5. That said trustees shall have full power and authority to employ a teacher or teachers in said normal school under such regulations as the said trustees may determine.

SEC. 6. That said board of trustees shall have full power to fill all vacancies by death, removal, or otherwise in said board: *Provided*, a majority vote of all the trustees shall be necessary to a choice.

SEC. 7. That the sum of five hundred dollars is hereby appropriated to the support of said school annually for two years, and no longer, commencing with the first day of January, one thousand eight hundred and eighty-eight, said sum to be paid out of the general education fund: *Provided*, That said sum thus appropriated shall be expended for the payment of services rendered for teaching and for no other purpose; said sum to be paid in semiannual payments upon warrants drawn by the State superintendent of public instruction upon receipt by said superintendent of report of trustees of said school showing the number of teachers employed, the amount paid to the teacher, the number of students in attendance during the term of six months next preceding the first day of July, one thousand eight hundred and eighty-eight, first day of January, one thousand eight hundred and eighty-nine, first day of July, one thousand eight hundred and eighty-nine, and the first day of January, one thousand eight hundred and ninety.

SEC. 8. That all property, real and personal, acquired by purchase, donation, or otherwise, as long as it is used for educational purposes, shall be exempt from taxation, whether on the part of the State or county.

SEC. 9. That no person shall sell any spiritous liquors within two miles of the location of said school, and any person violating this section shall be guilty of a misdemeanor, and upon conviction shall be fined not less than ten dollars nor more than thirty dollars, or imprisoned not less than ten days nor more than thirty days, or both at the discretion of the court.

SEC. 10. *Provided* that no person shall be admitted into said school as a student who has not attained the age of fifteen years; and that all those who shall enjoy the privileges of said school as students shall previously obligate to teach the youth of the Croatan race for a stated period.

SEC. 11. That this act shall be in force from and after its ratification.

In the General Assembly read three times, and ratified this 7th day of March. A.D. 1887.

[Laws of North Carolina, 1887—Chapter 400.]

Appendix B

MEMBERS OF THE BOARD OF TRUSTEES,
1887–2013

Allen, Curtis H., II '97 (ex officio)
Barrett, Wiley '69
Bass, Marion '65
Bell, James F. "Buddy" '58
Biggs, Murchison Bo
Blackwell, Breeden '68
Bleecker, Robert
Blue, Kellie '93
Bonner, Donald
Bowman, Phillip '01 (ex officio)
Brayboy, Isaac
Brewton, Terrance '95 (ex officio)
Britt, Joe Freeman
Britt, William Earl
Brooks, James Olin
Brooks, John
Brooks, Martin L.
Brooks, Tim
Brown, Ernest
Bullard, Becky
Bullard, Early

Bullard, Lester
Bullard, Sybil J.
Burch, Barry '09, Jr. (ex officio)
Burns, B.O.
Burns, Scott (ex officio)
Campbell, William '88 (ex officio)
Campbell, D.M. "Mac", Jr. '68
Carter, John L. '26, '29, '43
Caton, Robert "Bob"
Chavis, Benjamin
Chavis, Ernest
Coleman, Van '74 (ex officio)
Collins, Sybil (Lowry) '76
Conway, Percy Lee '73 (ex officio)
Cummings, Jay
Cummings, John
Cummings, McDuffie '74
Cummings, Robin
Davis, Brandon (ex officio)
Davis, Robert B.
Dial, Adolph L. '43

Dial, Herman
Dial, James E., Sr.
Emanuel, George '33
Epps, Frank
Evans, Wayne
Finch, Beth (Dail)
Freeman, Tommy "Brian" '92 (ex officio)
George, Fred
Gersh, Benjamin C. '99 (ex officio)
Gibson, M. Carr
Godwin, W.H.
Gospojevic, Marko '06 (ex officio)
Griswold, Kenneth '97 (ex officio)
Hafner, Nadean '05 (ex officio)
Hammond, Stephen A., Sr.
Hammonds, A.E.
Hammonds, James H.
Hammonds, Ronald
Hammonds, Steve, Jr.
Harris, Elias
Hatton, Veronica '03 (ex officio)
Hillman, James E. (ex officio)
Hostetler, Charles
Huffman, Joseph Chandler '94 (ex officio)
Humphrey, Dwight '10 (ex officio)
Hunt, Milton
Inscoe, Mark (ex officio)
Jacobs, Lonnie W. '25, '28
Jacobs, Marvin '09 (ex officio)
Jernigan, Lora Ann
Jones, John Robert
Jones, Thomas, II
Jones, Vanessa (ex officio)

Kennedy, Ken '78 (ex officio)
Lennon, Wayland, III '85 (ex officio)
Lewis, Henry G. '73
Little, Hal
Locklear, Anderson N.
Locklear, Arlinda
Locklear, Cheryl M. '75
Locklear, Gary '70
Locklear, Gaston
Locklear, George W.
Locklear, Harry W.
Locklear, Joanne '77
Locklear, Malachi
Locklear, Preston
Lowery, Dennis '64
Lowry, A.G.
Lowry, Burlin
Lowry, D.F. '05
Lowry, Derek '76 (ex officio)
Lowry, Donna '13
Lowry, Edmond
Lowry, Elmer T. '27
Lowry, Harvey '52
Lowry, Ira Pate '29
Lowry, James R.
Lowry, John R.
Lowry, Martin Luther, Sr.
Lowry, Ralph H.
Lowry, Zeb A. '25, '31
Mallard, Raymond B.
Marks, Leroy
Maynor, Carl L. '31
Maynor Locklear, Janie (Maynor) '66
McCormick, Brian J. '10, '12 (ex officio)
McDuffie, David (ex officio)

Appendix C

HEADS OF THE INSTITUTION

W.L. (William Luther) Moore, principal, 1888–1889

Ezra Bauder, principal, 1889–1890

W.L. (William Luther) Moore, principal, January–March 1891

Charles Stewart, principal, 1891–1894

D.B. (David Balharrie) Simpson, principal, 1894–1895

Isaac W. Lanner, principal, 1895–1896

P.B. (Philip Barbour) Hiden, principal, 1896–1898

G.W. Jones, principal, 1898–1899

O.(Oscar) R. Sampson, principal, 1899 (completed Jones' fall term)

T.C. (Thomas Calhoun) Henderson, principal, 1900–1904

M.E. Clark, principal, 1905

D.F. (Doctor Fuller) Lowry, principal, 1905–1906 (completed Clark's fall 1905 term)

T.M. (Thomas Moore) Seawell, principal, 1906–1907

H.L. (Henry Luther) Edens, principal, 1908–1912

O.V. (Otto Vetas) Hamrick Sr., principal, 1912–1914

H.A. (Henry Augustus) Neal, principal, 1914–1918

T.C. (Thomas Calhoun) Henderson, principal and later superintendent, 1918–1922

A.B. (Andrew Beckett) Riley, superintendent, 1922–1926

S.B. (Sherman Bryan) Smithey, superintendent, 1926–1929

J.E. (John Ephraim) Sawyer, superintendent, 1929–1935

G.G. (Grover Gaines) Maughon Sr., superintendent, 1935–1940

Dr. O.H. (Owens Hand) Browne, acting superintendent, 1940–1941; acting president, 1941–1942

Dr. Ralph D. Wellons, president, 1942–1956

Dr. Walter J. Gale, president, 1956–1962

Dr. English E. Jones, interim president, 1962–1963; president, 1963–1972; chancellor, 1972–1979; chancellor emeritus, 1979–1981

Dr. Paul R. Givens, chancellor, 1979–1989; chancellor emeritus, 1989–2004

Dr. Joseph B. Oxendine, chancellor, 1989–1999; chancellor emeritus, 1999–present

Dr. Allen C. Meadors, chancellor, 1999–2009; chancellor emeritus, 2009–present

Dr. Charles R. Jenkins, interim chancellor, 2009–2010

Dr. Kyle R. Carter, chancellor, 2010–present

Appendix D

LAND ACQUISITIONS, 1907–2013

A. E.L. and Lizzie Odum, 10 acres, 1907.

B. Edward Hunt and John Hunt, 5 acres, 1923.

C. Billy W. Lowry and Pates Supply Co. Inc. (Trustees), 5 acres, 1970.

D. Billy W. and Flora Lowry, 3 acres, 1930.

E. William H. and Crossie Lowry, 7 acres, 1930.

F. Crossie Lowry, James Lee and Etta Mae Locklear Lowry, Walter J. and Bertha Pinchbeck, Seavy and Nettie Brooks Lowry, and Raymond and Lockeye Lowry Deese, 5.7 acres, 1960.

G. Crossie Lowry and W.H. Lowry Heirs, 11.5 acres, 1967.

H. Robeson County Board of Education, 7.5 acres, 1981.

I. Wilbert and Leona Carter, 0.35 acre, 1972.

J. Orville Lowry, 0.35 acre, 1972.

K. Orville Lowry, 0.35 acre, 1972.

L. Letha Lowry, Linda Robertson, and Craig Lowry, 0.35 acre, 1975.

M. Letha Lowry, Linda Robertson, and Craig Lowry, 0.35 acre, 1975.

N. Letha Lowry, Linda Robertson, and Craig Lowry, 0.35 acre, 1975.

O. Harold and Ira Lee Lowry, 0.35 acre, 1975.

P. Dorsey and Gola Lowry, 0.35 acre, 1975.

Q. Dorsey and Gola Lowry, 0.35 acre, 1975.

R. Crossie Lowry and W.H. Lowry (Estate), 10.23 acres, 1972.

S. Stella Lowry (John R. Lowry Estate), 5.1 acres, 1972.

T. Raeford and Sallie Sampson, 1 acre, 1975.

U. Solomon L. Sanderson (Lifetime Estate), Clay B. Sanderson, Roderick D. Sanderson and Alex L. Sanderson, 1 acre, 2013.

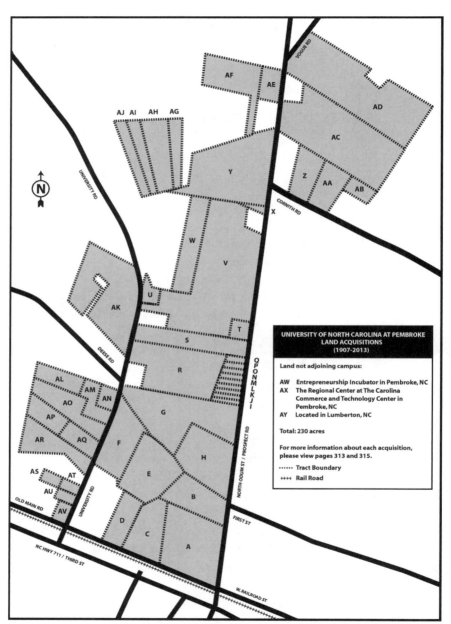

MAP AP.I. *Land acquisitions (1907–2013)*
Boundaries of tracts superimposed on 2013 map of campus.

V.   Walter and Wilma (Clark) Sanderson, 23 acres, 1974.

W.   John Calvin and Eula Mae Oxendine, 5 acres, 1976.

X.   Angela Woodell and Wayne S. Hawks, 0.37 acre, 2003.

Y.   Zimmie Chavis et. al., 13 acres, 2000.

Z.   Jerry Deese, 3.53 acres, 2013.

AA.   Jimmy Deese, 3.52 acres, 2012.

AB.   Jimmy Deese, 1.48 acres, 2013.

AC.   Tonya Deese Jacobs, 17.06 acres, 2012.

AD.   Corby and Theramae Deese, 19.8 acres, 2011.

AE.   Marvin C. Agent, Pamela Agent, Sherry Chavis and Ronnie Chavis, 1.73 acres, 2013.

AF.   Sherry (Lowry) Chavis and Pamela (Lowry) Agent, 5.72 acres, 2013.

AG.   Hughes D. and Mary Lowry, 2.15 acres, 2012.

AH.   Hughes D. and Mary Lowry, 4.33 acres, 2012.

AI.   Maitland Growe et. al, 2.15 acres, 2005.

AJ.   Dorsey Van and Jeannette Lowry et. al., 2.15 acres, 2005.

AK.   Edith Rose Deese and et. als., 12.8 acres, 2000.

AL.   Harrelton and Flora Margaret D. Woodell, 2.2 acres, 1996.

AM.   Henry E. and Mary Alice P. Teets, 1.8 acres, 1996.

AN.   Bertha L. Pinchbeck, 1 acre, 1996.

AO.   Bertha L. Pinchbeck, 4.3 acres, 1996.

AP.   Max E. Lowry, 2.3 acres, 1996.

AQ.   Harold B. and Laura L. Locklear, 2 acres, 1996.

AR.   Etta Mae Lowry, James Garnie and Annie Pearl Lowry, Sanford and Marie L. Lowry, Joan Lowry, Joel Brant Lowry, Kara Elizabeth Lowry, and Jamie Brant Ransom, 4.2 acres, 1996.

AS.   P.J. Smith, 0.5 acre, 2006.

AT.   James B. and Eleanor Ebert, 0.5 acre, 2005.

AU.   Kenneth P. Johnson, 0.5 acre, 2002.

AV.   Larry M. and Rose Marie Townsend, 0.75 acre, 2000.

AW.   Pembroke Furniture Company, Inc. and Pembroke Oil Company, Inc., 0.38 acre, 2013 (site of Entrepreneurship Incubator in Pembroke).

AX.   The Carolina and Commerce Technology Center, 12 acres, 2002 (site of The Regional Center at COMtech).

AY.   Robert T. and Patricia K. Godley and William C. and Ruth K. Godley, 4.15 acres, 2005 (located in Lumberton, NC).

Appendix E

UNC BOARD OF GOVERNORS AWARD FOR
EXCELLENCE IN TEACHING

1995   Dr. Bonnie Kelley, Department of Biology

1996   Dr. Kathryn Rileigh, Department of Psychology

1997   Dr. Harold Teague, Department of Chemistry and Physics

1998   Dr. David Eliades, Department of History

1999   Dr. Peter A. Wish, Department of Chemistry and Physics

2000   Dr. Richard Vela, Department of English, Theatre, and Foreign Languages

2001   Dr. Shelby Stephenson, Department of English, Theatre, and Foreign Languages

2002   Dr. Paul A. Flowers, Department of Chemistry and Physics

2003   Dr. Jeffery L Geller, Department of Philosophy and Religion

2004   Dr. Patricia Valenti, Department of English, Theatre, and Foreign Languages

2005   Dr. Nancy Barrineau, Department of English, Theatre, and Foreign Languages

2006   Dr. Robert W. Brown, Department of History

2007   Dr. Jose D'Arruda, Department of Chemistry and Physics

2008   Dr. Mark Canada, Department of English, Theatre, and Foreign Languages

2009   Dr. Susan Cannata, Department of English, Theatre, and Foreign Languages

2010   Dr. Beth Maisonpierre, Department of Music

2011   Dr. Joseph P. Lakatos, School of Business

2012   Dr. David Nikkel, Department of Philosophy and Religion

2013   Dr. Tim Ritter, Department of Chemistry and Physics

Appendix F

125TH ANNIVERSARY CELEBRATION
COMMITTEE

COCHAIRS

- Patricia Fields '97, '10, executive director, Givens Performing Arts Center
- Lawrence T. Locklear '05, '12, web publisher, University Communications and Marketing

HONORARY COCHAIRS

- Mickey Gregory '88, executive director, Lumberton Visitors Bureau
- Alphonzo McRae '74, vice president for Institutional Services, Robeson Community College
- Dr. Linda E. Oxendine, professor emeritus, American Indian Studies

Dorothy Blue '55, retired educator, Public Schools of Robeson County
Kellie Blue '93, Board of Trustees and finance director, Robeson County
Sandy Briscar, executive director, University Communications and Marketing
Sarah Carter, wife of Chancellor Kyle R. Carter
SallyAnn Clark, broadcast and emerging media manager, Mass Communication
Mia Goodman, student
Amira Hunt '91, clerk, town of Pembroke
Kim Hunt, past president, Pembroke Area Chamber of Commerce
Dr. Mary Ann Jacobs, chair, American Indian Studies

Wendy Lowery '99, '07, vice chancellor for advancement
Beatrice Maynor, Lumbee Tribe of North Carolina
Brian McCormick '10, '12, president, Student Government Association (2011–2012)
Robert Nunnery, president, Student Government Association (2012–2013)
Tasha Oxendine '95, '09, public relations officer, Public Schools of Robeson County
Mike Severy, director, Student Involvement and Leadership
Dr. Sara Simmons, professor, School of Education
Annette Straub, executive assistant, Enrollment
Dr. Richard Vela, professor, English, Theatre, and Foreign Languages
Mark Vesley, facility superintendent, Facilities Operations
Mary Helen Walker '94, '97, director, Disability Support Services

Appendix G

125TH ANNIVERSARY CELEBRATION EVENTS

UNC Pembroke held a fourteen-month-long celebration of its 125th Anniversary, which began with a kickoff on March 14, 2012, and concluded with the undergraduate Commencement ceremony on May 4, 2013. Heritage T-shirts, featuring each of the seven names the institution has had during its history, were sold throughout the celebration.

- March 12, 2012: Unfurling of 125th Anniversary banners hanging between the columns of Old Main
- March 14, 2012: 125th Anniversary Kickoff
- March 15, 2012: Announcement of establishment of Southeast American Indian Studies Program
- March 16, 2012: Annual Shamrock Ball hosted by the Pembroke Business and Professional Women's Organization
- March 17, 2012: Givens Performing Arts Center annual fund-raiser and silent auction
- March 27, 2012: Graduate Research Poster and Information Sessions
- April 19, 2012: 125th Anniversary Celebration Powwow
- April 26, 2012: Business Visions Sixteenth Annual Banquet
- May 4, 2012: School of Graduate Studies Commencement Ceremony
- May 5, 2012: Undergraduate Commencement Ceremony
- June 27, 2012: Hump Day Heritage Social
- July 6, 2012: Lumbee Book Talk during Lumbee Homecoming
  - Featured authors: Chancellor Emeritus Joseph B. Oxendine, Bruce Barton '86, Gloria (Barton) Gates, Arvis Boughman, Dr. Malinda (Maynor) Maynor Lowery, and Dr. Stan Knick

- Featured artists: Mardella Lowery—beadwork, Jordan McGirt—graphic art, Timmie Locklear—gourd and tile artist, Frankie Harris—wood carver, and Gloria Tara Lowery '66—pine needle baskets
- July 25, 2012: Hump Day Heritage Social
- August 14, 2012: University Address by Chancellor Kyle R. Carter
- August 16, 2012: 125th Anniversary Popsicle Party
- September 19–21, 2012: Sixth Annual Conference for American Indian Women of Proud Nations
- October 22–27, 2012: Homecoming
- October 22, 2012: "Reflections—A Review of UNCP's First 125 Years"
- October 27, 2012: "125th Choir" sang the national anthem and the alma mater before the football game against Newberry College
- November 8, 2012: "Dr. English E. Jones and James K. Braboy: Succeeding Against the Odds" sponsored by Friends of the Mary Livermore Library
- November 10, 2012: Second Annual Cruisin' Pembroke Street Festival
- December 7, 2012: School of Graduate Studies Commencement Ceremony
- December 8, 2012: Undergraduate Commencement Ceremony
- January 23, 2013: "Last Lecture"
  - Family members and former students of legendary individuals from the university's history shared advice they thought Professor James A. Jacobs '27, '29; Dr. Clifton Oxendine '24; Dr. Herbert G. Oxendine; and Virgie Mae Sutton would share if they could return for one lecture.
- January 25–26, 2013: River People Music and Culture Fest
- January 31, 2013: Sixty-First Annual Miss UNCP Scholarship Pageant
- February 12, 2013: Native American Speaker Series presented Dr. Brenda J. Child, an expert on Indian boarding schools in the early twentieth century and member of the Ojibwe Tribe
- February 18, 2013: 125th Anniversary Blood Drive
- February 25, 2013: Distinguished Speaker Series featured 2012 Olympic gold medalist Gabby Douglas
- February 27, 2013: Twenty-Fourth Annual National African American Read-In: A Literary Campaign
- March 4, 2013: Campus Conversation with Chancellor Kyle R. Carter
- March 5, 2013: Celebration of Old Main's Ninetieth Anniversary
  - Celebration of Old Main's Ninetieth Anniversary and recognition of

Judge L.R. Varser, Gov. James Holshouser, leaders of the Save Old Main Movement and members of the Save Old Main Commission
- March 6, 2013: "UNCP, Then and Now"
  - Mannequins dressed in period clothing from six eras in the university's history (1880s, 1920s, 1940s, 1950s, 1960s/1970s, and 1980s) were on display in the library.
- March 7, 2013
  - Founders' Day Ceremony
    - Recognized former and current members of the Board of Trustees, former chancellors, and Gloria Tara Lowery '66 for athletic logo design in 1992
  - Dedication of Heritage Oak in the Quad
  - Grand opening of Hawk Walk trail
- March 19, 2013
  - Fund-raising dinner to celebrate the history of *Pembroke Magazine*, UNC Pembroke's international literary magazine since 1969
    - The event featured Lumberton native and best-selling author Jill McCorkle and poet and former editor of *Pembroke Magazine* Shelby Stephenson. McCorkle read from her novel *Life after Life*.
  - Native American Speaker Series presented Dr. Kehente Horn-Miller, a scholar and member of the Kahnawà:ke Tribe.
- March 20, 2013: Guinness World Record Attempt for Longest Handshake Relay
- March 21, 2013: Alumni Regional Reception, Fayetteville, North Carolina
- March 22, 2013: Friends of the Library Benefit
  - The silent auction and dinner featured speakers Timothy Brayboy '64 and Betty Oxendine Mangum '60.
- March 23, 2013: 125th Fun Run
  - The event featured a three-mile run/walk from the center of the current campus to the site of the original campus and back, along with a one-mile run/walk through a portion of the Hawk Walk trail.
- March 25, 2013: Graduate Research Poster Session and School of Graduate Studies Open House
- March 27, 2013: "UNCP's African American Firsts: Celebrating Their Legacy!"

- April 3, 2013: Pembroke Undergraduate Research and Creativity (PURC) Center Symposium
- April 5–6, 2013: 110th Annual Meeting of the North Carolina Academy of Science
- April 10–12, 2013: UNC system Board of Governors meeting
- April 11–12, 2013: Ninth Annual Southeast Indian Studies Conference
- April 12–13, 2013: Relay for Life
- April 18, 2013: Braves Club Cash Bash presented by Southeastern Health
- April 20, 2013: Family Day
- April 28, 2013: UNCP Concert Band presented "Concerto Competition Winners," and premiere of composer James Hosay's *Sing, Pray, Shout: A Lumbee River Revival*
- May 3, 2013: School of Graduate Studies Commencement ceremony
- May 3–5, 2013: Lumbee Spring Powwow
- May 4, 2013: Undergraduate Commencement ceremony

Bibliography

UNIVERSITY OF NORTH CAROLINA AT PEMBROKE RECORDS

All UNC Pembroke records correspond to the previous names of the institution: Croatan Normal School (1887–1911); The Indian Normal School of Robeson County (1911–1913); The Cherokee Indian Normal School of Robeson County (1913–1941); Pembroke State College for Indians (1941–1949); Pembroke State College (1949–1969); Pembroke State University (1969–1996); and University of North Carolina at Pembroke (since 1996).

Academic Catalog
Athletic Record Book
Board of Trustees' Minutes
Chancellor Kyle R. Carter's Installation Program, 2011.
Chancellor's Report: Highlights of Chancellor's Activities and University Achievements (2010–2013)
Centennial Report 1887–1987
Deeds
Diamond Jubilee Program, 1963
Indianhead
Installation Address, Kyle R. Carter, 2011.
Installation Address, Paul R. Givens, 1979.
Long-Range Plan, 1967
Long-Range Plan, 1981–1986
Long-Range Planning Report, 1984–1989
Lumbee Tattler (1942)
PSU Today
PSU Yearbook-Athletics
Report on the UNCP Listening Tour, January 2011.

Self-Study Report, 1967
Self-Study Report, 1977–1979
Semicentennial Observation Program, 1937
The Chancellor's Reports
The President's Reports
UNCP Building Inventory as of Fall 2011
UNCP Today
University Address, Kyle R. Carter, 2010–2013

UNIVERSITY COMMUNICATIONS AND MARKETING ARCHIVES

Brave Bulletin, http://www.uncp.edu/ucm/
University Newswire, http://www.uncp.edu/news/

NATIVE AMERICAN RESOURCE CENTER

Hamilton McMillan Papers
John L. Carter Collection and Papers

SPECIAL COLLECTIONS, MARY LIVERMORE LIBRARY

Biographical Sketch of President English E. Jones, Pembroke State College
Elmer W. Hunt Photograph Collection
Revels, Ruth (Locklear). "I Am Old Main." 1972.

INTERVIEWS

Conducted by David K. Eliades and Linda E. Oxendine:
Mary M. Bell Deese '47, 1986
Clement Bullard '47, 1986
Johnny Bullard, 1986
Ziatta D. Bullard '43, 1986
Marvin Carter '26, 1986
Carrie M. Dial '53, 1986
Lucy S. Locklear '54, 1985

Mary H. Locklear '33, '53, 1985
Katie L. Lowery, 1985
Winford Lowry '47, 1986
Berteen (Oxendine) Prine, 1985

Conducted by Lawrence T. Locklear:
Dorothy L. Blue '55, 2013.
James C. Dial '54, 2007.
Joseph B. Oxendine, 2013.

GOVERNMENT RECORDS

US Census
Vital Records
    Georgia
    North Carolina
    South Carolina
    Tennessee
    Virginia

GOVERNMENT PUBLICATIONS

Cheyney, John L., Jr., ed. *North Carolina Government. 1585–1979: A Narrative and Statistical History*, 2nd ed. Raleigh: North Carolina Department of the Secretary of State, 1981.

McPherson, O.M. *Indians of North Carolina.* Washington, DC: Government Printing Office, 1915.

U.S. House of Representatives, 55th Congress, 3rd session. *Annual Reports of the Department of the Interior for the Fiscal Year ended June 30, 1898.* Indian Affairs. Vol. 2, Parts II and III. *Report of the Commissioner of Education.* Washington, DC: U.S. Government Printing Office, 1899.

U.S. House of Representatives, 58th Congress, 3rd session. *Annual Reports of the Department of the Interior for the Fiscal Year ended June 30, 1904. Indian Affairs.* Part 1. *Report of the Commissioner, and Appendixes.* Washington, DC: U.S. Government Printing Office, 1905.

STATE OF NORTH CAROLINA

Executive and Legislative Documents
Handbook
Journals. Constitutional Conventions of 1824, 1868, and 1875
Public Laws
Reports of the Supreme Court
State Superintendent of Public Instruction. Biennial Reports.
Vital Statistics

NORTH CAROLINA DEPARTMENT OF ARCHIVES AND HISTORY, RALEIGH, NC

Annual Report of the Auditor of the State of North Carolina
Department of Public Instruction. Division of Negro Education. "Papers."
———. Division of Professional Services. College Accreditation Inspection
    Reports, 1922–1952. "Cherokee Indian Normal School (1940)."
———. General Correspondence of the Superintendent, 1887–1951.
"Legislative Papers Relating to Education, 1798-1900."

UNIVERSITY OF NORTH CAROLINA SYSTEM

The Code
Focused-Growth Institutions of the University of North Carolina: A Progress Report.
    January 2005.
NC Commission on Higher Education Facilities. "North Carolina Facilities and
    Utilization Reports, Pembroke State University, 1984."

MISCELLANEOUS DOCUMENTS

Bruce Barton Collection. Personal.
Elmer Hunt Photographic Collection. Personal.
Free Will Baptist Historical Collection. Mount Olive College, Mount Olive, NC.
Lenoir-Rhyne University. *The Hacawa.* 1943.
McLean, A.W. "Historical Sketch of the Indians of Robeson County." McLean
    Collection, Robeson County Public Library, Lumberton, NC.
Sidney G. Gilbreath Papers, 1909–1938. Archives of Appalachia. East Tennessee
    State University. Johnson City, TN.

University of North Carolina at Chapel Hill. *Yackety Yack*. 1917.
Wake Forest University. *The Howler*. 1910.

NEWSPAPERS

Carolina Indian Voice (Pembroke, NC)
Charlotte Observer (Charlotte, NC)
Daily Press (Newport News, VA)
Greensboro Daily News (Greensboro, NC)
Fayetteville Observer (Fayetteville, NC)
Fayetteville Times (Fayetteville, NC)
Lumbee (Pembroke, NC)
Lumberton Post (Lumberton, NC)
News and Observer (Raleigh, NC)
Robesonian (Lumberton, NC)
Sylvan Valley News (Brevard, NC)
Times Herald (Newport News, VA)
Transylvania Times (Brevard, NC)

BOOKS AND ARTICLES

Barton, Bruce, Cynthia L. Hunt, and Linda E. Oxendine. *Pembroke: A Centennial Perspective 1895–1995*. N.p.: np, nd.
Barton, Lew. *The Most Ironic Story in American History*. Charlotte: Associated Printing Corporation, 1967.
Blu, Karen. *The Lumbee Problem*. New York: Cambridge University Press, 1980.
Brayboy, Tim, and Bruce Barton. *Playing Before an Overflow Crowd: The Story of Indian Basketball in Robeson, North Carolina, and Adjoining Counties*. Chapel Hill, NC: Chapel Hill Press, 2003.
Cathcart, William, ed. *The Baptist Encyclopedia. A Dictionary of the Doctrines, Ordinances, Usages, Confessions of Faith, Sufferings, Labors, and Successes, and of the General History of the Baptist Denomination in All Lands with Numerous Biographical Sketches of Distinguished American and Foreign Baptists, and a Supplement*. Philadelphia: Louis H. Everts, 1883. http://www.archive.org/stream/baptistencyclop01cath#page/n5/mode/2up.

Couper, William. *The Corps Forward. Biographical Sketches of VMI Cadets Who Found in the Battle of New Market*. Buena Vista, VA: Mariner Publishing, 2005.

Dial, Adolph L., and David K. Eliades. "The Lumbee Indians of North Carolina and Pembroke State University." *Indian Historian* (Winter 1971): 20–24.

———. *The Only Land I Know: A History of the Lumbee Indians*. 1975. Repr., Syracuse, NY: Syracuse University Press, 1996.

Elliott, Walker. "'I Told Him I'd Never Been to His Back Door for Nothing': The Lumbee Indian Struggle for Higher Education under Jim Crow." *North Carolina Historical Review* 90 (January 2013): 49-87.

Evans, William McKee. "The North Carolina Lumbees: From Assimilation to Revitalization." In *Southeastern Indians since the Removal Era*, ed. Walter L. Williams, 49–71. Athens: University of Georgia Press, 1979.

———. *To Die Game: The Story of the Lowry Band, Indian Guerillas of Construction*. 1971; Syracuse, NY: Syracuse University Press, 1995.

Locklear, Lawrence T. "Down by the Ol' Lumbee: An Investigation into the Origin and Use of the Word 'Lumbee' prior to 1952." *Native South* 3 (2010): 103–117.

Lockmiller, David A. *The Consolidation of the University of North Carolina*. Chapel Hill: University of North Carolina Press, 1942.

Lowery, Malinda Maynor. *Lumbee Indians in the Jim Crow South: Race, Identity, and the Making of a Nation*. Chapel Hill: University of North Carolina Press, 2010.

McMillan, Hamilton. *Sir Walter Raleigh's Lost Colony: An Historical Sketch of the Attempts of Sir Walter Raleigh to Establish a Colony in Virginia, with the Traditions of an Indian Tribe in North Carolina. Indicating the Fate of the Colony of Englishmen Left on Roanoke Island in 1587*. Raleigh, NC: Edwards and Broughton Company, 1888.

Norment, Mary C. *The Lowrie History as Acted in Part by Henry Berry Lowrie, the Great North Carolina Bandit, with Biographical Sketch of His Associates*. Lumberton, NC: Lumbee Publishing Company, 1909.

Oxendine, Clifton. "Pembroke State College for Indians." *North Carolina Historical Review* 22 (January 1945): 22–33.

Pelt, Michael. "A History of Ayden Seminary and Eureka College." N.p.: np, nd. http://www.moc.edu/images/uploads/library_files/Peltschools.pdf.

Patterson, Homer L. *Patterson's College and School Directory of the United States and*

Canada containing a complete list and description of all the schools, colleges and other institutions of higher education. A list of the college greek letter fraternities, their chapters, and where located. A list and description of the college newspapers and publications. A list of college, theological, law medical, state and public libraries, with name of librarian and number of bound volumes. Also a list of the state and county superintendents of public instruction, city superintendents, high school and graded high school principals. Chicago: American Educational Company, 1906. https://archive.org/details/pattersonscolle01pattgoog.

Pratt, Richard H. "The Advantages of Mingling Indians with Whites." In *Americanizing the American Indians: Writings by the "Friends of the Indian" 1880–1900, ed. Francis Paul Prucha, 260–271.* Cambridge, MA: Harvard University Press, 1973.

Presbyterian Church in the United States of America. *Minutes of the General Assembly of the Presbyterian Church in the United States of America. New Series, Vol. XII, August 1912. Proceedings, etc., of the 124th General Assembly.* Philadelphia: Office of the General Assembly, 1912. https://archive.org/stream/minutesofgeneral1912pres#page/n5/mode/2up.

Tyner, K. Blake. *Robeson County: Images of America.* Charleston, SC: Arcadia, 2003.

White, James Terry, ed. *The National Cyclopaedia of American Biography, Being the History of the United States as Illustrated in the Lives of the Founders, Builders, and Defenders of the Republic, and of the Men and Women Who Are Doing the Work and Moulding the Thought of the Present Rime, Edited by Distinguished Biographers, Selected from Each State, Revised and Approved by the Most Eminent Historians, Scholars, and Statesmen of the day.* Vol. 1 New York: James T. White & Company, 1898. http://babel.hathitrust.org/cgi/pt?id=nyp.33433016182630;view=1up;seq=456.

THESES AND DISSERTATIONS

Barclay, Russell B. "The Press and University Autonomy: How North Carolina's Major Newspapers Covered Their State University's Desegregation Controversy." PhD diss., Duke University, 1984.

Barnes, Bahson N. "A History of the Robeson County School System." Master's thesis, University of North Carolina at Chapel Hill, 1950.

Beckwith, Evalina G. "A Study of the Physical Equipment and Teaching Personnel of the Indian Schools of Robeson County." Master's thesis, University of North Carolina at Chapel Hill, 1931.

King, William E. "The Era of Progressive Reform in Southern Education: The Growth of Public Schools in North Carolina, 1885-1910." PhD diss., Duke University, 1970.

Oxendine, Clifton. "A Social and Economic History of the Indians of Robeson County, North Carolina." Master's thesis, George Peabody College, 1934.

Sider, Gerald M. "The Political History of the Lumbee Indians of Robeson County, North Carolina." PhD diss., New School for Social Research, 1971.

Thompson, Vernon Ray. "A History of the Education of the Lumbee Indians of Robeson County, North Carolina, 1885–1970." PhD diss., University of Miami, 1973.

Index

Pages on which illustrations appear are indicated in italic type.

David K. Eliades (1938–2007) was a professor of history and American Indian studies at the University of North Carolina at Pembroke from 1967 to 2001. A popular professor who specialized in southern Indians during the colonial era, Eliades won the 1998 UNC Board of Governors Award for Excellence in Teaching. He was awarded UNC Pembroke's first Distinguished Professor Award in 1983. A former chair of the History Department, Eliades was coordinator of the American Studies Program. Upon his retirement, Eliades was honored with the title of professor emeritus. Eliades coauthored two seminal works: *The Only Land I Know: A History of the Lumbee Indians* (1974) with Dr. Adolph L. Dial '43, and *Pembroke State University: A Centennial History* (1986) with Dr. Linda Ellen Oxendine. He earned a BA in journalism and history from the University of North Carolina at Chapel Hill in 1961, an MA in history from East Carolina University in 1963, and a PhD in history from the University of South Carolina in 1981.

Lawrence T. Locklear '05, '12 has been employed at the University of North Carolina at Pembroke since 1999, serving as the university web publisher between 2000 and 2014, and the program coordinator for the Southeast American Indian Studies Program since May 2014. He cochaired UNC Pembroke's 125th Anniversary Celebration Committee and was a corecipient of the inaugural Chancellor's Award of Excellence in 2013. In 2007 Locklear appeared in The History Channel's video documentary *Aftershock: Beyond the Civil War*, where he provided historical commentary about Lumbee hero Henry Berry Lowrie, his multiracial gang, and their fight for social and legal justice in Robeson County between 1864 and 1874. His essay "Down by the Ol' Lumbee: An Investigation into the Origin and Use of the Word 'Lumbee' prior to 1952" was published in *Native South* (2010). Between 2005 and 2008 Locklear served on the Lumbee Tribal Council, including two terms as speaker. He earned a BA in history from North Carolina State University in 1996, and a BA in American Indian studies and an MPA in public administration from UNC Pembroke in 2012 and 2005, respectively.

Linda E. Oxendine is a professor emeritus of American Indian studies at the University of North Carolina at Pembroke, where she taught from 1989 until her retirement in 2006. Oxendine taught part-time in American Indian Studies at UNC Pembroke until 2014. She served as the director and curator of UNC Pembroke's Native American Resource Center from 1982 to 1986 and chair of the American Indian Studies Department from 1989 to 2006. A noted Lumbee scholar, Oxendine coauthored *Pembroke State University: A Centennial History* (1986) with Dr. David K. Eliades. She has written about a variety of topics, including Indian education and Lumbee history and culture, and has worked with several tribal, state, and national agencies. In 2011 she was the recipient of the University of North Carolina at Chapel Hill's Distinguished Alumna Award. Oxendine earned a BA in mathematics from the University of North Carolina at Chapel Hill in 1967, an MA in educational administration from Penn State University in 1973, and a PhD in American studies from the University of Minnesota in 1992.